Learn Objective-C on the Mac

Penciled by MARK DALRYMPLE
Inked by SCOTT KNASTER

Apress®

Learn Objective-C on the Mac

Copyright © 2009 by Mark Dalrymple and Scott Knaster

ISBN-13 (pbk): 978-1-4302-1815-9

ISBN-13 (electronic): 978-1-4302-1816-6

Printed and bound in the United States of America 9 8 7 6 5 4 3 2

Lead Editors: Clay Andres and Dave Mark
Technical Reviewer: Jeff LaMarche
Editorial Board: Clay Andres, Steve Anglin, Mark Beckner, Ewan Buckingham, Tony Campbell, Gary Cornell,
    Jonathan Gennick, Michelle Lowman, Matthew Moodie, Jeffrey Pepper, Frank Pohlmann, Ben Renow-Clarke,
    Dominic Shakeshaft, Matt Wade, Tom Welsh
Project Manager: Denise Santoro Lincoln
Copy Editor: Heather Lang
Associate Production Director: Kari Brooks-Copony
Production Editor: Laura Esterman
Compositor/Artist/Interior Designer: Diana Van Winkle
Proofreader: Greg Teague
Indexer: Toma Mulligan
Cover Designer: Kurt Krames
Manufacturing Director: Tom Debolski

Distributed to the book trade worldwide by Springer-Verlag New York, Inc., 233 Spring Street, 6th Floor, New York, NY 10013. Phone 1-800-SPRINGER, fax 201-348-4505, e-mail orders-ny@springer-sbm.com, or visit http://www.springeronline.com.

For information on translations, please contact Apress directly at 2855 Telegraph Avenue, Suite 600, Berkeley, CA 94705. Phone 510-549-5930, fax 510-549-5939, e-mail info@apress.com, or visit http://www.apress.com.

Apress and friends of ED books may be purchased in bulk for academic, corporate, or promotional use. eBook versions and licenses are also available for most titles. For more information, reference our Special Bulk Sales–eBook Licensing web page at http://www.apress.com/info/bulksales.

The source code for this book is available to readers at http://www.apress.com.

For Jerri Shertzer—teacher, mentor, friend
—Mark

Contents at a Glance

Contents

About the Authors

 **Mark Dalrymple** is a longtime Mac and Unix programmer who has worked on cross-platform toolkits, Internet publishing tools, high-performance web servers, and end-user desktop applications. He's also the principal author of *Advanced Mac OS X Programming* (Big Nerd Ranch 2005). In his spare time, he plays trombone and bassoon and makes balloon animals.

 **Scott Knaster** is a legendary (that is, very old) Mac programmer and author of such best-selling books as *Take Control of Switching to the Mac* (TidBITS Publishing Inc. 2008) and *Macintosh Programming Secrets* (Addison-Wesley 1992). His book *How to Write Macintosh Software* (Addison-Wesley 1992) was required reading for Mac programmers for more than a decade. He lives in a house with other people and a dog.

About the Technical Reviewer

 **Jeff LaMarche** is a longtime Mac developer and certified Apple iPhone developer with more than 20 years of programming experience. He's written on Cocoa and Objective-C for *MacTech Magazine*, as well as articles for Apple's Developer Technical Services web site. He has experience working in enterprise software as both a developer for PeopleSoft, starting in the late 1990s, and later as an independent consultant.

Acknowledgments

If you've ever read a technical book, you've seen the acknowledgments and understand that even though there are (in this case) two names on the front cover, a lot of other folks behind the scenes make the whole process work.

In particular, we'd like to single out Denise Santoro Lincoln, who was our primary wrangler. We gave her "polenta" of problems, which she handled with taste, grace, and humor. Thanks also to Clay Andres and Jeff LaMarche, who helped make sure we didn't tell you any lies. Zillions of thanks to Laura Esterman, our production editor, for turning mere piles of text into this awesome tome that you're reading and to Heather Lang for warping (temporarily, we hope) her mind sufficiently to think like we do and still perform a masterful copy editing job.

Mark would like to thank Aaron Hillegass for introducing him to all of this Objective-C and Cocoa stuff many moons ago and for introducing him to Scott and Dave. Without Aaron, none of this would have happened. Also, Mark gives a shout out to Greg Miller for introducing him to the coolness of KVC and NSPredicate. And Scott just wants to thank Mark for doing all the real work.

Finally, impossibly enormous thanks go out to Dave Mark. Without his vision, dogged persistence, and awesome nagging, this book would not have seen the light of day.

Preface

One of the dangers of being a programmer for a long time is that you can lose that spark of delight that got you interested in programming the first place. Luckily, shiny new technologies come along all the time that can reignite that interest, and Mac OS X is chock full of shiny stuff.

Objective-C is a programming language that blends C's speed and ubiquity with an elegant object-oriented environment and provides a buzzword-laden cornucopia of programming good times. Objective-C is the gateway drug for many of Apple's niftiest technologies, such as the Cocoa toolkit and the iPhone SDK. Once you've mastered the Objective-C language, you're well on your way to conquering the rest of the platform. And from there, you can try to take over the world.

Chapter 1

Hello

Welcome to *Learn Objective-C on the Mac*! This book is designed to teach you the basics of the Objective-C language. Objective-C is a superset of C and is the language used by many (if not most) applications that have a true Mac OS X look and feel.

This book teaches you the Objective-C language and introduces you to its companion, Apple's Cocoa toolkit. Cocoa is written in Objective-C and contains all the elements of the Mac OS X user interface, plus a whole lot more. Once you learn Objective-C in this book, you'll be ready to dive into Cocoa with a full-blown project or another book such as *Learn Cocoa on the Mac* or *Beginning iPhone Development*, both by Dave Mark and Jeff LaMarche (Apress 2009).

In this chapter, we'll let you know the basic information you need before you get started with this book. We'll also serve up a bit of history about Objective-C and give you a thumbnail sketch of what's to come in future chapters.

Before You Start

Before you read this book, you should have some experience with a C-like programming language such as C++, Java, or venerable C itself. Whatever the language, you should feel comfortable with its basic principles. You should know what variables and functions are and understand how to control your program's flow using conditionals and loops. Our focus is the features Objective-C adds to its base language, C, along with some goodies chosen from Apple's Cocoa toolkit.

Are you coming to Objective-C from a non-C language? You'll still be able to follow along, but you might want to take a look at Appendix A or check out *Learn C on the Mac* by Dave Mark (Apress 2009).

Where the Future Was Made Yesterday

Cocoa and Objective-C are at the heart of Apple's Mac OS X operating system. Although Mac OS X is relatively new, Objective-C and Cocoa are much older. Brad Cox invented Objective-C in the early 1980s to meld the popular and portable C language with the elegant Smalltalk language. In 1985, Steve Jobs founded NeXT, Inc., to create powerful, affordable workstations. NeXT chose Unix as its operating system and created NextSTEP, a powerful user interface toolkit developed in Objective-C. Despite its features and a small, loyal following, NextSTEP achieved little commercial success.

When Apple acquired NeXT in 1996 (or was it the other way around?), NextSTEP was renamed Cocoa and brought to the wider audience of Macintosh programmers. Apple gives away its development tools—including Cocoa—for free, so any Mac programmer can take advantage of them. All you need is a bit of programming experience, basic knowledge of Objective-C, and the desire to dig in and learn stuff.

You might wonder, "If Objective-C and Cocoa were invented in the '80s—in the days of *Alf* and *The A-Team*, not to mention stuffy old Unix—aren't they old and moldy by now?" Absolutely not! Objective-C and Cocoa are the result of years of effort by a team of excellent programmers, and they have been continually updated and enhanced. Over time, Objective-C and Cocoa have evolved into an incredibly elegant and powerful set of tools. Objective-C is also the key to writing applications for the iPhone. So now, twenty-some years after NeXT adopted Objective-C, all the cool kids are using it.

What's Coming Up

Objective-C is a superset of C. Objective-C begins with C, and then adds a couple of small but significant additions to the language. If you've ever looked at C++ or Java, you may be surprised at how small Objective-C really is. We'll cover Objective-C's additions to C in detail in this book's chapters:

- Chapter 2, "Extensions to C," focuses on the basic features that Objective-C introduces.

- In Chapter 3, "An Introduction to Object-Oriented Programming," we kick off the learning by showing you the basics of object-oriented programming.

- Chapter 4, "Inheritance," describes how to create classes that gain the features of their parent classes.

- Chapter 5, "Composition," discusses techniques for combining objects so they can work together.

- Chapter 6, "Source File Organization," presents real-world strategies for creating your program's sources.

- Chapter 7, "More about Xcode," shows you some shortcuts and power-user features to help you get the most out of your programming day.

- We take a brief respite from Objective-C in Chapter 8, "A Quick Tour of the Foundation Kit," to impress you with some of Cocoa's cool features using one of its two primary frameworks.

- You'll spend a lot of time in your Cocoa applications dealing in Chapter 9, "Memory Management" (sorry about that).

- Chapter 10, "Object Initialization," is all about what happens when objects are born.

- Chapter 11, "Properties," gives you the lowdown on Objective-C's new dot notation and an easier way to make object accessors.

- Chapter 12, "Categories," describes the supercool Objective-C feature that lets you add your own methods to existing classes—even those you didn't write.

- Chapter 13, "Protocols," tells about a form of inheritance in Objective-C that allows classes to implement packaged sets of features.

- Chapter 14, "Introduction to the Application Kit," gives you a taste of the gorgeous applications you can develop in Cocoa using its other primary framework.

- Chapter 15, "File Loading and Saving," shows you how to save and retrieve your data.

- Chapter 16, "Key-Value Coding," gives you ways to deal with your data indirectly.

- And finally, in Chapter 17, "NSPredicate," we show you how to slice and dice your data.

If you're coming from another language like Java or C++, or from another platform like Windows or Linux, you may want to check out Appendix A, "Coming to Objective-C from Other Languages," which points out some of the mental hurdles you'll need to jump to embrace Objective-C.

Summary

Mac OS X programs are written in Objective-C, using technology from way back in the 1980s that has matured into a powerful set of tools. In this book, we'll start by assuming you know something about C programming and go from there.

We hope you enjoy the ride!

Chapter 2

Extensions to C

*O*bjective-C is nothing more than the C language with some extra features drizzled on top—it's delicious! In this chapter, we'll cover some of those key extras as we take you through building your first Objective-C program.

The Simplest Objective-C Program

You've probably seen the C version of the classic Hello World program, which prints out the text "Hello, world!" or a similar pithy remark. Hello World is usually the first program that neophyte C programmers learn. We don't want to buck tradition, so we're going to write a similar program here called Hello Objective-C.

Building Hello Objective-C

As you work through this book, we're assuming you have Apple's Xcode tools installed. If you don't already have Xcode, or if you've never used it before, an excellent section in Chapter 2 of Dave Mark's *Learn C on the Mac* (Apress 2009) walks you through the steps of acquiring, installing, and creating programs with Xcode.

In this section, we'll step through the process of using Xcode to create your first Objective-C project. If you are already familiar with Xcode, feel free to skip ahead; you won't hurt our feelings. Before you go, be sure to expand the *Learn ObjC Projects* archive from this book's archive (which you can download from the Source Code/Download page of the Apress web site). This project is located in the *02.01 - Hello Objective-C* folder.

To create the project, start by launching Xcode. You can find the Xcode application in */Developer/Applications*. We put the Xcode icon in the Dock for easy access. You might want to do that too.

Once Xcode finishes launching, choose **New Project** from the **File** menu. Xcode shows you a list of the various kinds of projects it can create. Use your focus to ignore most of the intriguing project types there, and choose *Command Line Utility* on the left-hand side of the window and *Foundation Tool* on the right-hand side, as shown in Figure 2-1. Click the *Choose* button.

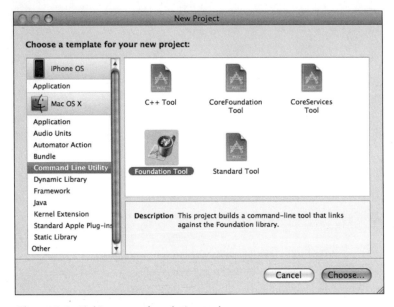

Figure 2-1. *Making a new foundation tool*

Xcode drops a sheet and asks you to name the project. You can choose any name you want, but as you can see in Figure 2-2, we called it Hello Objective-C. We're putting it into one of our *Projects* directories here to keep things organized, but you can put it anywhere you want.

After you click *Save*, Xcode shows you its main window, called the project window (see Figure 2-3). This window displays the pieces that compose your project along with an editing pane. The highlighted file, *Hello Objective-C.m*, is the source file that contains the code for Hello Objective-C.

Hello Objective-C.m contains boilerplate code, kindly provided by Xcode for each new project. We can make our Hello Objective-C application a little simpler than the sample Xcode supplies. Delete everything in *Hello Objective-C.m* and replace it with this code:

```
#import <Foundation/Foundation.h>

int main (int argc, const char *argv[])
{
  NSLog (@"Hello, Objective-C!");

  return (0);

} // main
```

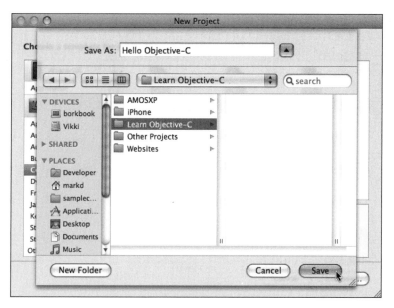

Figure 2-2. *Name the new foundation tool*

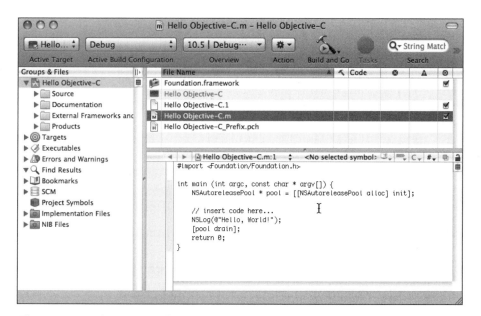

Figure 2-3. *XCode's main window*

If you don't understand all the code right now, don't worry about it. We'll go through this program in excruciating, line-by-line detail soon.

Source code is no fun if you can't turn it into a running program. Build and run the program by clicking the *Build and Go* button or pressing ⌘**R**. If there aren't any nasty syntax errors, Xcode compiles and links your program and then runs it. Open the Xcode console window (by selecting **Console** from the **Run** menu or pressing ⌘⇧R), which displays your program's output, as shown in Figure 2-4.

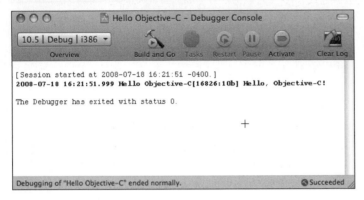

Figure 2-4. *Running Hello Objective-C*

And there you have it: your first working Objective-C program. Congratulations! Let's pull it apart and see how it works.

Deconstructing Hello Objective-C

Here, again, are the contents of *Hello Objective-C.m*:

```
#import <Foundation/Foundation.h>

int main (int argc, const char *argv[])
{
    NSLog (@"Hello, Objective-C!");

    return (0);

} // main
```

Xcode uses the *.m* extension to indicate a file that holds Objective-C code and will be processed by the Objective-C compiler. File names ending in *.c* are handled by the C compiler, and *.cpp* files are the province of the C++ compiler. (In Xcode, all this compiling is handled by the GNU Compiler Collection [GCC], a single compiler that understands all three variations of the language.)

The *main.m* file contains two lines of code that should be familiar to you already if you know plain C: the declaration of main() and the return (0) statement at the end. Remember that Objective-C really is C at heart, and the syntax for declaring main() and returning a value is the same as in C. The rest of the code looks slightly different from regular C. For example, what is that wacky #import thing? To find out, read on!

NOTE

The .*m* extension originally stood for "messages" when Objective-C was first introduced, referring to a central feature of Objective-C that we'll talk about in future chapters. Nowadays, we just call them dot-m files.

That Wacky #import Thing

Just like C, Objective-C uses **header files** to hold the declarations of elements such as structs, symbolic constants, and function prototypes. In C, you use the #include statement to inform the compiler that it should consult a header file for some definitions. You can use #include in Objective-C programs for the same purpose, but you probably never will. Instead, you'll use #import, like this:

```
#import <Foundation/Foundation.h>
```

#import is a feature provided by the GCC compiler, which is what Xcode uses when you're compiling Objective-C, C, and C++ programs. #import guarantees that a header file will be included only once, no matter how many times the #import directive is actually seen for that file.

NOTE

In C, programmers typically use a scheme based on the #ifdef directive to avoid the situation where one file includes a second file, which then, recursively, includes the first.

In Objective-C, programmers use #import to accomplish the same thing.

The #import <Foundation/Foundation.h> statement tells the compiler to look at the Foundation.h header file in the Foundation framework.

What's a framework? We're glad you asked. A framework is a collection of parts—header files, libraries, images, sounds, and more—collected together into a single unit. Apple ships technologies such as Cocoa, Carbon, QuickTime, and OpenGL as sets of frameworks. Cocoa consists of a pair of frameworks, Foundation and Application Kit (also known as AppKit), along with a suite of supporting frameworks, including Core Animation and Core Image, which add all sorts of cool stuff to Cocoa.

The Foundation framework handles features found in the layers beneath the user interface, such as data structures and communication mechanisms. All the programs in this book are based on the Foundation framework.

> **NOTE**
>
> Once you finish this book, your next step along the road to becoming a Cocoa guru is to master Cocoa's Application Kit, which contains Cocoa's high-level features: user interface elements, printing, color and sound management, AppleScript support, and so on. To find out more, check out *Learn Cocoa on the Mac* by Dave Mark and Jeff LaMarche (Apress 2009).

Each framework is a significant collection of technology, often containing dozens or even hundreds of header files. Each framework has a master header file that includes all the framework's individual header files. By using #import on the master header file, you have access to all the framework's features.

The header files for the Foundation framework take up nearly a megabyte of disk storage, and contain more than 14,000 lines of code, spread across over a hundred files. When you include the master header file with #import <Foundation/Foundation.h>, you get that whole vast collection. You might think wading through all that text for every file would take the compiler a lot of time, but Xcode is smart: it speeds up the task by using precompiled headers, a compressed and digested form of the header that's loaded quickly when you #import it.

If you're curious about which headers are included with the Foundation framework, you can peek inside its *Headers* directory (*/System/Library/Frameworks/Foundation.framework/Headers/*). You won't break anything if you browse the files in there; just don't remove or change anything.

NSLog() and @"strings"

Now that we have used #import on the master header file for the Foundation framework, you're ready to write code that takes advantage of some Cocoa features. The first (and only) real line of code in Hello Objective-C uses the NSLog() function, like so:

```
NSLog (@"Hello, Objective-C!");
```

This prints "Hello, Objective-C!" to the console. If you've used C at all, you have undoubtedly encountered printf() in your travels. NSLog() is a Cocoa function that works very much like printf().

Just like printf(), NSLog() takes a string as its first argument. This string can contain format specifiers (such as %d), and the function takes additional parameters that match the format specifiers. printf() plugs these extra parameters into the string before it gets printed.

As we've said before, Objective-C is just C with a little bit of special sauce, so you're welcome to use `printf()` instead of `NSLog()` if you want. We recommend `NSLog()`, however, because it adds features such as time and date stamps, as well as automatically appending the newline (`'\n'`) character for you.

You might be thinking that `NSLog()` is kind of a strange name for a function. What is that "NS" doing there? It turns out that Cocoa prefixes all its function, constant, and type names with "NS". This prefix tells you the function comes from Cocoa instead of some other toolkit.

The prefix helps prevent **name collisions**, big problems that result when the same identifier is used for two different things. If Cocoa had named this function `Log()`, there's a good chance the name would clash with a `Log()` function created by some innocent programmer somewhere. When a program containing `Log()` is built with Cocoa included, Xcode complains that `Log()` is defined multiple times, and sadness results.

Now that you have an idea why a prefix is a good idea, you might wonder about the specific choice: why "NS" instead of "Cocoa," for example? Well, the "NS" prefix dates back from the time when the toolkit was called NextSTEP and was the product of NeXT Software (formerly NeXT, Inc.), which was acquired by Apple in 1996. Rather than break compatibility with code already written for NextSTEP, Apple just continued to use the "NS" prefix. It's a historical curiosity now, like your appendix.

Cocoa has staked its claim on the NS prefix, so obviously, you should not prefix any of your own variables or function names with "NS". If you do, you will confuse the readers of your code, making them think your stuff actually belongs to Cocoa. Also, your code might break in the future if Apple happens to add a function to Cocoa with the same name as yours. There is no centralized prefix registry, so you can pick your own prefix. Many people prefix names with their initials or company names. To make our examples a little simpler, we won't use a prefix for the code in this book.

Let's take another look at that `NSLog()` statement:

```
NSLog (@"Hello, Objective-C!");
```

Did you notice the at sign before the string? It's not a typo that made it past our vigilant editors. The at sign is one of the features that Objective-C adds to standard C. A string in double quotes preceded by an at sign means that the quoted string should be treated as a Cocoa `NSString` element.

So what's an `NSString` element? Peel the "NS" prefix off the name and you see a familiar term: "String". You already know that a string is a sequence of characters, usually human-readable, so you can probably guess (correctly) that an `NSString` is a sequence of characters in Cocoa.

NSString elements have a huge number of features packed into them and are used by Cocoa any time a string is needed. Here are just a few of the things an NSString can do:

- Tell you its length

- Compare itself to another string

- Convert itself to an integer or floating-point value

That's a whole lot more than you can do with C-style strings. We'll be using and exploring NSString elements much more in Chapter 8.

WATCH THOSE STRINGS

One mistake that's easy to make is to pass a C-style string to NSLog() instead of one of the fancy NSString @"strings" elements. If you do this, the compiler will give you a warning:

```
main.m:46: warning: passing arg 1 of `NSLog' from
        incompatible pointer type
```

If you run this program, it might crash. To catch problems like this, you can tell Xcode to always treat warnings as errors. To do that, select the top item in the Xcode *Groups & Files* list, choose **File ➤ Get Info**, select the *Build* tab, type *error* into the search field, and check the *Treat Warnings as Errors* checkbox, as shown in the following image. Also make sure that the *Configuration* pop-up menu at the top says *All Configurations*.

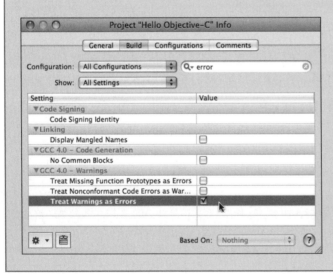

Here's another cool fact about NSString: the name itself highlights one of the nice features of Cocoa. Most Cocoa elements are named in a very straightforward manner, striving to describe the features they implement. For instance, NSArray provides arrays; NSDateFormatter helps you format dates in different ways; NSThread gives you tools for multithreaded programming; and NSSpeechSynthesizer lets you hear speech.

Now, we'll get back to stepping through our little program. The last line of the program is the return statement that ends the execution of main() and finishes the program:

```
return (0);
```

The zero value returned says that our program completed successfully. This is just the way return statements work in C.

Congratulations, again! You've just written, compiled, run, and dissected your first Objective-C program.

Are You the Boolean Type?

Many languages have a Boolean type, which is, of course, a fancy term for variables that store true and false values. Objective-C is no exception.

C has a Boolean data type, bool, which can take on the values true and false. Objective-C provides a similar type, BOOL, which can have the values YES and NO. Objective-C's BOOL type, incidentally, predates C's bool type by over a decade. The two different Boolean types can coexist in the same program, but when you're writing Cocoa code, you'll be using BOOL.

NOTE

BOOL in Objective-C is actually just a type definition (typedef) for the signed character type (signed char), which uses 8 bits of storage. YES is defined as 1 and NO as 0 (using #define).

Objective-C doesn't treat BOOL as a true Boolean type that can hold only YES or NO values. The compiler considers BOOL to be an 8-bit number, and the values of YES and NO are just a convention. This causes a subtle gotcha: if you inadvertently assign an integer value that's more than 1 byte long, such as a short or an int value, to a BOOL variable, only the lowest byte is used for the value of the BOOL. If that byte happens to be zero (as with 8960, which in hexadecimal is 0x2300), the BOOL value will be zero, the NO value.

Mighty BOOL in Action

To show mighty BOOL in action, we move on to our next project, *02.02 - BOOL Party*, which compares pairs of integers to see if they're different. Aside from `main()`, the program defines two functions. The first, `areIntsDifferent()`, takes two integer values and returns a BOOL: YES if the integers are different and NO if they are the same. A second function, `boolString()`, takes a BOOL parameter and returns the string @"YES" if the parameter is YES and @"NO" if the parameter is NO. This is a handy function to have around when you want to print out a human-readable representation of BOOL values. `main()` uses these two functions to compare integers and print out the results.

Creating the project for BOOL Party is exactly the same process as making the project for Hello Objective-C:

1. Launch Xcode, if it's not already running.

2. Select **New Project** from the **File** menu.

3. Choose *Command Line Utility* on the left and *Foundation Tool* on the right.

4. Click *Choose*.

5. Type *BOOL Party* as the *Project Name*, and click *Save*.

Edit *BOOL Party.m* to make it look like this:

```
#import <Foundation/Foundation.h>

// returns NO if the two integers have the same
// value, YES otherwise

BOOL areIntsDifferent (int thing1, int thing2)
{
  if (thing1 == thing2) {
    return (NO);
  } else {
    return (YES);
  }

} // areIntsDifferent


// given a NO value, return the human-readable
// string "NO". Otherwise return "YES"

NSString *boolString (BOOL yesNo)
{
  if (yesNo == NO) {
    return (@"NO");
```

```
  } else {
    return (@"YES");
  }

} // boolString


int main (int argc, const char *argv[])
{
  BOOL areTheyDifferent;

  areTheyDifferent = areIntsDifferent (5, 5);

  NSLog (@"are %d and %d different? %@",
      5, 5, boolString(areTheyDifferent));

  areTheyDifferent = areIntsDifferent (23, 42);

  NSLog (@"are %d and %d different? %@",
      23, 42, boolString(areTheyDifferent));

  return (0);

} // main
```

Build and run your program. You'll need to bring up the *Console* window to see the output, by choosing **Console** from the **Run** menu, or using the keyboard shortcut ⌘⇧R. In the *Run Debugger Console* window, you should see output like the following:

```
2008-07-20 16:47:09.528 02 BOOL Party[16991:10b] are 5 and 5 different? NO
2008-07-20 16:47:09.542 02 BOOL Party[16991:10b] are 23 and 42 different?
YES

The Debugger has exited with status 0.
```

Once again, let's pull this program apart, function by function, and see what's going on. The first function in our tour is areIntsDifferent():

```
BOOL areIntsDifferent (int thing1, int thing2)
{
  if (thing1 == thing2) {
    return (NO);
  } else {
    return (YES);
  }

} // areIntsDifferent
```

The `areIntsDifferent()` function that takes two integer parameters and returns a BOOL value. The syntax should be familiar to you from your C experience. Here you can see `thing1` being compared to `thing2`. If they're the same, NO is returned (since they're not different). If they're different, YES is returned. That's pretty straightforward, isn't it?

WON'T GET BOOLED AGAIN

Experienced C programmers might be tempted to write the `areIntsDifferent()` function as a single statement:

```
BOOL areIntsDifferent_faulty (int thing1, int thing2)
{
   return (thing1 - thing2);
} // areIntsDifferent_faulty
```

They'd do so operating under the assumption that a nonzero value is the same as YES. But that's not the case. Yes, this function returns a value, as far as C is concerned, that is true or false, but callers of functions returning BOOL will expect either YES or NO to be returned. If a programmer tries to use this function as follows, it will fail, since 23 minus 5 is 18:

```
if (areIntsDifferent_faulty(23, 5) == YES) {
   // ....
}
```

While the preceding function may be a true value in C, it is not equal to YES (a value of 1) in Objective-C.

It's a good idea never to compare a BOOL value directly to YES, because too-clever programmers sometimes pull stunts similar to `areIntsDifferent_faulty()`. Instead, write the preceding if statement like this:

```
if (areIntsDifferent_faulty(5, 23)) {
   // ....
}
```

Comparing directly to NO is always safe, since falsehood in C has a single value: zero.

The second function, `boolString()`, maps a numeric BOOL value to a string that's readable by mere humans:

```
NSString *boolString (BOOL yesNo)
{
  if (yesNo == NO) {
    return (@"NO");
  } else {
    return (@"YES");
  }

} // boolString
```

The if statement in the middle of the function should come as no surprise. It just compares yesNo to the constant NO, and returns @"NO" if they match. Otherwise, yesNo must be a true value, so it returns @"YES".

Notice that the return type of boolString() is a pointer to an NSString. This means the function returns one of the fancy Cocoa strings that you saw earlier when you first met NSLog(). If you look at the return statements, you'll see the at sign in front of the returned values, a dead giveaway that they're NSString values.

main() is the final function. After the preliminaries of declaring the return type and arguments for main(), there is a local BOOL variable:

```
int main (int argc, const char *argv[])
{
  BOOL areTheyDifferent;
```

The areTheyDifferent variable holds onto the YES or NO value returned by areIntsDifferent(). We could simply use the function's BOOL return value directly in an if statement, but there's no harm in adding an extra variable like this to make the code easier to read. Deeply nested constructs are often confusing and hard to understand, and they're a good place for bugs to hide.

The Comparison Itself

The next two lines of code compare a couple of integers with areIntsDifferent() and store the return value into the areTheyDifferent variable. NSLog() prints out the numeric values and the human-readable string returned by boolString():

```
  areTheyDifferent = areIntsDifferent (5, 5);

  NSLog (@"are %d and %d different? %@",
      5, 5, boolString(areTheyDifferent));
```

As you saw earlier, NSLog() is basically a Cocoa-flavored printf() function that takes a format string and uses the additional parameters for values to plug in the format specifiers. You can see that the two fives will replace the two %d format placeholders in our call to NSLog().

At the end of the string we're giving to NSLog(), you see another at sign. This time, it's %@. What's that all about? boolString() returns an NSString pointer. printf() has no idea how to work with an NSString, so there is no format specifier we can use. The makers of NSLog() added the %@ format specifier to instruct NSLog() to take the appropriate argument, treat it as an NSString, use the characters from that string, and send it out to the console.

NOTE

We haven't officially introduced you to objects yet, but here's a sneak preview: when you print the values of arbitrary objects with NSLog(), you'll use the %@ format specification. When you use this specifier, the object supplies its own NSLog() format via a method named description. The description method for NSString simply prints the string's characters.

The next two lines are very similar to those you just saw:

```
areTheyDifferent = areIntsDifferent (23, 42);

NSLog (@"are %d and %d different? %@",
    23, 42, boolString(areTheyDifferent));
```

The function compares the values 23 and 42. This time, because they're different, areIntsDifferent() returns YES, and the user sees text stating the monumental fact that 23 and 42 are different values.

Here's the final return statement, which wraps up our BOOL Party:

```
return (0);

} // main
```

In this program, you saw Objective-C's BOOL type, and the constants YES and NO for indicating true and false values. You can use BOOL in the same way you use types such as int and float: as variables, parameters to functions, and return values from functions.

Summary

In this chapter, you wrote your first two Objective-C programs, and it was fun! You also met some of Objective-C's extensions to the language, such as #import, which tells the compiler to bring in header files and to do so only once. You learned about NSString literals, those strings preceded by an at sign, such as @"hello". You used the important and versatile NSLog(), a function Cocoa provides for writing text to the console, and the NSLog() special format specifier, %@, that lets you plug NSString values into NSLog() output. You also gained the secret knowledge that when you see an at sign in code, you know you're looking at an Objective-C extension to the C language.

Stay tuned for our next chapter, in which we'll enter the mysterious world of object-oriented programming.

Chapter 3

Introduction to Object-Oriented Programming

*i*f you've been using and programming computers for any length of time, you've probably heard the term "object-oriented programming" more than once. **Object-oriented programming**, frequently shortened to its initials, OOP, is a programming technique originally developed for writing simulation programs. OOP soon caught on with developers of other kinds of software, such as those involving graphical user interfaces. Before long, "OOP" became a major industry buzzword. It promised to be the magical silver bullet that would make programming simple and joyous.

Of course, nothing can live up to that kind of hype. Like most pursuits, OOP requires study and practice to gain proficiency, but it truly does make some kinds of programming tasks easier and, in some cases, even fun. In this book, we'll be talking about OOP a lot, mainly because Cocoa is based on OOP concepts, and Objective-C is a language that is designed to be object oriented.

So what is OOP? OOP is a way of constructing software composed of objects. Objects are like little machines living inside your computer and talking to each other in order to get work done. In this chapter, we'll look at some basic OOP concepts. After that, we'll examine the style of programming that leads to OOP, describing the motivation behind some OOP features. We'll wrap up with a thorough description of the mechanics of OOP.

NOTE

Like many "new" technologies, the roots of OOP stretch way back into the mists of time. OOP evolved from Simula in the 1960s, Smalltalk in the 1970s, Clascal in the 1980s, and other related languages. Modern languages such as C++, Java, Python, and of course, Objective-C draw inspiration from these older languages.

As we dive into OOP, stick a Babel fish in your ear, and be prepared to encounter some strange terminology along the way. OOP comes with a lot of fancy-sounding lingo that makes it seem more mysterious and difficult than it actually is. You might even think that computer scientists create long, impressive-sounding words to show everyone how smart they are, but of course, they don't all do that. Well, don't worry. We'll explain each term as we encounter it.

Before we get into OOP itself, let's take a look at a key concept of OOP: indirection.

It's All Indirection

An old saying in programming goes something like this, "There is no problem in computer science that can't be solved by adding another level of indirection." **Indirection** is a fancy word with a simple meaning—instead of using a value directly in your code, use a pointer to the value. Here's a real-word example: you might not know the phone number of your favorite pizza place, but you know that you can look in the phone book to find it. Using the phone book like this is a form of indirection.

Indirection can also mean that you ask another person to do something rather than doing it yourself. Let's say you have a box of books to return to your friend Andrew who lives across town. You know that your next-door neighbor is going to visit Andrew tonight. Rather than driving across town, dropping off the books, and driving back, you ask your friendly neighbor to deliver the box. This is another kind of indirection: you have someone else do the work instead of doing it yourself.

In programming, you can take indirection to multiple levels, writing code that consults other code, which accesses yet another level of code. You've probably had the experience of calling a technical support line. You explain your problem to the support person, who then directs you to the specific department that can handle your problem. The person there then directs you to the second-level technician with the skills to help you out. And if you're like us, at this point, you find out you called the wrong number, and you have to be transferred to some other department for help. This runaround is a form of indirection. Luckily, computers have infinite patience and can handle being sent from place to place to place looking for an answer.

Variables and Indirection

You might be surprised to find out that you have already used indirection in your programs. The humble variable is a real-world use of indirection. Consider this small program that prints the numbers from one to five. You can find this program in the *Learn ObjC Projects* folder, in *03.01 Count-1*:

```
#import <Foundation/Foundation.h>

int main (int argc, const char *argv[])
{
  NSLog (@"The numbers from 1 to 5:");

  int i;
  for (i = 1; i <= 5; i++) {
    NSLog (@"%d\n", i);
  }

  return (0);

} // main
```

Count-1 has a for loop that runs five times, using NSLog () to display the value of i each time around. When you run this program, you see output like this:

```
2008-07-20 11:54:20.463 03.01 Count-1[17985:10b] The numbers from 1 to 5:
2008-07-20 11:54:20.466 03.01 Count-1[17985:10b] 1
2008-07-20 11:54:20.466 03.01 Count-1[17985:10b] 2
2008-07-20 11:54:20.466 03.01 Count-1[17985:10b] 3
2008-07-20 11:54:20.467 03.01 Count-1[17985:10b] 4
2008-07-20 11:54:20.467 03.01 Count-1[17985:10b] 5
```

Now, suppose you want to upgrade your program to print the numbers from one to ten. You have to edit your code in two places, which are highlighted in bold in the following listing, and then rebuild the program (this version is in the folder *03.02 Count-2*):

```
#import <Foundation/Foundation.h>

int main (int argc, const char * argv[])
{
  NSLog (@"The numbers from 1 to 10:");

  int i;
  for (i = 1; i <= 10; i++) {
    NSLog (@"%d\n", i);
  }
```

```
    return (0);

} // main
```

Count-2 produces this output:

```
2008-07-20 11:55:35.909 03.02 Count-2[18001:10b] The numbers from 1 to 10:
2008-07-20 11:55:35.926 03.02 Count-2[18001:10b] 1
2008-07-20 11:55:35.927 03.02 Count-2[18001:10b] 2
2008-07-20 11:55:35.928 03.02 Count-2[18001:10b] 3
2008-07-20 11:55:35.935 03.02 Count-2[18001:10b] 4
2008-07-20 11:55:35.936 03.02 Count-2[18001:10b] 5
2008-07-20 11:55:35.936 03.02 Count-2[18001:10b] 6
2008-07-20 11:55:35.939 03.02 Count-2[18001:10b] 7
2008-07-20 11:55:35.939 03.02 Count-2[18001:10b] 8
2008-07-20 11:55:35.940 03.02 Count-2[18001:10b] 9
2008-07-20 11:55:35.940 03.02 Count-2[18001:10b] 10
```

Modifying the program in this way is obviously not a very tricky change to make: you can do it with a simple search-and-replace action, and only two places need to be changed. However, doing a similar search and replace in a larger program, consisting of, say, tens of thousands of lines of code would be a lot trickier. We would have to be careful about simply replacing 5 with 10: no doubt, there would be other instances of the number five that aren't related to this and so shouldn't be changed to ten.

Solving this problem is what variables are for. Rather than sticking the upper loop value (five or ten) directly in the code, we can solve this problem by putting the number in a variable, thus adding a layer of indirection. When you add the variable, instead of telling the program to "go through the loop five times," you're telling it to "go look in this variable named count, which will say how many times to run the loop." Now, the program is called Count-3 and looks like this:

```
#import <Foundation/Foundation.h>

int main (int argc, const char * argv[])
{
  int count = 5;

  NSLog (@"The numbers from 1 to %d:", count);

  int i;
  for (i = 1; i <= count; i++) {
    NSLog (@"%d\n", i);
  }
```

```
    return (0);

} // main
```

The program's output should be unsurprising:

```
2008-07-20 11:58:12.135 03.03 Count-3[18034:10b] The numbers from 1 to 5:
2008-07-20 11:58:12.144 03.03 Count-3[18034:10b] 1
2008-07-20 11:58:12.144 03.03 Count-3[18034:10b] 2
2008-07-20 11:58:12.145 03.03 Count-3[18034:10b] 3
2008-07-20 11:58:12.146 03.03 Count-3[18034:10b] 4
2008-07-20 11:58:12.151 03.03 Count-3[18034:10b] 5
```

NOTE

The NSLog() time stamp and other information take up a lot of space, so for clarity, we'll leave that information out of future listings.

If you want to print the numbers from 1 to 100, you just have to touch the code in one obvious place:

```
#import <Foundation/Foundation.h>

int main (int argc, const char * argv[])
{
  int count = 100;

  NSLog (@"The numbers from 1 to %d:", count);

  int i;
  for (i = 1; i <= count; i++) {
    NSLog (@"%d\n", i);
  }

  return (0);

} // main
```

By adding a variable, our code is now much cleaner and easier to extend, especially when other programmers need to change the code. To change the loop values, they won't have to scrutinize every use of the number five to see if they need to modify it. Instead, they can just change the count variable to get the result they want.

Indirection Through Filenames

Files provide another example of indirection. Consider Word-Length-1, a program that prints a list of words along with their lengths; it is in the *03.04 Word-Length-1* folder. This vital program is the key technology for your new Web 2.0 start-up, Length-o-words.com. Here's the listing:

```
#import <Foundation/Foundation.h>

int main (int argc, const char * argv[])
{
  const char *words[4] = { "aardvark", "abacus",
            "allude", "zygote" };
  int wordCount = 4;

  int i;
  for (i = 0; i < wordCount; i++) {
    NSLog (@"%s is %d characters long",
        words[i], strlen(words[i]));
  }

  return (0);

} // main
```

The `for` loop determines which word in the `words` array is being processed at any time. The `NSLog()` function inside the loop prints out the word using the `%s` format specifier. We use `%s`, because `words` is an array of C strings rather than of `@"NSString"` objects. The `%d` format specifier takes the integer value of the `strlen()` function, which calculates the length of the string, and prints it out along with the word itself.

When you run Word-Length-1, you see informative output like this:

```
aardvark is 8 characters long
abacus is 6 characters long
allude is 6 characters long
zygote is 6 characters long
```

NOTE

We're leaving out the time stamp and process ID that `NSLog()` adds to the output of Word-Length-1.

Now suppose the venture capitalists investing in Length-o-words.com want you to use a different set of words. They've scrutinized your business plan and have concluded that you can sell to a broader market if you use the names of country music stars.

Because we stored the words directly in the program, we have to edit the source, replacing the original word list with the new names. When we edit, we have to be careful with the punctuation, such as the quotes in Joe Bob's name and the commas between entries. Here is the updated program, which can be found in the *03.05 Word-Length-2* folder:

```
#import <Foundation/Foundation.h>

int main (int argc, const char * argv[])
{
  const char *words[4]
    = { "Joe-Bob \"Handyman\" Brown",
        "Jacksonville \"Sly\" Murphy",
        "Shinara Bain",
        "George \"Guitar\" Books" };
  int wordCount = 4;

  int i;
  for (i = 0; i < wordCount; i++) {
    NSLog (@"%s is %d characters long",
        words[i], strlen(words[i]));
  }

  return (0);

} // main
```

Because we were careful with the surgery, the program still works as we expect:

```
Joe-Bob "Handyman" Brown is 24 characters long
Jacksonville "Sly" Murphy is 25 characters long
Shinara Bain is 12 characters long
George "Guitar" Books is 21 characters long
```

Making this change required entirely too much work: we had to edit *Word-Length-2*.m, fix any typos, and then rebuild the program. If the program runs on a web site, we then have to retest and redeploy the program to upgrade to Word-Length-2.

Another way to construct this program is to move the names completely out of the code and put them all into a text file, one name on each line. Let's all say it together: this is indirection. Rather than putting the names directly in the source code, the program looks for the names elsewhere. The program reads a list of names from a text file and proceeds to print them out, along with their lengths. The project files for this new program live in the *03.06 Word-Length-3* folder, and the code looks like this:

```
#import <Foundation/Foundation.h>

int main (int argc, const char * argv[])
{
  FILE *wordFile = fopen ("/tmp/words.txt", "r");
  char word[100];

  while (fgets(word, 100, wordFile)) {
    // strip off the trailing \n
    word[strlen(word) - 1] = '\0';

    NSLog (@"%s is %d characters long",
        word, strlen(word));
  }

  fclose (wordFile);

  return (0);

} // main
```

Let's stroll through Word-Length-3 and see what it's doing. First, fopen() opens the *words. txt* file for reading. Next, fgets() reads a line of text from the file and places it into word. The fgets() call preserves the newline character that separates each line, but we really don't want it: if we leave it, it will be counted as a character in the word. To fix this, we replace the newline character with a zero, which indicates the end of the string. Finally, we use our old friend NSLog() to print out the word and its length.

NOTE

> Take a look at the path name we used with fopen(). It's */tmp/words.txt*. This means that *words.txt* is a file that lives in the */tmp* directory, the Unix temporary directory, which gets emptied when the computer reboots. You can use */tmp* to store scratch files that you want to mess around with but really don't care about keeping. For a real, live program, you'd put your file in a more permanent location, such as the home directory.

Before you run the program, use your text editor to create the file *words.txt* in the */tmp* directory. Type the following names into the file:

```
Joe-Bob "Handyman" Brown
Jacksonville "Sly" Murphy
Shinara Bain
George "Guitar" Books
```

To save a file to the */tmp* directory from a text editor, type the file's text, choose Save, press the slash key (/), type *tmp*, and press Enter.

If you prefer, instead of typing the names, you can copy *words.txt* from the *03.06 Word-Length-3* directory into */tmp*. To see */tmp* in the Finder, choose *Go* ➤ *Go to Folder*.

TIP

> If you're using our prebuilt Word-Length-3 project, we've done a little Xcode magic to copy the *words. txt* file to */tmp* for you. See if you can discover what we did. Here's a hint: look in the *Targets* area in the *Groups & Files* pane.

When you run Word-Length-3, the program's output looks just as it did before:

```
Joe-Bob "Handyman" Brown is 24 characters long
Jacksonville "Sly" Murphy is 25 characters long
Shinara Bain is 12 characters long
George "Guitar" Books is 21 characters long
```

Word-Length-3 is a shining example of indirection. Rather than coding the words directly into your program, you're instead saying, "Go look in */tmp/words.txt* to get the words." With this scheme, we can change the set of words anytime we want, just by editing this text file, without having to change the program. Go ahead and try it out: add a couple of words to your *words.txt* file and rerun the program. We'll wait for you here.

This approach is better, because text files are easier to edit and far less fragile than source code. You can get your nonprogrammer friends to use TextEdit to do the editing. Your marketing staff can keep the list of words up to date, which frees you to work on more interesting tasks.

As you know, people always come along with new ideas for upgrading or enhancing a program. Maybe your investors have decided that counting the length of cooking terms is the new path to profit. Now that your program looks at a file for its data, you can change the set of words all you want without ever having to touch the code.

Despite great advances in indirection, Word-Length-3 is still rather fragile, because it insists on using a full path name to the words file. And that file itself is in a precarious position: if the computer reboots, */tmp/words.txt* vanishes. Also, if others are using the program on your machine with their own */tmp/words.txt* file, they could accidentally stomp on your copy. You could edit the program each time to use a different path, but we already know that that's no fun, so let's add another indirection trick to make our lives easier.

Instead of looking in */tmp/words.txt* to get the words, we'll change the program and tell it to "go look at the first launch parameter of the program to figure out the location of the words file." Here is the Word-Length-4 program (which can be found in the *03.07 Word-Length-4* folder). It uses a command-line parameter to specify the file name. The changes we made to Word-Length-3 are highlighted:

```
#import <Foundation/Foundation.h>

int main (int argc, const char * argv[])
{
   if (argc == 1) {
     NSLog (@"you need to provide a file name");
     return (1);
   }

   FILE *wordFile = fopen (argv[1], "r");
   char word[100];

   while (fgets(word, 100, wordFile)) {
     // strip off the trailing \n
     word[strlen(word) - 1] = '\0';

     NSLog (@"%s is %d characters long",
         word, strlen(word));
   }

   fclose (wordFile);

   return (0);

} // main
```

The loop that processes the file is the same as in Word-Length-3, but the code that sets it up is new and improved. The if statement verifies that the user supplied a path name as a launch parameter. The code consults the argc parameter to main(), which holds the number of launch parameters. Because the program name is always passed as a launch parameter, argc is always 1 or greater. If the user doesn't pass a file path, the value of argc is 1, and we have no file to read, so we print an error message and stop the program.

If the user was thoughtful and provided a file path, argc is greater than one. We then look in the argv array to see what that file path is. argv[1] contains the filename the user has given us. (In case you're curious, the argv[0] parameter holds the name of the program.)

If you're running the program in Terminal, it's easy to specify the name of the file on the command line, like so:

```
$ ./Word-Length-4 /tmp/words.txt
Joe-Bob "Handyman" Brown is 24 characters long
Jacksonville "Sly" Murphy is 25 characters long
Shinara Bain is 12 characters long
George "Guitar" Books is 21 characters long
```

SUPPLYING A FILE PATH IN XCODE

If you're editing the program along with us in Xcode, supplying a file path as you run it is a little more compli-cated. **Launch arguments**, also called **command-line parameters**, are a little trickier to control from Xcode than from Terminal. Here's what you need to do to change the launch arguments:

First, in the Xcode files list, expand *Executables*, and double-click the program name (*Word-Length-4*), as shown in the following screen shot:

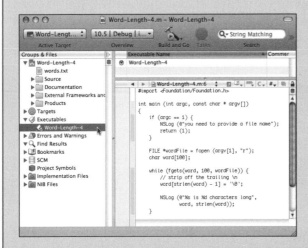

Next, as shown in the following screen shot, click the plus sign in the *Arguments* section, and type the launch argument—in this case, the path to the *words.txt* file:

(Continued)

Now, when you run the program, Xcode passes your launch argument into Word-Length-4's `argv` array. Here's what you'll see when you run the program:

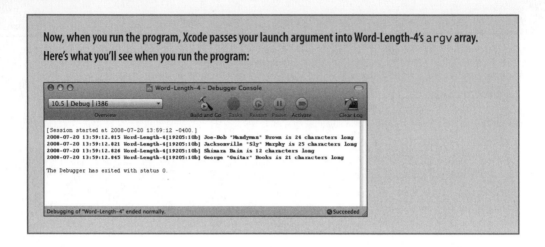

Just for fun, run your program with */usr/share/dict/words*, which has over 230,000 words in it. Your program can handle huge amounts of data! When you get tired of watching words whiz by in the Xcode console window, click the red stop sign to make the program stop.

Because you're supplying arguments at runtime, everybody can use your program to get the length of *any* set of words they want to, even absurdly large sets of words. Users can change the data without changing the code, just as nature intended. This is the essence of indirection: it's telling us where to get the data we need.

Using Indirection in Object-Oriented Programming

Object-oriented programming is all about indirection. OOP uses indirection for accessing data, just as we did in the previous examples by employing variables, files, and arguments. The real revolution of OOP is that it uses indirection for calling *code*. Rather than calling a function directly, you end up calling it indirectly.

Now that you know that, you're an expert in OOP. Everything else is a side effect of this indirection.

Procedural Programming

To complete your appreciation of the flexibility of OOP, we'll take a quick look at procedural programming, so you can get an idea of the kinds of problems that OOP was created to solve. Procedural programming has been around a long, long time, since just after the invention of dirt. Procedural programming is the kind typically taught in introductory programming books and classes. Most programming in languages like BASIC, C, Tcl, and Perl is procedural.

In procedural programs, data is typically kept in simple structures, such as C struct elements. There are also more complex data structures such as linked lists and trees. When you call a function, you pass the data to the function, and it manipulates the data. Functions are the center of the procedural programming experience: you decide which functions you want to use, and then you call those functions, passing in the data they need.

Consider a program that draws a bunch of geometric shapes on the screen. Thanks to the magic of computers, you can do more than consider it—you'll find the source code to this program in the *03.08 Shapes-Procedural* folder. For simplicity's sake, the Shapes-Procedural program doesn't actually draw shapes on the screen, it just quaintly prints out some shape-related text.

Shapes-Procedural uses plain C and the procedural programming style. The code starts out by defining some constants and a structure.

After the obligatory inclusion of the foundation headers is an enumeration that specifies the different kinds of shapes that can be drawn: circle, square, and something vaguely egg-shaped:

```
#import <Foundation/Foundation.h>
typedef enum {
    kCircle,
    kRectangle,
    kOblateSpheroid
} ShapeType;
```

Next is an enum that defines the colors that can be used to draw the shape:

```
typedef enum {
    kRedColor,
    kGreenColor,
    kBlueColor
} ShapeColor;
```

After that, we have a structure that describes a rectangle, which specifies the area on the screen where the shape will be drawn:

```
typedef struct {
    int x, y, width, height;
} ShapeRect;
```

Finally, we have a structure that pulls all these things together to describe a shape:

```
typedef struct {
    ShapeType type;
    ShapeColor fillColor;
    ShapeRect bounds;
} Shape;
```

Next up in our example, `main()` declares an array of shapes we're going to draw. After declaring the array, each shape structure in the array is initialized by assigning its fields. The following code gives us a red circle, a green rectangle, and a blue spheroid:

```
int main (int argc, const char * argv[])
{
  Shape shapes[3];

  ShapeRect rect0 = { 0, 0, 10, 30 };
  shapes[0].type = kCircle;
  shapes[0].fillColor = kRedColor;
  shapes[0].bounds = rect0;

  ShapeRect rect1 = { 30, 40, 50, 60 };
  shapes[1].type = kRectangle;
  shapes[1].fillColor = kGreenColor;
  shapes[1].bounds = rect1;

  ShapeRect rect2 = { 15, 18, 37, 29 };
  shapes[2].type = kOblateSpheroid;
  shapes[2].fillColor = kBlueColor;
  shapes[2].bounds = rect2;

  drawShapes (shapes, 3);

  return (0);

} // main
```

A HANDY C SHORTCUT

The rectangles in the Shapes-Procedural program's `main()` method are declared using a handy little C trick: when you declare a variable that's a structure, you can initialize all the elements of that structure at once.

```
ShapeRect rect0 = { 0, 0, 10, 30 };
```

The structure elements get values in the order they're declared. Recall that ShapeRect is declared like this:

```
typedef struct {
  int x, y, width, height;
} ShapeRect;
```

The preceding assignment to `rect0` means that `rect0.x` and `rect0.y` will both have the value 0; `rect0.width` will be 10; and `rect0.height` will be 30.

This technique lets you reduce the amount of typing in your program without sacrificing readability.

After initializing the shapes array, `main()` calls the `drawShapes()` function to draw the shapes.

`drawShapes()` has a loop that inspects each Shape structure in the array. A `switch` statement looks at the `type` field of the structure and chooses a function that draws the shape. The program calls the appropriate drawing function, passing parameters for the screen area and color to use for drawing. Check it out:

```
void drawShapes (Shape shapes[], int count)
{
  int i;

  for (i = 0; i < count; i++) {

    switch (shapes[i].type) {

    case kCircle:
      drawCircle (shapes[i].bounds,
           shapes[i].fillColor);
      break;

    case kRectangle:
      drawRectangle (shapes[i].bounds,
            shapes[i].fillColor);
      break;

    case kOblateSpheroid:
      drawEgg (shapes[i].bounds,
          shapes[i].fillColor);
      break;
    }
  }

} // drawShapes
```

Here is the code for `drawCircle()`, which just prints out the bounding rectangle and the color passed to it:

```
void drawCircle (ShapeRect bounds,
       ShapeColor fillColor)
{
  NSLog (@"drawing a circle at (%d %d %d %d) in %@",
      bounds.x, bounds.y,
      bounds.width, bounds.height,
      colorName(fillColor));

} // drawCircle
```

The colorName() function called inside NSLog() simply does a switch on the passed-in color value and returns a literal NSString such as @"red" or @"blue":

```
NSString *colorName (ShapeColor colorName)
{
  switch (colorName) {
    case kRedColor:
      return @"red";
      break;
    case kGreenColor:
      return @"green";
      break;
    case kBlueColor:
      return @"blue";
      break;
  }

  return @"no clue";

} // colorName
```

The other draw functions are almost identical to drawCircle, except that they draw a rectangle and an egg.

Here is the output of Shapes-Procedural (minus the time stamp and other information added by NSLog()):

```
drawing a circle at (0 0 10 30) in red
drawing a rectangle at (30 40 50 60) in green
drawing an egg at (15 18 37 29) in blue
```

This all seems pretty simple and straightforward, right? When you use procedural programming, you spend your time connecting data with the functions designed to deal with that type of data. You have to be careful to use the right function for each data type: for example, you must call drawRectangle() for a shape of type kRectangle. It's disappointingly easy to pass a rectangle to a function meant to work with circles.

Another problem with coding like this is that it can make extending and maintaining the program difficult. To illustrate, let's enhance Shapes-Procedural to add a new kind of shape: a triangle. You can find the modified program in the *03.09 Shapes-Procedural-2* project. We have to modify the program in at least four different places to accomplish this task.

First, we'll add a kTriangle constant to the ShapeType enum:

```
typedef enum {
  kCircle,
  kRectangle,
  kOblateSpheroid,
  kTriangle
} ShapeType;
```

Then, we'll implement a drawTriangle() function that looks just like its siblings:

```
void drawTriangle (ShapeRect bounds,
          ShapeColor fillColor)
{
  NSLog (@"drawing triangle at (%d %d %d %d) in %@",
      bounds.x, bounds.y,
      bounds.width, bounds.height,
      colorName(fillColor));

} // drawTriangle
```

Next, we'll add a new case to the switch statement in drawShapes(). This will test for kTriangle and will call drawTriangle() if appropriate:

```
void drawShapes (Shape shapes[], int count)
{
  int i;

  for (i = 0; i < count; i++) {

    switch (shapes[i].type) {

    case kCircle:
      drawCircle (shapes[i].bounds,
          shapes[i].fillColor);
      break;

    case kRectangle:
      drawRectangle (shapes[i].bounds,
          shapes[i].fillColor);
      break;

    case kOblateSpheroid:
      drawEgg (shapes[i].bounds,
          shapes[i].fillColor);
      break;
```

```
      case kTriangle:
        drawTriangle (shapes[i].bounds,
                shapes[i].fillColor);
        break;
      }
    }

} // drawShapes
```

Finally, we'll add a triangle to the shapes array. Don't forget to increase the number of shapes in the shapes array:

```
int main (int argc, const char * argv[])
{
  Shape shapes[4];

  ShapeRect rect0 = { 0, 0, 10, 30 };
  shapes[0].type = kCircle;
  shapes[0].fillColor = kRedColor;
  shapes[0].bounds = rect0;

  ShapeRect rect1 = { 30, 40, 50, 60 };
  shapes[1].type = kRectangle;
  shapes[1].fillColor = kGreenColor;
  shapes[1].bounds = rect1;

  ShapeRect rect2 = { 15, 18, 37, 29 };
  shapes[2].type = kOblateSpheroid;
  shapes[2].fillColor = kBlueColor;
  shapes[2].bounds = rect2;

  ShapeRect rect3 = { 47, 32, 80, 50 };
  shapes[3].type = kTriangle;
  shapes[3].fillColor = kRedColor;
  shapes[3].bounds = rect3;

  drawShapes (shapes, 4);

  return (0);

} // main
```

OK, let's take a look at Shapes-Procedural-2 in action:

```
drawing a circle at (0 0 10 30) in red
drawing a rectangle at (30 40 50 60) in green
drawing an egg at (15 18 37 29) in blue
drawing a triangle at (47 32 80 50) in red
```

Adding support for triangles wasn't too bad, but our little program only does one kind of action—drawing shapes. The more complex the program, the trickier it is to extend. For example, let's say the program does more messing around with shapes; suppose it computes their areas and determines if the mouse pointer lies within them. In that case, you'll have to modify every function that performs an action on shapes, touching code that has been working perfectly and possibly introducing errors.

Here's another scenario that's fraught with peril: adding a new shape that needs more information to describe it. For example, a rounded rectangle needs to know its bounding rectangle as well as the radius of the rounded corners. To support rounded rectangles, you could add a radius field to the Shape structure, which is a waste of space, because the field won't be used by other shapes, or you could use a C union to overlay different data layouts in the same structure, which complicates things by making all shapes dig into the union to get to their interesting data.

OOP addresses these problems elegantly. As we teach our program to use OOP, we'll see how OOP handles the first problem, modifying already-working code to add new kinds of shapes.

Implementing Object Orientation

Procedural programs are based on functions. The data orbits around the functions. Object orientation reverses this point of view, placing a program's data at the center, with the functions orbiting around the data. Instead of focusing on functions in your programs, you concentrate on the data.

That sounds interesting, but how does it work? In OOP, data contains references to the code that operates on it, using indirection. Rather than telling the drawRectangle() function to "go draw a rectangle using this shape structure," you instead ask a rectangle to "go draw yourself" (gosh, that sounds rude, but it's really not). Through the magic of indirection, the rectangle's data knows how to find the function that will perform the drawing.

So what exactly is an object? It's nothing more than a fancy C struct that has the ability to find code it's associated with, usually via a function pointer. Figure 3-1 shows four Shape objects: two squares, a circle, and a spheroid. Each object is able to find a function to do its drawing.

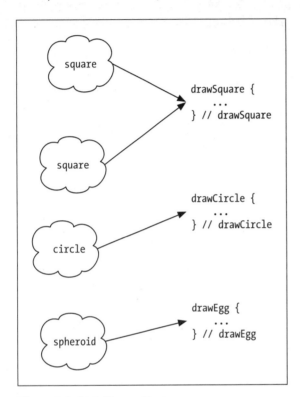

Figure 3-1. *Basic Shape objects*

Each object has its own draw() function that knows how to draw its specific shape. For example, a Circle object's draw() knows to draw a circle. A Rectangle's draw() knows to draw four straight lines that form a rectangle.

The Shapes-Object program (available at *03.10 - Shapes-Object*) does the same stuff as Shapes-Procedural but uses Objective-C's object-oriented features to do it. Here's drawShapes() from Shapes-Object:

```
void drawShapes (id shapes[], int count)
{
  int i;

  for (i = 0; i < count; i++) {
    id shape = shapes[i];
    [shape draw];
  }

} // drawShapes;
```

This function contains a loop that looks at each shape in the array. In the loop, the program tells the shape to draw itself.

Notice the differences between this version of drawShapes() and the original. For one thing, this one is a lot shorter! The code doesn't have to ask each individual shape what kind it is.

Another change is shapes[], the first argument to the function: it's now an array of id objects. What is an id? Is it a psychological term referring to the part of the mind in which innate instinctive impulses and primary processes are manifest? Not in this case: it stands for **identifier**, and it's pronounced "eye dee." An id is a generic type that's used to refer to any kind of object. Recall that an object is just a C struct with some code attached, so an id is actually a pointer to one of these structures; in this case, the structures make various kinds of shapes.

The third change to drawShapes() is the body of the loop:

```
id shape = shapes[i];
[shape draw];
```

The first line looks like ordinary C. The code gets the id—that is, a pointer to an object— from the shapes array and sticks it into the variable named shape, which has the type id. This is just a pointer assignment: it doesn't actually copy the entire contents of the shape. Take a look at Figure 3-2 to see the various shapes available in Shapes-Object. shapes[0] is a pointer to the red circle; shapes[1] is a pointer to a green rectangle; and shapes[2] is a pointer to a blue egg.

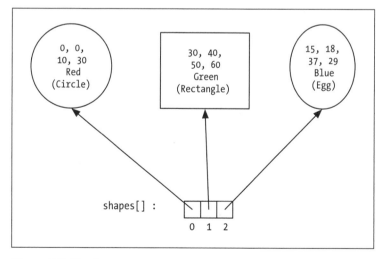

Figure 3-2. *The shapes array*

Now we've come to the last line of code in the function:

```
[shape draw];
```

This is seriously weird. What's going on? We know that C uses square brackets to refer to array elements, but we're don't seem to be doing anything with arrays here. In Objective-C, square brackets have an additional meaning: they're used to tell an object what to do. Inside the square brackets, the first item is an object, and the rest is an action that you want the object to perform. In this case, we're telling an object named shape to perform the action draw. If shape is a circle, a circle is drawn. If shape is a rectangle, we'll get a rectangle.

In Objective-C, telling an object to do an action is called **sending a message** (although some folks also say "calling a method"). The code [shape draw] sends the message draw to the object shape. One way to pronounce [shape draw] is "send draw to shape." How the shape actually does the drawing is up to the shape's implementation.

When you send a message to an object, how does the necessary code get called? This happens with the assistance of behind-the-scenes helpers called **classes**.

Take a look at Figure 3-3 please. The left side of the figure shows that this is the circle object at index zero of the shapes array, last seen in Figure 3-2. The object has a pointer to its class. The class is a structure that tells how to be an object of its kind. In Figure 3-3, the Circle class has a pointer to code for drawing circles, for calculating the area of circles, and other stuff required in order to be a good Circle citizen.

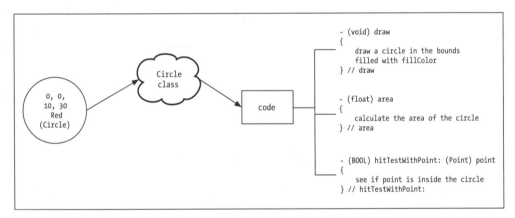

Figure 3-3. *A circle and its class*

What's the point of having class objects? Wouldn't it be simpler just to have each object point directly to its code? Indeed, it would be simpler, and some OOP systems do just that. But having class objects is a great advantage: if you change the class at runtime, all objects of that class automatically pick up the changes (we'll discuss this more in later chapters).

Figure 3-4 shows how the draw message ends up calling the right function for the circle object.

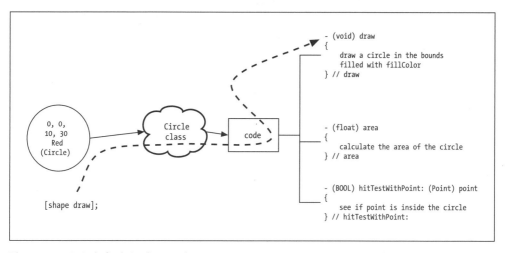

Figure 3-4. *A circle finds its draw code.*

Here are the steps illustrated in Figure 3-4:

1. The object that is the target of the message (the red circle in this case) is consulted to see what its class is.

2. The class looks through its code and finds out where the draw function is.

3. Once it's found, the function that draws circles is executed.

Figure 3-5 shows what happens when you call [shape draw] on the second shape in the array, which is the green rectangle.

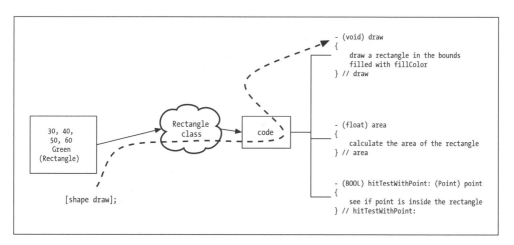

Figure 3-5. *A rectangle finds its draw code.*

The steps used in Figure 3-5 are nearly identical those in the previous image:

1. The target object of the message (the green rectangle) is consulted to see what its class is.

2. The rectangle class checks its pile of code and gets the address of the draw function.

3. Objective-C runs the code that draws a rectangle.

This program shows some very cool indirection in action! In the procedural version of the program, we had to write code that determined which function to call. Now, that decision is made behind the scenes by Objective-C, as it asks the objects which class they belong to. This reduces the chance of calling the wrong function and makes our code easier to maintain.

Time Out for Terminology

Before we dig into the rest of the Shapes-Object program, let's take a moment to go over some object-oriented terminology. We've already talked about some of these terms; others are brand new.

- A **class** is a structure that represents an object's type. An object refers to its class to get various information about itself, particularly what code to run to handle each action. Simple programs might have a handful of classes; moderately complex ones will have a couple of dozen. Objective-C style encourages developers to capitalize class names.

- An **object** is structure containing values and a hidden pointer to its class. Running programs typically have hundreds or thousands of objects. Objective-C variables that refer to objects are typically not capitalized.

- **Instance** is another word for "object." For example, a circle object can also be called an instance of class Circle.

- A **message** is an action that an object can perform. This is what you send to an object to tell it to do something. In the [shape draw] code, the draw message is sent to the shape object to tell it to draw itself. When an object receives a message, its class is consulted to find the proper code to run.

- A **method** is code that runs in response to a message. A message, such as draw, can invoke different methods depending on the class of the object.

- The **method dispatcher** is the mechanism used by Objective-C to divine which method will be executed in response to a particular message. We'll get out our shovels and dig a lot more into the Objective-C method dispatch mechanism in the next chapter.

Those are the key OOP terms you'll need for the rest of this book. In addition, there are a couple of generic programming terms that will soon become very important:

- The **interface** is the description of the features provided by a class of objects. For example, the interface for class `Circle` declares that circles can accept the draw message.

NOTE

The concept of interfaces is not limited to OOP. For example, header files in C provide interfaces for libraries such as the standard I/O library (which you get when you `#include <stdio.h>`), and the math library (`#include <math.h>`). Interfaces do not provide implementation details, and the general idea is that you shouldn't care about them.

- The **implementation** is the code that makes the interface work. In our examples, the implementation for the circle object holds the code for drawing a circle on the screen. When you send the draw message to a circle object, you don't know or care how the function works, just that it draws a circle on the screen.

OOP in Objective-C

If your brain is starting to hurt now, that's OK. We've been filling it up with a lot of new stuff, and assimilating all the terms and technology will take awhile. While your subconscious is chewing on the previous couple of sections, let's take a look at the rest of the code for Shapes-Object, including some new syntax for declaring classes.

The @interface Section

Before you can create objects of a particular class, the Objective-C compiler needs some information about that class. Specifically, it has to know about the data members of the object (that is, what the C `struct` for the object looks like) and which features it provides. You use the `@interface` directive to give this information to the compiler.

NOTE

In Shapes-Object, we put everything into its *Shapes-Object.m* file. In larger programs, you'll use multiple files, giving each class its own set of files. We'll explore ways of organizing classes and files in Chapter 6.

Here is the interface for the Circle class:

```
@interface Circle : NSObject
{
  ShapeColor  fillColor;
  ShapeRect   bounds;
}

- (void) setFillColor: (ShapeColor) fillColor;

- (void) setBounds: (ShapeRect) bounds;

- (void) draw;

@end // Circle
```

This code includes some syntax we haven't talked about yet, so let's do that. A lot of information is packed into these few lines. Let's pull them apart.

The first line looks like this:

```
@interface Circle : NSObject
```

As we said in Chapter 2, whenever you see an at sign in Objective-C, you're looking at an extension to the C language. @interface Circle says to the compiler, "Here comes the interface for a new class named Circle."

NOTE

NSObject in the @interface line tells the compiler that the Circle class is based on the NSObject class. This statement says that every Circle is also an NSObject, and every Circle will inherit all the behaviors that are defined by class NSObject. We'll explore inheritance in much greater detail in the next chapter.

After starting to declare a new class, we tell the compiler about the various pieces of data that circle objects need:

```
{
  ShapeColor  fillColor;
  ShapeRect   bounds;
}
```

The stuff between the curly braces is a template used to churn out new Circle objects. It says that when a new Circle object is created, it will be made up of two elements. The first, fillColor, of type ShapeColor, is the color used to draw the circle. The second, bounds, is the circle's bounding rectangle. Its type is `ShapeRect`. This rectangle tells where the circle will be drawn on the screen.

You specify `fillColor` and bounds in the class declaration. Then, every time a `Circle` object is created, it includes these two elements. So, every object of class `Circle` has its own `fillColor` and its own bounds. The `fillColor` and bounds values are called **instance variables** for objects of class `Circle`.

The closing brace tells the compiler we're done specifying the instance variables for `Circle`.

What follows are some lines that look kind of like C function prototypes:

```
- (void) draw;

- (void) setFillColor: (ShapeColor) fillColor;

- (void) setBounds: (ShapeRect) bounds;
```

In Objective-C, these are called **method declarations**. They're a lot like good old-fashioned C function prototypes, which are a way of saying, "Here are the features I support." The method declarations give the name of each method, the method's return type, and any arguments.

Let's start out with the simplest one, `draw`:

```
- (void) draw;
```

The leading dash signals that this is the declaration for an Objective-C method. That's one way you can distinguish a method declaration from a function prototype, which has no leading dash. Following the dash is the return type for the method, enclosed in parentheses. In our case, `draw` just draws and won't be returning anything. Objective-C uses `void` to indicate that there's no return value.

Objective-C methods can return the same types as C functions: standard types (`int`, `float`, and `char`), pointers, object references, and structures.

The next method declarations are more interesting:

```
- (void) setFillColor: (ShapeColor) fillColor;

- (void) setBounds: (ShapeRect) bounds;
```

Each of these methods takes a single argument. `setFillColor:` takes a color for its argument. Circles use this color when they draw themselves. `setBounds:` takes a rectangle. Circles use this rectangle to define their bounds.

GET YOUR INFIX HERE

Objective-C uses a syntax technique called **infix notation**. The name of the method and its arguments are all intertwined. For instance, you call a single-argument method like this:

```
[circle setFillColor: kRedColor];
```

A method that takes two arguments is called like this:

```
 [textThing setStringValue: @"hello there"
        color: kBlueColor];
```

The `setStringValue:` and `color:` thingies are the names of the arguments (and are actually part of the method name—more on that later), and `@"hello there"` and `kBlueColor` are the arguments being passed.

This syntax differs from C, in which you call a function with its name followed by all its arguments, like so:

```
setTextThingValueColor (textThing, @"hello there",
        kBlueColor);
```

We really like the infix syntax, although it does look a little weird at first. It makes the code very readable, and it's easy to match arguments with what they do. With C and C++ code, you'll sometimes have four or five arguments to a function, and knowing exactly which argument does what without consulting the documentation can be difficult.

The `setFillColor:` declaration starts out with the usual leading dash and the return type in parentheses:

```
- (void)
```

As with the draw method, the leading dash says, "This is the declaration for a new method." The (void) says that this method will not return anything. Let's continue with the code:

```
setFillColor:
```

The name of the method is `setFillColor:`. The trailing colon is part of the name. It's a clue to compilers and humans that a parameter is coming next.

```
 (ShapeColor) fillColor;
```

The type of the argument is specified in parentheses, and in this case, it's one of our ShapeColor values (kRedColor, kBlueColor, and so on). The name that follows, fillColor, is the parameter name. You use this name to refer to the parameter in the body of the method. You can make your code easier to read by choosing meaningful parameter names, rather than naming them after your pets or favorite superheroes.

CALLIN' ALL COLONS

It's important to remember that the colon is a very significant part of the method's name. The method

```
- (void) scratchTheCat;
```

is distinct from

```
- (void) scratchTheCat: (CatType) critter;
```

A common mistake made by many freshly minted Objective-C programmers is to indiscriminantly add a colon to the end of a method name that has no arguments. In the face of a compiler error, you might be tempted to toss in an extra colon and hope it fixes things. The rule to follow is this: If a method takes an argument, it has a colon. If it takes no arguments, it has no colons.

The declaration of setBounds: is exactly the same as the one for setFillColor:, except that the type of the argument is ShapeRect rather than ShapeColor.

The last line tells the compiler we're finished with the declaration of the Circle class:

```
@end // Circle
```

Even though it's not required, we advocate putting comments on all @end statements noting the class name. This makes it easy to know what you're looking at if you've scrolled to the end of a file or you're on the last page of a long printout.

That's the complete interface for the Circle class. Now anyone reading the code knows that that this class has a couple of instance variables and three methods. One method sets the bounds; one sets the color; and the third draws the shape.

Now that we have the interface done, it's time to write the code that makes this class actually do stuff. You didn't think we were done, did you?

The @implementation Section

The @interface section, which we just discussed, defines a class's public interface. The interface is often called the API, which is a TLA for "application programming interface" (and TLA is a TLA for "three-letter acronym"). The actual code to make objects work is found in the @implementation section.

Here is the implementation for class Circle in its entirety:

```
@implementation Circle

- (void) setFillColor: (ShapeColor) c
{
  fillColor = c;
```

```
} // setFillColor


- (void) setBounds: (ShapeRect) b
{
  bounds = b;
} // setBounds


- (void) draw
{
  NSLog (@"drawing a circle at (%d %d %d %d) in %@",
      bounds.x, bounds.y,
      bounds.width, bounds.height,
      colorName(fillColor));
} // draw

@end // Circle
```

Now we'll examine the code in detail, in our customary fashion. The implementation for Circle starts out with this line:

```
@implementation Circle
```

@implementation is a compiler directive that says you're about to present the code for the guts of a class. The name of the class appears after @implementation. There is no trailing semicolon on this line, because you don't need semicolons after Objective-C compiler directives.

The definitions of the individual methods are next. They don't have to appear in the same order as they do in the @interface directive. You can even define methods in an @implementation that don't have a corresponding declaration in the @interface. You can think of these as private methods, used just in the implementation of the class.

NOTE

> You might think that defining a method solely in the @implementation directive makes it inaccessible from outside the implementation, but that's not the case. Objective-C doesn't really have private methods. There is no way to mark a method as being private and preventing other code from calling it. This is a side effect of Objective-C's dynamic nature.

setFillColor: is the first method defined:

```
- (void) setFillColor: (ShapeColor) c
{
  fillColor = c;
} // setFillColor
```

The first line of the definition of setFillColor: looks a lot like the declaration in the @interface section. The main difference is that this one doesn't have a semicolon at the end. You may notice that we renamed the parameter to simply c. It's OK for the parameter names to differ between the @interface and the @implementation. In this case, if we had left the parameter name as fillColor, it would have hidden the fillColor instance variable and generated a warning from the compiler.

NOTE

Why exactly do we have to rename fillColor? We already have an instance variable named fillColor defined by the class. We can refer to that variable in this method—it's in scope. So, if we define another variable with the same name, the compiler will cut off our access from the instance variable. Using the same variable name hides the original variable. We avoid this problem by using a new name for the parameter. We could have named the instance variable something else, like myFillColor, and then we could have kept fillColor as the parameter name. As you'll see later in Chapter 16, Cocoa can do some magic if we name our instance variable similar to how we name our methods.

In the @interface section, we used the name fillColor in the method declaration because it tells the reader exactly what the argument is for. In the implementation, we have to distinguish between the parameter name and the instance variable name, and it's easiest to simply rename the parameter.

The body of the method is one line:

```
fillColor = c;
```

If you're extra curious, you might wonder where the instance variables are stored. When you call a method in Objective-C, a secret hidden parameter called self is passed to the receiving object that refers to the receiving object. For example, in the code [circle setFillColor: kRedColor], the method passes circle as its self parameter. Because self is passed secretly and automatically, you don't have to do it yourself. Code inside a method that refers to instance variables works like this:

```
self->fillColor = c;
```

By the way, passing hidden arguments is yet another example of indirection in action (bet you thought we were all done talking about indirection, huh?). Because the Objective-C runtime can pass different objects as the hidden self parameter, it can change which objects get their instance variables changed.

NOTE

The Objective-C runtime is the chunk of code that supports applications, including ours, when users are running them. The runtime performs important tasks like sending messages to objects and passing parameters. You'll learn more about the runtime in future chapters, starting with Chapter 9.

The second method, setBounds:, is just like our setFillColor: method:

```
- (void) setBounds: (ShapeRect) b
{
  bounds = b;
} // setBounds
```

This code sets a circle object's bounding rectangle to be the rectangle that's passed in.

The last method is our draw method. Note that there's not a colon at the end of the method's name, which tells us that it doesn't take any arguments:

```
- (void) draw
{
  NSLog (@"drawing a circle at (%d %d %d %d) in %@",
      bounds.x, bounds.y,
      bounds.width, bounds.height,
      colorName(fillColor));
} // draw
```

The draw method uses the hidden self parameter to find the values of its instance variables, just as setFillColor: and setBounds: did. This method then uses NSLog() to print out the text for all the world to see.

The @interface and @implementation for the other classes (Rectangle and OblateSphereoid) are nearly identical to those for Circle.

Instantiating Objects

Now we're ready for the final, meaty part of Shapes-Object, in which we create lovely shape objects, such as red circles and green rectangles. The big-money word for this process is **instantiation**. When you instantiate an object, memory is allocated, and then that memory is initialized to some useful default values—that is, something other than the random values you get with freshly allocated memory. When the allocation and initialization steps are done, we say that a new object **instance** has been created.

NOTE

> Because an object's local variables are specific to that instance of the object, we call them **instance variables**, often shortened to "ivars."

To create a new object, we send the new message to the class we're interested in. Once the class receives and handles the new message, we'll have a new object instance to play with.

One of the nifty features of Objective-C is that you can treat a class just like an object and send it messages. This is handy for behavior that isn't tied to one particular object but is global to the class. The best example of this kind of message is allocating a new object. When you want a new circle, it's appropriate to ask the Circle class for that new object, rather than asking an existing circle.

Here is Shapes-Object's main() function, which creates the circle, rectangle, and spheroid:

```
int main (int argc, const char * argv[])
{
  id shapes[3];

  ShapeRect rect0 = { 0, 0, 10, 30 };
  shapes[0] = [Circle new];
  [shapes[0] setBounds: rect0];
  [shapes[0] setFillColor: kRedColor];

  ShapeRect rect1 = { 30, 40, 50, 60 };
  shapes[1] = [Rectangle new];
  [shapes[1] setBounds: rect1];
  [shapes[1] setFillColor: kGreenColor];

  ShapeRect rect2 = { 15, 19, 37, 29 };
  shapes[2] = [OblateSphereoid new];
  [shapes[2] setBounds: rect2];
  [shapes[2] setFillColor: kBlueColor];

  drawShapes (shapes, 3);

  return (0);

} // main
```

You can see that Shapes-Object's `main()` is very similar to Shapes-Procedural's. There are a couple of differences, though. Instead of an array of shapes, Shapes-Object has an array of `id` elements (which you probably remember are pointers to any kind of object). You create individual objects by sending the new message to the class of object you want to create:

```
...
shapes[0] = [Circle new];
...
shapes[1] = [Rectangle new];
...
shapes[2] = [OblateSphereoid new];
...
```

Another difference is that Shapes-Procedural initializes objects by assigning `struct` members directly. Shapes-Object, on the other hand, doesn't muck with the object directly. Instead, Shapes-Object uses messages to ask each object to set its bounding rectangle and fill color:

```
...
[shapes[0] setBounds: rect0];
[shapes[0] setFillColor: kRedColor];
...
[shapes[1] setBounds: rect1];
[shapes[1] setFillColor: kGreenColor];
...
[shapes[2] setBounds: rect2];
[shapes[2] setFillColor: kBlueColor];
...
```

After this initialization frenzy, the shapes are drawn using the `drawShapes()` function we looked at earlier, like so:

```
drawShapes (shapes, 3);
```

Extending Shapes-Object

Remember when we added triangles to the Shapes-Procedural program? Let's do the same for Shapes-Object. The task should be a lot neater this time. You can find the project for this in the *03.11 Shapes-Object-2* folder of *Learn ObjC Projects*.

We had to do a lot of stuff to teach Shapes-Procedural-2 about triangles: edit the `ShapeType` enum, add a `drawTriangle()` function, add a triangle to the list of shapes, and modify the `drawShapes()` function. Some of the work was pretty invasive, especially the surgery done to `drawShapes()`, in which we had to edit the loop that controls the drawing of all shapes, potentially introducing errors.

With Shapes-Object-2, we only have to do two things: create a new `Triangle` class, and then add a `Triangle` object to the list of objects to draw.

Here is the `Triangle` class, which happens to be exactly the same as the `Circle` class with all occurrences of "Circle" changed to "Triangle":

```
@interface Triangle : NSObject
{
  ShapeColor   fillColor;
  ShapeRect    bounds;
}

- (void) setFillColor: (ShapeColor) fillColor;
- (void) setBounds: (ShapeRect) bounds;

- (void) draw;

@end // Triangle


@implementation Triangle

- (void) setFillColor: (ShapeColor) c
{
  fillColor = c;
} // setFillColor


- (void) setBounds: (ShapeRect) b
{
  bounds = b;
} // setBounds


- (void) draw
{
  NSLog (@"drawing a triangle at (%d %d %d %d) in %@",
      bounds.x, bounds.y,
      bounds.width, bounds.height,
      colorName(fillColor));
} // draw

@end // Triangle
```

> **NOTE**
>
> One drawback to **cut and paste programming**, like our `Triangle` class, is that it tends to create a lot of duplicated code, like the `setBounds:` and `setFillColor:` methods. We'll introduce you to inheritance in the next chapter, which is a fine way to avoid redundant code like this.

Next, we need to edit `main()` so it will create the new triangle. First, change the size of the shapes array from 3 to 4 so it will have enough room to store the new object:

```
id shapes[4];
```

After that, add a block of code that creates a new `Triangle`, just like we create a new `Rectangle` or `Circle`:

```
ShapeRect rect3 = { 47, 32, 80, 50 };
shapes[3] = [Triangle new];
[shapes[3] setBounds: rect3];
[shapes[3] setFillColor: kRedColor];
```

And finally, update the call to `drawShapes()` with the new length of the shapes array:

```
drawShapes (shapes, 4);
```

And that's it. Our program now understands triangles:

```
drawing a circle at (0 0 10 30) in red
drawing a rectangle at (30 40 50 60) in green
drawing an egg at (15 19 37 29) in blue
drawing a triangle at (47 32 80 50) in red
```

Note that we were able to add this new functionality without touching the `drawShapes()` function or any other functions that deal with shapes. That's the power of object-oriented programming at work.

> **NOTE**
>
> The code in Shapes-Object-2 provides an example of object-oriented programming guru Bertrand Meyer's Open/Closed Principle, which says that software entities should be open for extension but closed for modification. The `drawShapes()` function is open to extension: just add a new kind of shape object to the array to draw. `drawShapes()` is also closed to modification: we can extend it without modifying it. Software that adheres to the Open-Closed Principle tends to be more robust in the face of change, because you don't have to edit code that's already working correctly.

Summary

This is a big, head-space chapter—one with lots of concepts and ideas—and it's a long chapter, too. We talked about the powerful concept of indirection and showed that you've already been using indirection in your programs, such as when you deal with variables and files. Then we discussed procedural programming and showed you some of the limitations caused by its "functions first, data second" view of the world.

We introduced object-oriented programming, which uses indirection to tightly associate data with code that operates on it. This permits a "data first, functions second" style of programming. We talked about messages, which are sent to objects. The objects handle these messages by executing methods, the chunks of code that make the object sing and dance. You also learned that every method call includes a hidden parameter named `self`, which is the object itself. By using this `self` parameter, methods find and manipulate the object's data. The implementation for the methods and a template for the object's data are defined by the object's class. You create a new object by sending the new message to the class.

Coming up in our next chapter is inheritance, a feature that lets you leverage the behavior of existing objects so you can write less code to do your work. Hey, that sounds great! We'll see you there!

Chapter 4

Inheritance

When you write an object-oriented program—and we hope you're going to write *a lot* of them—the classes and objects you create have relationships with each other. They work together to make your program do its thing.

Two aspects of OOP are most important when dealing with relationships between classes and objects. The first is **inheritance**, the subject of this chapter. When you create a new class, it's often useful to define the new class in terms of its differences from another, already existing class. Using inheritance, you can define a class that has all the capabilities of a parent class: it *inherits* those capabilities.

The other OOP technique used with related classes is **composition**, in which objects contain references to other objects. For example, a car object in a racing simulator might have four tire objects that it uses during game play. When your object keeps references to others, you can take advantage of features offered by the others: that's composition. We'll cover composition in the next chapter.

Why Use Inheritance?

Remember our old friend the Shapes-Object program from the previous chapter? It contained several classes that had very similar interfaces and implementations. And, of course, they're similar because we created them by cutting and pasting.

We'll jog your memory by presenting the interfaces for the Circle and Rectangle classes:

```
@interface Circle : NSObject
{
  ShapeColor  fillColor;
  ShapeRect   bounds;
```

```
}

- (void) setFillColor: (ShapeColor) fillColor;
- (void) setBounds: (ShapeRect) bounds;
- (void) draw;
@end // Circle

@interface Rectangle : NSObject
{
  ShapeColor  fillColor;
  ShapeRect   bounds;
}

- (void) setFillColor: (ShapeColor) fillColor;
- (void) setBounds: (ShapeRect) bounds;
- (void) draw;
@end // Rectangle
```

The interfaces for these classes are much alike, very, *very* much alike. In fact, except for the class names, they're identical twins.

The implementations of Circle and Rectangle are also very similar. Recall from the previous chapter that setFillColor: and setBounds: are identical in the two classes:

```
@implementation Circle
- (void) setFillColor: (ShapeColor) c
{
  fillColor = c;
} // setFillColor

- (void) setBounds: (ShapeRect) b
{
  bounds = b;
} // setBounds

// ...

@end // Circle

@implementation Rectangle
- (void) setFillColor: (ShapeColor) c
{
```

```
  fillColor = c;
} // setFillColor

- (void) setBounds: (ShapeRect) b
{
  bounds = b;
} // setBounds

// ...

@end // Rectangle
```

These methods do exactly the same job; they set the `fillColor` and bounds instance variables. However, the implementations of `Circle` and `Rectangle` are not identical. For example, the draw method's signature, that is, the method's name and parameters, is the same in both classes, but the implementations differ:

```
@implementation Circle

// ...

- (void) draw
{
  NSLog (@"drawing a circle at (%d %d %d %d) in %@",
        bounds.x, bounds.y,
        bounds.width, bounds.height,
        colorName(fillColor));
} // draw
@end // Circle

@implementation Rectangle

// ...

- (void) draw
{
  NSLog (@"drawing rect at (%d %d %d %d) in %@",
        bounds.x, bounds.y,
        bounds.width, bounds.height,
        colorName(fillColor));
} // draw
@end // Rectangle
```

Shapes-Object clearly duplicates a lot of code and behavior between the `Circle` and `Rectangle` classes. Figure 4-1 is a diagram of the classes.

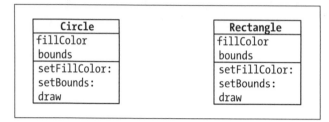

Figure 4-1. *Shapes-Object architecture without inheritance*

<u>NOTE</u>

In Figure 4-1, the name of the class is at the top of each box. The middle section gives the instance variables, and the bottom shows the methods provided by the class. This kind of diagram is defined by the Unified Modeling Language (UML), which is a common way to diagram classes, their contents, and their relationships.

There's a lot of duplication in Figure 4-1, and that just smells like inefficiency. When you're programming, duplication like this suggests bad architecture. You have twice as much code to maintain, and you have to make changes in two (or more) places when you modify code, which greatly increases your chances of introducing errors. If you forget to make a change in one of these places, weird bugs can occur.

Wouldn't it be nice if all this duplicated stuff could be consolidated in one place? And it would be nicer still if we could maintain the ability to have custom methods where we need them, such as when we have to draw circles and rectangles. We need a system that allows us to tell the compiler, "The `Circle` class is just like this other thing, with a couple of tweaks here and there." Well, you probably already figured out that the powerful OOP feature for exactly this is inheritance.

Figure 4-2 shows how our architecture looks after we sprinkle in some inheritance. We have created Shape, a brand new class, to hold the common instance variables and declare the methods. Class Shape holds the implementation of `setFillColor:` and `setBounds:`.

Take a look (in Figure 4-2) at our spiffy new `Circle` and `Rectangle` classes. They're a lot smaller than they were before. All the common elements got pulled up into Shape. The only things left in `Circle` and `Rectangle` are elements that make them unique, the `draw` method in particular. We now say that `Circle` and `Rectangle` *inherit* from Shape.

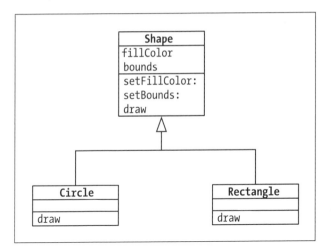

Figure 4-2. *Improved Shapes-Object architecture using inheritance*

Just as you might have inherited features like your hair color, shape of your nose, or your desire to use a Mac from your biological parents, inheritance in OOP means that a class acquires features from another class, its parent or **superclass**. Circle and Rectangle, because they inherit from Shape, pick up Shape's two instance variables.

In addition to instance variables, inheritance also brings methods along for the ride. Every Circle and every Rectangle knows how to respond to setFillColor: and setBounds:. They inherit that ability from class Shape.

Inheritance Syntax

Let's take a look at the syntax we've been using to declare a new class:

```
@interface Circle : NSObject
```

The identifier following the colon is the class you're inheriting from. You can inherit from no class in Objective-C, but if you're using Cocoa, you'll want to inherit from NSObject, because it provides a lot of useful features (you also get those features when you inherit from a class that inherits from NSObject). We'll cover more of NSObject's features when we talk about memory management in Chapter 9.

INHERIT THE ONE

Some languages, such as C++, include a feature called *multiple inheritance*, in which a class can inherit directly from two or more classes. Objective-C does not support multiple inheritance. If you tried to use multiple inheritance in Objective-C, which might look something like the following statement, you would make the compiler very unhappy:

```
@interface Circle : NSObject, PrintableObject
```

You can get many of the benefits of multiple inheritance by using other features of Objective-C, such as categories (see Chapter 12) and protocols (see Chapter 13).

Now that you've discovered inheritance and we're fixing up our architecture so that our classes inherit from Shape, the interfaces for Circle and Rectangle change to look like the following listing (you can find the code for this program in *04.01 Shapes-Inheritance*):

```
@interface Circle : Shape

@end // Circle

@interface Rectangle : Shape

@end // Rectangle
```

You can't get much simpler than that. When code is simple, bugs have no place to hide.

Notice that we don't declare the instance variables any more: we get them from Shape as part of our inheritance. You'll notice we didn't include the curly braces for the missing instance variables: if you don't have any ivars, you can omit the braces. We also don't declare the methods we get from Shape (setBounds: and setFillColor:).

Now lets look at the code that makes Shape do its thing. Here's the declaration of Shape:

```
@interface Shape : NSObject
{
  ShapeColor  fillColor;
  ShapeRect   bounds;
}

- (void) setFillColor: (ShapeColor) fillColor;
- (void) setBounds: (ShapeRect) bounds;
- (void) draw;
@end // Shape
```

You can see that Shape ties up in one neat package all the stuff that was duplicated in different classes before.

The implementation of Shape is lovely and unsurprising:

```
@implementation Shape
- (void) setFillColor: (ShapeColor) c
{
  fillColor = c;
} // setFillColor

- (void) setBounds: (ShapeRect) b
{
  bounds = b;
} // setBounds

- (void) draw
{
} // draw
@end // Shape
```

Although the draw method doesn't do anything, we define it anyway so that all of Shape's subclasses can implement their versions. It's OK to have an empty body, or one that returns a dummy value, for a method definition.

Now let's examine the implementation of Circle. As you probably figured out, it's a lot simpler now:

```
@implementation Circle
- (void) draw
{
  NSLog (@"drawing a circle at (%d %d %d %d) in %@",
         bounds.x, bounds.y,
         bounds.width, bounds.height,
         colorName(fillColor));
```

```
} // draw
@end // Circle
```

Here's the new, simplified `Rectangle` implementation:

```
@implementation Rectangle
- (void) draw
{
  NSLog (@"drawing rect at (%d %d %d %d) in %@",
        bounds.x, bounds.y,
        bounds.width, bounds.height,
        colorName(fillColor));
} // draw
@end // Rectangle
```

The `Triangle` and `OblateSpheroid` classes are similarly skinnier. Take a look at the *04.01 Shapes-Inheritance* folder for details.

You can now run Shapes-Inheritance and see that it works exactly as it did before. Notice this fascinating fact: we didn't have to touch any of the code in `main()` that sets up and uses the objects. That's because we didn't change which methods the objects respond to, and we didn't modify their behavior.

NOTE

> Moving and simplifying code this way is called **refactoring**, a subject which is quite trendy in the OOP community. When you refactor, you move code around to improve the architecture, as we did here to eliminate duplicate code, without changing the code's behavior or results. A typical development cycle involves adding some features to your code and then refactoring to take out any duplication.
>
> You might be surprised to learn that object-oriented programs often become simpler after new features are *added*, which is exactly what happened when we added the Shapes class.

Time Out for Terminology

What would new technology be without new terms to learn? Here are the words you'll need to be fully inheritance literate:

- The **superclass** is the class you're inheriting from. The superclass of `Circle` is Shape. The superclass of Shape is NSObject.

- **Parent class** is another word for "superclass." For example, Shape is the parent class of `Rectangle`.

- The **subclass** is the class doing the inheriting. Circle is a subclass of Shape, and Shape is a subclass of NSObject.

■ **Child class** is another word for "subclass." Circle is a child class of Shape. It's your choice whether to use subclass/superclass or parent class/child class. You'll come across both pairs in the real world. In this book, we use superclass and subclass, possibly because we're more nerdy than parental.

- You **override** an inherited method when you want to change its implementation. Circle has its own draw method, so we say it overrides draw. Objective-C makes sure that the appropriate class's implementation of an overridden method is called when the code runs.

How Inheritance Works

We did major surgery to Shapes-Object, taking all that code out of Circle and Rectangle and moving it into Shape. It's very cool that the rest of the program still works, without modification. Creating and initializing all the different shapes in main() didn't change, and the drawShapes() function is the same, yet the program still works:

- drawing a circle at (0 0 10 30) in red
- drawing a rect at (30 40 50 60) in green
- drawing an egg at (15 19 37 29) in blue
- drawing a triangle at (47 32 80 50) in red

Here, you can see another aspect of the power of OOP: you can make radical changes to a program, and if you're careful, things will still work when you're done. Of course, you can do that with procedural programming, but your chances of success are usually higher with OOP.

Method Dispatching

How do objects know which methods to run when they receive messages? For example, setFillColor:'s code has been moved out of the Circle and Rectangle classes, so how does the Shape code know what to do when you send setFillColor: to a Circle object? Here's the secret: when code sends a message, the Objective-C method dispatcher searches for the method in the current class. If the dispatcher doesn't find the method in the class of the object receiving the message, it looks at the object's superclasses.

Figure 4-3 shows how method dispatching works for code sending the setFillColor: message to a Circle object, using the old, pre–Shape version of our program. To handle code like [shape setFillColor: kRedColor], the Objective-C method dispatcher looks at the object receiving the message; in this case, it's an object of class Circle. The object has a pointer to its class, and the class has a pointer to its code. The dispatcher uses these pointers to find the right code to run.

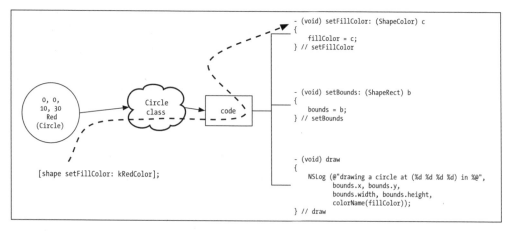

Figure 4-3. *Method dispatch without inheritance*

Check out Figure 4-4, which shows our snazzy new inheritance-enhanced structure. In this code, class Circle has a reference to its superclass, Shape. The Objective-C method dispatcher uses this information to find the right implementation of a method when a message comes in.

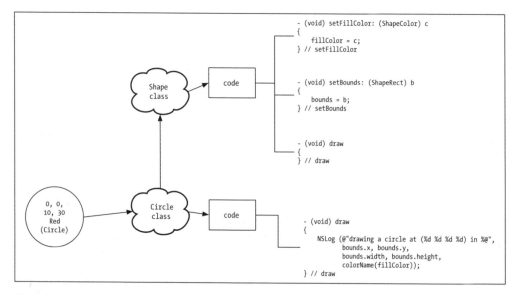

Figure 4-4. *Inheritance and class code*

Figure 4-5 shows the method dispatch process when inheritance is involved. When you send the setFillColor: message to the Circle object, the dispatcher first consults the Circle class to see if it can respond to setFillColor: with its own code. In this case, the answer is no: the dispatcher discovers that Circle has no definition for setFillColor:, so it's time to look in the superclass, Shape. The dispatcher then roots around in Shape and finds the definition of setFillColor:, and it runs that code.

This action of saying, "I can't find it here, I'll go look in the superclass," is repeated for every class in the inheritance chain, as necessary. If a method can't be found in either the Circle or Shape class, the dispatcher checks class NSObject, because it's the next superclass in the chain. If the method doesn't exist in NSObject, the most super of the superclasses, you'll get a runtime error (and you would also have gotten a compile-time warning).

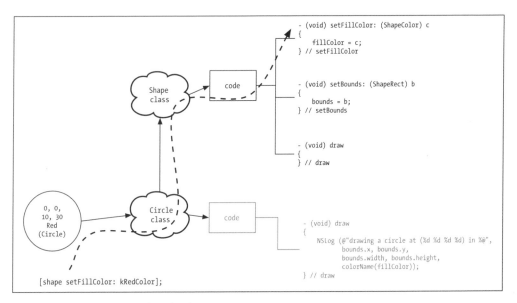

Figure 4-5. *Method dispatch with inheritance*

Instance Variables

We've spent time discussing how methods are called in response to messages. Now, let's look at how Objective-C accesses instance variables. How does Circle's draw method find the bounds and fillColor instance variables declared in Shape?

When you create a new class, its objects inherit the instance variables from its superclasses, and then (optionally) add their own instance variables. To see how instance variable inheritance works, let's invent a new shape that adds a new instance variable. This new class,

RoundedRectangle, needs a variable to hold the radius to use when drawing the corners of the rectangle. The class definition goes a little something like this:

```
@interface RoundedRectangle : Shape
{
    int radius;
}

@end // RoundedRectangle
```

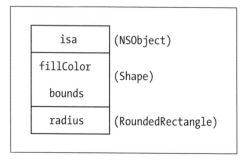

Figure 4-6 shows the memory layout of a rounded rectangle object. NSObject declares one instance variable, called isa, which holds the pointer to the object's class.

Figure 4-6. *Object instance variable layout*

Next are the two instance variables declared by Shape: fillColor and bounds. Finally, there's radius, the instance variable that RoundedRectangle declares.

NOTE

The NSObject instance variable is called isa because inheritance sets up an "is a" relationship between the subclass and the superclass; that is, a Rectangle *is a* Shape, and a Circle *is a* Shape. Code that uses a Shape can also use a Rectangle or Circle instead.

The ability to use a more specific kind of object (a Rectangle or Circle) instead of a general type (Shape) is called **polymorphism**, a Greek word meaning "many shapes," appropriately enough.

Remember that every method call gets a hidden parameter, called self, which is a pointer to the object that receives the message. Methods use the self parameter to find the instance variables they use.

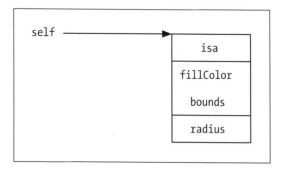

Figure 4-7 shows self pointing to a rounded rectangle object. self points to the first instance variable of the first class in the chain of inheritance. For RoundedRectangle, the inheritance chain starts with NSObject, then con-

Figure 4-7. *The self parameter pointing to a circle object*

tinues with Shape, and finally ends with RoundedRectangle, so self points to isa, the first instance variable. The Objective-C compiler knows the layout of the instance variables in an object because it has seen the @interface declarations for each of these classes. With this important knowledge, the compiler can generate code to find any instance variable.

CAUTION: FRAGILE!

The compiler works its magic by using a "base plus offset" mechanism. Given the base address of an object—that is, the memory location of the first byte of the first instance variable—the compiler can find all other instance variables by adding an offset to that address.

For example, if the base address of the rounded rectangle object is 0x1000, the isa instance variable is at 0x1000 + 0, which is 0x1000. isa is a 4-byte value, so the next instance variable, fillColor, starts at an offset of four, at 0x1000 + 4, or 0x1004. Every instance variable has an offset from the object's base.

When you access the fillColor instance variable in a method, the compiler generates code to take the value that self holds and add the value of the offset (4, in this case) to point to the location where the variable's value is stored.

This does lead to problems over time. These offsets are now hard-coded into the program generated by the compiler. Even if Apple's engineers wanted to add another instance variable to NSObject, they couldn't, because that would change all of the instance variable offsets. This is called the **fragile base class problem**. Apple has fixed this problem with the new 64-bit Objective-C runtime introduced with Leopard, which uses indirection for determining ivar locations.

Overriding Methods

When you're making your own fresh subclasses, you often add your own methods. Sometimes, you'll add a new method that introduces a unique feature to your class. Other times, you'll replace or enhance an existing method defined by one of your new class's superclasses.

For instance, you could start with the Cocoa NSTableView class, which shows a scrolling list of stuff for users to click, and add a new behavior, such as announcing the contents of the list with a speech synthesizer. You might add a new method called speakRows that feeds the contents of the table to the speech synthesizer.

Or, instead of adding an entirely new feature, you might create a subclass that tweaks an existing behavior inherited from one of its superclasses. In Shapes-Inheritance, Shape already does most of what we want a shape to do by setting the fill color and bounds of the shape, but Shape doesn't know how to draw anything. And it can't know how to draw: Shape is a generic, abstract class, and every shape is drawn differently. So when we want to make a Circle class, we subclass Shape and write a draw method that knows how to draw a circle.

When we created Shape, we knew that all its subclasses would have to draw, even though we didn't know exactly what they would do to implement their drawing. So we gave Shape a draw method, but made it empty so that every subclass could do its own thing. When classes such as `Circle` and `Rectangle` implement their own draw methods, we say that they have **overridden** the draw method.

When a draw message is sent to a circle object, the method dispatcher runs the overridden method—`Circle`'s implementation of draw. Any implementation of draw defined by a super-class, such as Shape, is completely ignored. That's fine in this case—Shape has no code in its implementation of draw. But other times, you might *not* want to ignore the superclass's version of a method. For more on this, read on.

I Feel Super!

Objective-C provides a way to override a method and still call the superclass's implementation—useful when you want to let the superclass do its thing and perform some additional work before or after. To call the inherited method implementation, you use super as the target for a method call.

 For example, let's suppose we just learned that some cultures are offended by red circles, and we want to sell our Shapes-Inheritance software in those countries. Instead of drawing red circles, as we've been doing all along, we want all the circles to be drawn in green. Because this limitation affects only circles, one way to do this is to modify `Circle` so that all circles are drawn green. Other shapes drawn in red aren't a problem, so we don't need to eliminate them. Why not just bash `Circle`'s fill color methods directly? Here, we could. You don't always have this luxury, though; for example, you don't have the code for the class you want to modify.

Remember that `setFillColor:` is defined in class Shape. We can therefore fix the problem for circles only by overriding `setFillColor:` in the `Circle` class. We'll look at the color parameter, and if it's red, we'll change it to green. We'll then use super to tell the superclass (Shape) to store this changed color into the `fillColor` instance variable (the complete code listing for this program is in *04.02 Shapes-Green-Circles*).

The `@interface` section of `Circle` doesn't change, because we're not adding any new methods or instance variables. We only need to add code to the `@implementation` section:

```
@implementation Circle
- (void) setFillColor: (ShapeColor) c
{
  if (c == kRedColor) {
    c = kGreenColor;
  }

  [super setFillColor: c];
} // setFillColor
// and the rest of the Circle @implementation
// is unchanged
@end // Circle
```

In this new implementation of setFillColor:, we examine the ShapeColor parameter to see if it's red. If so, we change it to green. Next, we ask the superclass to do the work of putting the color in the instance variable with the code [super setFillColor: c].

Where does super come from? It's not a parameter or an instance variable, but instead a bit of magic provided by the Objective-C compiler. When you send a message to super, you're asking Objective-C to send the message to the class's superclass. If it's not defined there, Objective-C continues looking up the inheritance chain in the usual fashion.

Figure 4-8 shows the flow of execution for Circle's setFillColor:. The circle object is sent the setFillColor: message. The method dispatcher finds the custom version of setFillColor: that's implemented by class Circle.

After Circle's version of setFillColor: does its check for kRedColor and changes the color if needed, the superclass's method is invoked by calling [super setFillColor: c]. The super call runs Shape's version of the setFillColor: method.

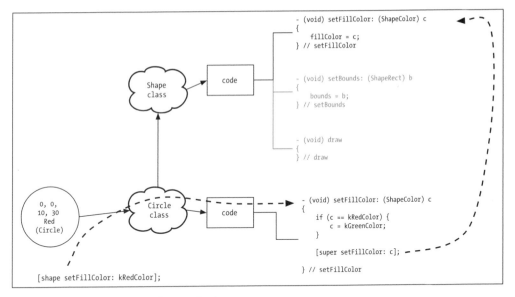

Figure 4-8. *Calling the superclass method*

NOTE

When you override a method, invoking the superclass method is almost always a good idea, in case it's doing more work than you're aware of. In this case, we have access to the source for Shape, so we know that all Shape does in its setFillColor: is stick the new color into an instance variable. But if we weren't so well versed in Shape, we wouldn't know if Shape was doing something else. And even though we know what Shape does now, we might not if the class is changed or enhanced later. By calling the inherited method, we make sure we get all the features it implements.

Summary

Inheritance is a vital concept in object-oriented programming, as many advanced techniques of OOP involve it. In this chapter, you met inheritance and saw how it was used to beautify and simplify the Shapes-Object code. We discussed how new classes can be made from existing classes, and you saw how instance variables of a superclass appear in subclasses.

We went over the Objective-C method dispatch machinery and noted how it crawls up the inheritance chain looking for the method to run in response to a particular message. Finally, we introduced the super keyword and showed how you can use it to take advantage of a superclass's code in an overridden method.

You'll get to know composition in the next chapter, which is another way of having different objects collaborate to get work done. It might not be quite as geeky-cool as inheritance, but it's very important, so we'll see you there.

Chapter 5

Composition

*i*n the previous chapter, you got hip to inheritance, a way to set up a relationship between two classes that removes the need for a lot of duplicated code. And we (briefly) mentioned that you can also set up relationships using composition, which is the subject of this chapter. You can use composition to combine objects so they can work together. In a typical program, you'll use both inheritance and composition when creating your own classes, so it's important to have a good handle on both concepts.

What Is Composition?

Composition in programming is like composition in music: you're bringing individual components together and making them work to build something bigger. In music, you might bring together a bassoon part and an oboe part in creating a symphony. In software, you might bring together a pedal object and a tire object as part of a virtual unicycle.

In Objective-C, you compose by including pointers to objects as instance variables. So, our virtual unicycle would have a pointer to a Pedal object and a pointer to a Tire object and would look something like this:

```
@interface Unicycle : NSObject
{
    Pedal *pedal;
    Tire *tire;
}

@end // Unicycle
```

Through composition, a Unicycle consists of a Pedal and a Tire.

Car Talk

Let's put the Shapes program aside for awhile (are those sighs of relief we hear?) and take a look at modeling an automobile. A car, in our simplified model, has an engine and four tires. Rather than wading through the physics modeling of actual tires and engines, we'll use a couple of classes that have only a method to print out which part they represent: tire objects will say that they're tires, and the engine object will say that it's an engine. In a real program, the tires would have attributes like air pressure and handling ability, and the engine would have variables like horsepower and gas mileage. The code for this program can be found in *05.01 CarParts*.

Like the Shapes program, CarParts has everything in its *mainCarParts.m*. CarParts starts out by importing the Foundation framework header:

```
#import <Foundation/Foundation.h>
```

The Tire class follows; there's not much to it except a description method:

```
@interface Tire : NSObject
@end // Tire
@implementation Tire

- (NSString *) description
{
    return (@"I am a tire. I last a while");
} // description

@end // Tire
```

NOTE

You can leave out the curly braces in your class definitions if you don't have any instance variables.

The only method in Tire is `description`, and it wasn't declared in the interface. Where did it come from? How can anybody know to use `description` with a Tire if it's not included in the interface? It happens with the help of a little Cocoa magic.

Customizing for NSLog()

Remember that NSLog() lets you use the %@ format specifier to print objects. When NSLog() processes the %@ specifier, it asks the corresponding object in the parameter list for its description. Speaking technically, NSLog() sends the description message to the object, and the object's description method builds an NSString and returns it. NSLog() then includes that string in its output. By supplying a description method in your class, you can customize how your objects are printed by NSLog().

In your description methods, you can return a literal NSString, such as @"I am a cheese Danish object", or you can construct a string that describes all sorts of information about the object, such as the fat content and calories for the cheese Danish. The description method for Cocoa's NSArray class, which manages a collection of objects, provides information about the array itself, such as the number of objects it contains and descriptions of each object it contains. These descriptions, naturally, are acquired by sending the description message to each of the objects the array contains.

Getting back to CarParts, let's have a look at the Engine class. Like Tire, it has just a description method. In a real program, your engine would have methods such as start and accelerate and instance variables like RPMs. But we're here to see a simple example of composition at work, so we've given Engine just a description:

```
@interface Engine : NSObject
@end // Engine


@implementation Engine

- (NSString *) description
{
    return (@"I am an engine.  Vrooom!");
} // description

@end // Engine
```

The last part is the car itself, which has an engine and a C array of four tires. The car uses composition to assemble itself. Car also has a method called print that uses NSLog() to print out the tires and engine:

```
@interface Car : NSObject
{
    Engine *engine;
    Tire *tires[4];
}

- (void) print;

@end // Car
```

The engine and tires instance variables are the composition, because tires and engine are instance variables of Car. You can say that Car is *composed* of four tires and an engine. Of course, people don't usually talk like that, so you can also say that Car has four tires and an engine.

Each car object allocates memory for *pointers* to the engine and tires. An entire engine and four tires aren't embedded into the car, just references to other objects floating around in memory. When a new Car is allocated, these pointers are initialized to nil (a zero value) indicating that the car does not have an engine or any tires. You can picture it just sitting up on blocks.

Let's take a look at the implementation of the Car class. First is an init method, which initializes the instance variables. The init method creates an engine and four tires to outfit the car. When you create a new object with new, two steps actually happen under the hood. First, the object is allocated, meaning that a chunk of memory is obtained that will hold your instance variables. The init method is then called automatically to get the object into a workable state.

```
@implementation Car

- (id) init
{
    if (self = [super init]) {
        engine = [Engine new];

        tires[0] = [Tire new];
        tires[1] = [Tire new];
        tires[2] = [Tire new];
        tires[3] = [Tire new];
    }

    return (self);

} // init
```

The init method for Car makes a new engine and assigns it to the engine instance variable. init then creates four new tires and assigns them to the tires array.

Next comes Car's print method:

```
- (void) print
{
    NSLog (@"%@", engine);

    NSLog (@"%@", tires[0]);
    NSLog (@"%@", tires[1]);
    NSLog (@"%@", tires[2]);
    NSLog (@"%@", tires[3]);

} // print

@end // Car
```

ABOUT THAT IF STATEMENT . . .

This line of code in the `init` method looks a little odd:

```
if (self = [super init]) {
```

We'll explain what's happening here. You need to call `[super init]` so that the superclass (`NSObject`, in this case) can do any one-time initialization that it needs to do. The `init` method returns a value (of type `id`, a generic object pointer) representing the object that was initialized.

Assigning the result of `[super init]` back to `self` is a standard Objective-C convention. We do this in case the superclass, as part of its initialization work, returns a different object than the one originally created. We'll explore this in depth in a later chapter when we cover `init` methods in more detail, so for now, please just nod and smile over this line of code, and we'll move on.

The `print` method uses `NSLog()` to print out the instance variables. Remember that `%@` simply calls the `description` method of each object, and the results are displayed. In a real program, you would use the tires and the engine to figure out how well the car was holding the road.

The last part of *CarParts.m* is the `main()` function, the *driver* of this program. (Sorry about that.) `main()` creates a new car, tells it to do its thing by asking the car to print itself, and then exits.

```
int main (int argc, const char * argv[])
{
    Car *car;

    car = [Car new];
    [car print];

    return (0);

} // main
```

Build and run CarParts, and you should see output similar to this:

```
I am an engine.  Vrooom!
I am a tire. I last a while.
I am a tire. I last a while.
I am a tire. I last a while.
I am a tire. I last a while.
```

It won't win any car awards, but it works!

Accessor Methods

Programmers are rarely satisfied with the programs they write, because software is never finished. There's always one more bug to fix, one more feature to add, or one more way to make the program bigger, stronger, or faster. So it's no surprise that CarParts isn't perfect yet. We can improve it and make its code more flexible by using accessor methods. The code for this new version can be found in the *05.02 CarParts-Accessors* folder.

An experienced programmer looking at Car's `init` method might say, "Why is the car creating its own tires and engine?" The program would be much better if you could customize the car to use different kinds of tires (such as snow tires for the winter months) or various types of engines (fuel injected rather than carbureted).

It would be nice if we could instruct the car to use a particular tire or engine. We could then let users mix and match car parts to create custom vehicles.

We can make this happen by adding accessor methods. An **accessor** method is one that reads or changes a specific attribute for an object. For instance, `setFillColor:` in Shapes-Object is an accessor method. If we added a new method to change the engine in a Car object, it would be an accessor method. This particular kind of accessor method is called a **setter** method, because it sets a value on an object. You might hear the term **mutator** used for a method that changes an object state.

You've probably already guessed that another kind of accessor method is a **getter**. A getter method provides a way for code that uses an object to access its attributes. In a racing game, the physics logic would want to access attributes of the car's tires to figure out if the car will skid on wet pavement at its current speed.

NOTE

You should always use any provided accessor methods when manipulating another object's attributes—never reach into an object and change values directly. For example, `main()` should not directly access the Car's engine instance variable (using `car->engine`) to change its engine. Instead, your code should use a setter method to make the change.

Accessor methods are yet another example of indirection at work. By accessing the car's engine indirectly via an accessor method, you're allowing for flexibility in the car's implementation.

Let's add some setter and getter methods to Car so the code that uses it has control over the kinds of tires and engine used. Here is the new interface for Car, with the new items in bold:

```
@interface Car : NSObject
{
    Engine *engine;
    Tire *tires[4];
}

- (Engine *) engine;

- (void) setEngine: (Engine *) newEngine;


- (Tire *) tireAtIndex: (int) index;

- (void) setTire: (Tire *) tire
        atIndex: (int) index;

- (void) print;

@end // Car
```

The set of instance variables hasn't changed, but there are two new pairs of methods: `engine` and `setEngine:` deal with the engine attributes, and `tireAtIndex:` and `setTire:atIndex:` work with the tires. Accessor methods almost always come in pairs, one to set the value and one to get it. Occasionally, having only a getter (for a read-only attribute, like the size of a file on disk) or only a setter (like setting a secret password) might make sense, but most often, you'll be writing both setters and getters.

Cocoa has conventions for naming accessor methods. When you're writing accessor methods for your own classes, you should follow these conventions so that you and other people reading your code won't get confused.

Setter methods are named after the attribute they change, preceded by the word "set." Here are examples of names of setter methods: `setEngine:`, `setStringValue:`, `setFont:`, `setFillColor:`, and `setTextLineHeight:`.

Getter methods are simply named after the attribute they return. The getters corresponding to the preceding setters would be named `engine`, `stringValue`, `font`, `fillColor`, and `textLineHeight`. Don't use the word "get" in the name of the method. For example, methods named `getStringValue` and `getFont` would violate the convention. Some languages, such as Java, have different conventions that use "get" in the name of accessor methods, but if you're writing Cocoa code, don't use it.

The word "get" has a special meaning in Cocoa: in a Cocoa method name, it means the method returns a value via a pointer that you pass in as a parameter. For example, NSData (a Cocoa class for objects that store an arbitrary sequence of bytes) has a method called getBytes:, which takes a parameter that is the address of a memory buffer for holding the bytes. NSBezierPath (used for drawing) has a method called getLineDash:count:phase:, which takes a pointer to a float array for the line dash pattern, a pointer to an integer for the number of elements in the dash pattern, and a pointer to a float for the place in the pattern to start drawing.

If you use "get" in your accessor method names, experienced Cocoa programmers using your code will expect to provide pointers as arguments to your method and will then be confused when they discover that it's just a simple accessor. It's best not to confuse the programmers.

Setting the Engine

The first pair of accessor methods affect the engine:

```
- (Engine *) engine;

- (void) setEngine: (Engine *) newEngine;
```

Code that uses Car objects calls engine to access the engine and setEngine: to change it. Here is what the implementation of these methods look like:

```
- (Engine *) engine
{
    return (engine);
} // engine


- (void) setEngine: (Engine *) newEngine
{
    engine = newEngine;
} // setEngine
```

The getter method engine returns the current value of the engine instance variable. Remember that all object interaction in Objective-C happens via pointers, so the engine method returns a pointer to the engine object that the Car contains.

Similarly, the setter method setEngine: sets the value of the engine instance variable to the value that's pointed in. The actual engine itself is not copied, just the value of the pointer that points to the engine. Here's another way to say this: after you call setEngine: on a car object, only one engine exists in the world, not two engines.

NOTE

In the interests of full disclosure, we'll state that there are a couple of problems with the Engine getter and setter in the areas of memory management and object ownership. Throwing memory and object life cycle management at you right now would be both confusing and frustrating, so we'll defer the discussion of the absolutely correct way to write accessor methods until Chapter 8.

To actually use these accessors, you write code like this:

```
Engine *engine = [Engine new];
[car setEngine: engine];

NSLog (@"the car's engine is %@", [car engine]);
```

Setting the Tires

The accessor methods for the tires are a little more sophisticated:

```
- (void) setTire: (Tire *) tire
         atIndex: (int) index;

- (Tire *) tireAtIndex: (int) index;
```

Because a car has multiple spots for tires (one on each of the four corners of the vehicle), Car objects contain an array of tires. Rather than exposing the tires array to the world, an indexed accessor is used. When setting a tire for a car, you tell the car not only which tire to use but also which position on the car to use for each tire. Likewise, when accessing a tire for a car, you ask for the tire in a particular location.

Here is the implementation of tire accessors:

```
- (void) setTire: (Tire *) tire
         atIndex: (int) index
{
    if (index < 0 || index > 3) {
        NSLog (@"bad index (%d) in setTire:atIndex:",
                index);
        exit (1);
    }

    tires[index] = tire;

} // setTire:atIndex:


- (Tire *) tireAtIndex: (int) index
```

```
{
    if (index < 0 || index > 3) {
        NSLog (@"bad index (%d) in tireAtIndex:",
                index);
        exit (1);
    }

    return (tires[index]);

} // tireAtIndex:
```

The tire accessors have some common code that checks to make sure the array index for the tires instance variable is a valid value. If it's outside of the range of 0 through 3, the program prints a complaint and exits. This code is what's known as **defensive programming**, and it's a good idea. Defensive programming catches errors, such as using a bad index for a tire location, early in the development cycle.

We have to check the validity of the array index because tires is a C-style array, and the compiler doesn't do any error checking on the index used when accessing the array. We could write tires[-5] or tires[23] without a compiler complaint. Of course, the array has only four elements, so using –5 or 23 for the index will access random memory and lead to bugs and program crashes.

After the index check, the tires array is manipulated to put the new tire in its proper place. Code that uses these accessors looks like this:

```
Tire *tire = [Tire new];

[car setTire: tire
      atIndex: 2];

NSLog (@"tire number two is %@",
        [car tireAtIndex: 2]);
```

Tracking Changes to Car

There are a couple of details left to clean up before we can declare CarParts-Accessors to be done.

The first detail is Car's init method. Because Car now has accessors for its engine and tires, its init method doesn't need to create any. The code that creates the car is responsible for outfitting the engine and tires. In fact, we can remove the init method entirely, since there's no need to do that work in Car any more. People who get a new car will get one without tires or an engine, but these can easily be made (sometimes, life in software is so much easier than it is out here in the real world).

Because Car no longer creates its own moving parts, main() must be updated to create them. Change your main() function to look like this:

```
int main (int argc, const char * argv[])
{
    Car *car = [Car new];

    Engine *engine = [Engine new];
    [car setEngine: engine];

    int i;
    for (i = 0; i < 4; i++) {
        Tire *tire = [Tire new];

        [car setTire: tire
              atIndex: i];
    }

    [car print];

    return (0);

} // main
```

main() creates a new car, as it did in its previous incarnation. Then, a new Engine is made and placed in the car. Then a for loop spins around four times. Each time through the loop, a new tire is created, and the car is told to use the new tire. Finally, the car is printed and the program exits.

From the user's point of view, the program hasn't changed at all:

```
I am an engine.  Vrooom!
I am a tire. I last a while.
I am a tire. I last a while.
I am a tire. I last a while.
I am a tire. I last a while.
```

As with Shapes-Object, we've refactored the program, improving the internal structure but leaving the external behavior the same.

Extending CarParts

Now that Car has accessors, let's take advantage of them. Instead of the stock engine and tires, we'll implement variations on these parts. We'll use inheritance to make the new kinds of engines and tires, and then use Car's accessors (that's composition) to give the car its new moving pieces. The code for this program can be found in the *05.03 CarParts-2* folder.

First is a new kind of engine, a Slant6 (if you prefer a V8 or a ThreeFiftyOneWindsor, go for it).

```
@interface Slant6 : Engine
@end // Slant6


@implementation Slant6

- (NSString *) description
{
    return (@"I am a slant-6. VROOOM!");
} // description

@end // Slant6
```

A Slant6 is a kind of engine, so it makes sense for us to subclass Engine. Remember that inheritance sets up a relationship that allows us to pass subclasses (Slant6) where the super-class (Engine) is expected. Because Car takes an argument of type Engine for the setEngine: method, we can safely pass in a Slant6.

Slant6 overrides description to make it print a new message. Because Slant6 does not invoke the superclass's description method (that is, it doesn't include [super description]), it com-pletely replaces its inherited description.

The steps for implementing a new class of tires, called AllWeatherRadial, are a lot like the ones we used for Slant6. We subclass an existing class (Tire) and provide a new description method:

```
@interface AllWeatherRadial : Tire
@end // AllWeatherRadial


@implementation AllWeatherRadial

- (NSString *) description
{
    return (@"I am a tire for rain or shine.");
} // description

@end // AllWeatherRadial
```

And finally, we tweak `main()` to use the new engine and tire types (the changed code is in bold):

```
int main (int argc, const char * argv[])
{
    Car *car = [Car new];

    int i;
    for (i = 0; i < 4; i++) {
        Tire *tire = [AllWeatherRadial new];

        [car setTire: tire
            atIndex: i];
    }

    Engine *engine = [Slant6 new];
    [car setEngine: engine];

    [car print];

    return (0);

} // main
```

We added two new classes and slightly changed two lines of code. We didn't touch `Car` at all. Our `Car` happily uses whatever kind of engine and tires you devise without having to change `Car` itself. The behavior of the program is now radically different:

```
I am a slant-6. VROOOM!
I am a tire for rain or shine.
I am a tire for rain or shine.
I am a tire for rain or shine.
I am a tire for rain or shine.
```

Composition or Inheritance?

CarParts-2 uses both inheritance and composition, the two new tools in your utility belt introduced here and in the previous chapter. A good question—no, a great question—to ask is, "When do I use inheritance, and when do I use composition?"

Inheritance sets up an "is a" relationship. A triangle *is a* shape. `Slant6` *is an* engine. `AllWeatherRadial` *is a* tire. When you can say, "X is a Y," you can use inheritance.

Composition, on the other hand, sets up a "has a" relationship. A shape *has a* fill color. A car *has an* engine, and it *has a* tire. In contrast, a car is not an engine, and a car is not a tire. When you can say, "X has a Y," you should use composition.

Programmers new to object-oriented programming often make the mistake of trying to use inheritance for everything, such as having `Car` inherit from `Engine`. Inheritance is a fun new toy, but it's not appropriate for every situation. You can create a working program with such a structure, because you can access stuff that makes an engine work from inside the `Car` code. But it doesn't make sense to people reading the code. A car is an engine? Huh? So, use inheritance only when it's appropriate.

Here's an example of how your thinking might go when designing your data structures: when creating new objects, take some thinking time to figure out when inheritance should be used and when composition should be used. For instance, in designing car stuff, you might think, "A car has tires, and an engine, and a transmission." So you'd use composition and make instance variables in your `Car` class for all of those.

In other circumstances, you would use inheritance. For instance, you might need the idea of a licensed vehicle, that is, one requires some kind of license before it is legal to use. An automobile, motorcycle, and tractor-trailer rig would all be licensed vehicles. An automobile *is a* licensed vehicle, and a motorcycle *is a* licensed vehicle—sounds like a good job for inheritance. So you'd probably have a `LicensedVehicle` class that holds things like the municipality and license number (using composition!), and `Automobile`, `MotorCycle`, and so on would inherit from `LicensedVehicle`.

Summary

Composition, the technique of creating objects that have references to other objects, is a fundamental concept of OOP. For instance, a car object has references to the engine object and four tire objects. During this chapter's discussion of composition, we introduced accessor methods, which provide a way for outside objects to change attributes while keeping the instance variables shielded.

Accessor methods and composition go hand in hand, because you usually write accessor methods for each object that's being composed. You also learned about two types of accessor methods: setter methods tell an object what to change an attribute to, and getter methods ask an object for the value of an attribute.

In this chapter, you also heard about Cocoa rules for naming accessor methods. In particular, we cautioned you to not use "get" in the name of accessor methods that return an attribute value.

In the next chapter, we'll take a breather from all this fabulous OOP theory so we can look at how to split classes among multiple source files, rather than keeping everything in one big file.

Chapter 6

Source File Organization

So far, every project we've talked about has had all its source code crammed into its *main.m* file. The `main()` function and all the `@interface` and `@implementation` sections for our classes are piled into the same file. That structure's fine for small programs and quick hacks, but it doesn't scale to larger projects. As your program gets bigger, you'll have a ponderous file to scroll through, making it harder to find stuff. Back in your school days (assuming you're finished with them), you didn't put every term paper into the same word processing document (assuming you had word processors). You kept each paper in its own document, with a descriptive name. Likewise, it's a good idea to split your program's source code into multiple files, and you can give each one a helpful name. Compartmentalizing your program into smaller files gives you a chance to find important bits of code more quickly, and it helps others get a quick overview when they look at your project. Putting your code in multiple files also makes sending the source for an interesting class to a friend easier: you just pack up a couple of files rather than your entire project. In this chapter, we'll discuss strategies and ideas for keeping various bits of your program in separate files.

Split Interface and Implementation

As you've seen, the source code for Objective-C classes is divided into two parts. One part is the interface, which provides the public view of the class. The interface contains all the information necessary for someone to use the class. By showing the compiler the `@interface` section, you'll be able to use objects of that class, call class methods, compose objects into another class, and make subclasses.

The other part of a class's source is the implementation. The @implementation section tells the Objective-C compiler how to make the class actually work. This section contains the code that implements the methods declared in the interface.

Because of the natural split in the definition of a class into interface and implementation, a class's code is often split into two files along the same lines. One part holds the interface components: the @interface directive for the class, any public struct definitions, enum constants, #defines, extern global variables, and so on. Because of Objective-C's C heritage, this stuff typically goes into a header file, which has the same name as the class with a .h at the end. For example, class Engine's header file would be called *Engine.h*, and Circle's header file would be *Circle.h*.

All the implementation details, such as the @implementation directive for the class, definitions of global variables, private structs, and so on, go into a file with the same name as the class and a .m at the end (sometimes called a **dot-m file**). *Engine.m* and *Circle.m* would be the implementation files for those classes.

NOTE

If you use *.mm* for the file extension, you're telling the compiler you've written your code in Objective-C++, which lets you use C++ and Objective-C together.

Making New Files in Xcode

When you build a new class, Xcode makes your life easier by automatically creating the *.h* and *.m* files for you. When you choose File ➤ New File in Xcode, you get a window like the one shown in Figure 6-1 that presents you with a list of the kinds of files that Xcode knows how to create.

Select *Objective-C class*, and click *Next*. You'll get another window asking you to fill in the name, as shown in Figure 6-2.

You can see a bunch of other things in that window. There's a checkbox you can use to have Xcode create *Engine.h* for you. If you had multiple projects open, you could use the *Add to project* pop-up menu to choose which project should get the new files. We won't discuss the *Targets* section right now, except to say that complex projects can have multiple targets, each having its own configuration of source files and different build rules.

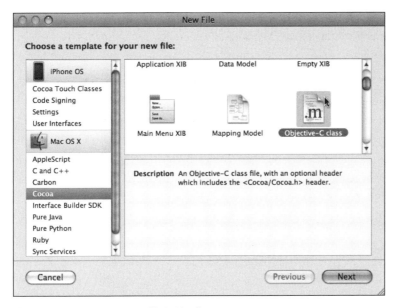

Figure 6-1. *Creating a new file in Xcode*

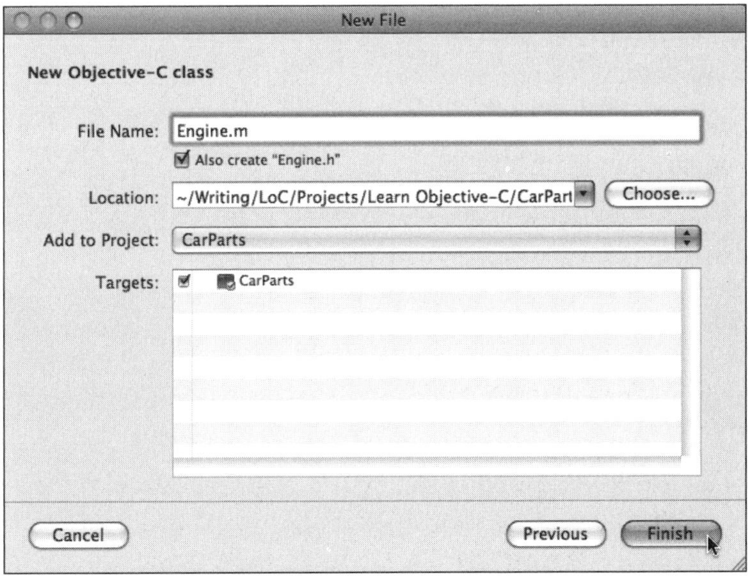

Figure 6-2. *Naming the new files*

Once you click the *Finish* button, Xcode adds the appropriate files to the project and displays the results in the project window, as shown in Figure 6-3.

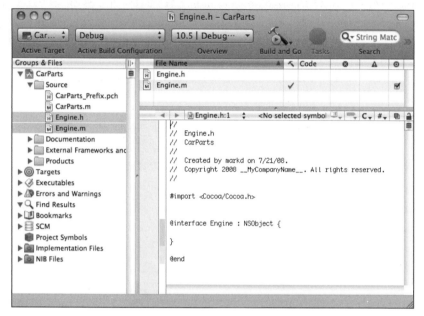

Figure 6-3. *The new files displayed in the Xcode project window*

Xcode puts the new files into the selected folder in the *Groups & Files* pane (if you had *Source* selected before creating the files, the files would go into that folder). These folders (called *Groups* by Xcode) provide a way to organize the source files in your project. For example, you can make one group for your user interface classes and another for your data-manipulation classes to make your project easier to navigate. When you set up groups, Xcode doesn't actually move any files or create any directories on your hard drive. The group relationship is just a lovely fantasy maintained by Xcode. If you want, you can set up a group so that it points to a particular place in the file system. Xcode will then put newly created files into that directory for you.

Once you've created the files, you can double-click them in the list to edit them. Xcode helpfully includes some of the standard boilerplate code, stuff you'll always need to have in these files, such as #import <Cocoa/Cocoa.h>, as well as empty @interface and @implementation sections for you to fill in.

NOTE

> So far in this book, we've had #import <Foundation/Foundation.h> in our programs because we're using only that part of Cocoa. But it's OK to use #import <Cocoa/Cocoa.h> instead. That statement brings in the Foundation framework headers for us, along with some other stuff.

Breaking Apart the Car

CarParts-Split, found in the *06.01CarParts-Split* project folder, takes all the classes out of the *CarParts-Split.m* file and moves them into their own files. Each class lives in its own header (*.h*) and implementation (*.m*) files. Let's see what it takes to create this project ourselves. We'll start with two classes that inherit from NSObject: Tire and Engine. Choose *New File*, and then pick *Objective-C Class*, and enter the name *Tire*. Do the same with *Engine*. Figure 6-4 shows the four new files in the project list.

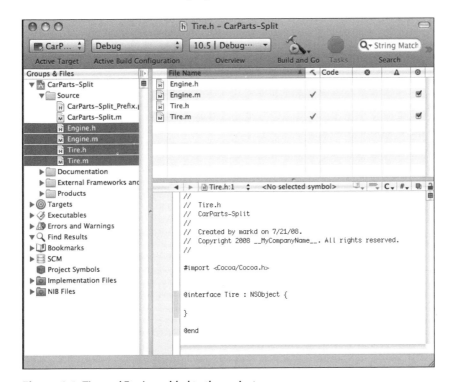

Figure 6-4. *Tire and Engine added to the project*

Now, cut Tire's @interface from *CarParts-Split.*m, and paste it into *Tire.h*. The file should look like this:

```
#import <Cocoa/Cocoa.h>

@interface Tire : NSObject
@end // Tire
```

Next, we'll cut the Tire @implementation from *CarParts-Split.m* and paste it into *Tire.m*. You'll also need to add an #import "Tire.h" at the top. This is what *Tire.m* should look like:

```
#import "Tire.h"
```

```
@implementation Tire

- (NSString *) description
{
    return (@"I am a tire. I last a while");
} // description

@end // Tire
```

The first #import of the file is interesting. It's not importing the *Cocoa.h* or *Foundation.h* header files, as we've done before. Instead, it imports the header file for the class. This is standard procedure, and you'll end up doing this in virtually every project you create. The compiler needs the layout of instance variables in the class so it can generate the proper code, but it doesn't automatically know there is a header file to go along with this source file. So, we need to inform the compiler by adding the #import "Tire.h" statement. When compiling, if you encounter an error message like "Cannot find interface definition for Tire," that usually means you forgot to #import the class's header file.

NOTE

Notice that there are two different ways of doing imports: with quotation marks and with angle brackets. For example, there's #import <Cocoa/Cocoa.h> and #import "Tire.h". The version with angle brackets is used for importing system header files. The quotes version indicates a header file that's local to the project. If you see a header file name in angle brackets, it's read-only for your project, because it's owned by the system. When a header file name is in quotes, you know that you (or someone else on the project) can make changes to it.

Now, do the same procedure for class Engine. Cut the Engine @interface out of *CarParts-Split*.m, and paste it into *Engine.h*. *Engine.h* now looks like this:

```
#import <Cocoa/Cocoa.h>

@interface Engine : NSObject
@end // Engine
```

Next, cut the @implementation from Engine, and paste it into *Engine.m*, which should now look like the following:

```
#import "Engine.h"

@implementation Engine

- (NSString *) description
{
```

```
    return (@"I am an engine. Vrooom!");
} // description

@end // Engine
```

If you try to compile the program now, *CarParts-Split.m* will report errors due to the missing declarations of Tire and Engine. Those are pretty easy to fix. Just add the following two lines to the top of *CarParts-Split*.m, just after the #import <Foundation/Foundation.h> statement:

```
#import "Tire.h"
#import "Engine.h"
```

NOTE

Remember that #import is like #include, a command that's handled by the C preprocessor. In this case, the C preprocessor is essentially just doing cut and paste, sticking the contents of *Tire.h* and *Engine.h* into *CarParts-Split.m* before continuing.

You can build and run CarParts-Split now, and you'll find its behavior unchanged from the original version, which is the one that uses AllWeatherRadials and Slant6:

```
I am a tire for rain or shine
I am a tire for rain or shine
I am a tire for rain or shine
I am a tire for rain or shine
I am a slant-6. VROOM!
```

Using Cross-File Dependencies

A **dependency** is a relationship between two entities. Issues with dependencies pop up frequently during program design and development. Dependencies can exist between two classes: for example, Slant6 depends on Engine because of their inheritance relationship. If Engine changes, such as by adding a new instance variable, Slant6 will need to be recompiled to adapt to the change.

Dependencies can exist between two or more files. *CarParts-Split.m* is dependent on *Tire.h* and *Engine.h*. If either of those files change, *CarParts-Split.m* will need to be recompiled to pick up the changes. For instance, *Tire.h* might have a constant called kDefaultTirePressure with a value of 30 psi. The programmer who wrote *Tire.h* might decide that the default tire pressure should be changed to 40 psi in the header file. *CarParts-Split.m* now needs to be recompiled to use the new value of 40 rather than the old value of 30.

Importing a header file sets up a strong dependency relationship between the header file and the source file that does the importing. If the header file changes, all the files dependent on that header file must be recompiled. This can lead to a cascade of changes in the files that need to be recompiled. Imagine you have a hundred *.m* files, all of which include the same header file—let's call it *UserInterfaceConstants.h*. If you make a change to *UserInterfaceConstants.h*, all 100 of the *.m* files will be rebuilt, which can take a significant amount of time, even with a cluster of souped-up, Intel-based Xserves at your disposal.

The recompilation issue can get even worse, because dependencies are transitive: header files can be dependent on each other. For example, if *Thing1.h* imports *Thing2.h*, which in turn imports *Thing3.h*, any change to *Thing3.h* will cause files that import *Thing1.h* to be recompiled. Although compilation can take a long time, at least Xcode keeps track of all dependencies for you.

Recompiling on a Need-to-Know Basis

But there's good news: Objective-C provides a way to limit the effects of dependency-caused recompilations. Dependency issues exist because the Objective-C compiler needs certain pieces of information to be able to do its work. Sometimes, the compiler needs to know everything about a class, such as its instance variable layout and which classes it ultimately inherits from. But sometimes, the compiler only needs to know the name of the class, rather than its entire definition.

For example, when objects are composed (as you saw in the last chapter), the composition uses pointers to objects. This works because all Objective-C objects use dynamically allocated memory. The compiler only needs to know that a particular item is a class. It then knows that the instance variable is the size of a pointer, which is always the same for the whole program.

Objective-C introduces the `@class` keyword as a way to tell the compiler, "This thing is a class, and therefore I'm only going to refer to it via a pointer." This calms the compiler down: it doesn't need to know more about the class, just that it's something referred to by a pointer.

We'll use `@class` while moving class Car into its own file. Go ahead and make the *Car.h* and *Car.m* files with Xcode, just as you did with `Tire` and `Engine`. Copy and paste the `@interface` for Car into *Car.h*, which now looks like this:

```
#import <Cocoa/Cocoa.h>


@interface Car : NSObject
{
```

```
  Tire *tires[4];
  Engine *engine;
}

- (void) setEngine: (Engine *) newEngine;

- (Engine *) engine;


- (void) setTire: (Tire *) tire
         atIndex: (int) index;

- (Tire *) tireAtIndex: (int) index;

- (void) print;

@end // Car
```

If we now try using this header file, we'll get errors from the compiler stating that it doesn't understand what Tire or Engine is. The message will most likely be error: parse error before "Tire", which is compiler-speak for "I don't understand this."

We have two choices for how to fix this error. The first is to just #import *Tire.h* and *Engine.h*, which will give the compiler oodles of information about these two classes.

But there's a better way. If you look carefully at the interface for Car, you'll see that it only refers to Tire and Engine by pointer. This is a job for @class. Here is what *Car.h* looks like with the @class lines added:

```
#import <Cocoa/Cocoa.h>

@class Tire;
@class Engine;

@interface Car : NSObject
{
  Tire *tires[4];
  Engine *engine;
}

- (void) setEngine: (Engine *) newEngine;

- (Engine *) engine;


- (void) setTire: (Tire *) tire
         atIndex: (int) index;
```

```
- (Tire *) tireAtIndex: (int) index;

- (void) print;

@end // Car
```

That's enough information to tell the compiler everything it needs to know to handle the @interface for Car.

NOTE

@class sets up a **forward reference**. This is a way to tell the compiler, "Trust me; you'll learn eventually what this class is, but for now, this is all you need to know."

@class is also useful if you have a **circular dependency**. That is, class A uses class B, and class B uses class A. If you try having each class #import the other, you'll end up with compilation errors. But if you use @class B in *A.h* and @class A in *B.h*, the two classes can refer to each other happily.

Making the Car Go

That takes care of Car's header file. But *Car.m* needs more information about Tires and Engines. The compiler has to see which classes Tire and Engine inherit from so it can do some checking to make sure the objects can respond to messages sent to them. To do this, we'll import *Tire.h* and *Engine.h* in *Car.m*. We also need to cut the @implementation for Car out of *CarParts-Split.m*. *Car.m* now looks like this:

```
#import "Car.h"
#import "Tire.h"
#import "Engine.h"

@implementation Car

- (void) setEngine: (Engine *) newEngine
{
  engine = newEngine;
} // setEngine


- (Engine *) engine
{
  return (engine);
} // engine


- (void) setTire: (Tire *) tire
         atIndex: (int) index
```

```
{
  if (index < 0 || index > 3) {
    NSLog (@"bad index (%d) in setTire:atIndex:",
        index);
    exit (1);
  }

  tires[index] = tire;

} // setTire:atIndex:


- (Tire *) tireAtIndex: (int) index
{
  if (index < 0 || index > 3) {
    NSLog (@"bad index (%d) in setTire:atIndex:",
        index);
    exit (1);
  }

  return (tires[index]);

} // tireAtIndex:


- (void) print
{
  NSLog (@"%@", tires[0]);
  NSLog (@"%@", tires[1]);
  NSLog (@"%@", tires[2]);
  NSLog (@"%@", tires[3]);

  NSLog (@"%@", engine);

} // print

@end // Car
```

You can build and run the program again and get the same output as before. Yep, we're refactoring again (shh, don't tell anybody). We've been improving the internal structure of our program while keeping its behavior the same.

Importation and Inheritance

We need to liberate two more classes from *CarParts-Split*.m: Slant6 and AllWeatherRadial. These are a little trickier to handle because they inherit from classes we've created: Slant6 inherits from Engine, and AllWeatherRadial inherits from Tire. Because we're inheriting

from these classes rather than just using pointers to the classes, we can't use the @class
trick in their header files. We'll have to use #import "Engine.h" in *Slant6.h* and #import
"Tire.h" in *AllWeatherRadial.h*.

 So why, exactly, can't we just use @class here? Because the compiler needs to know all
about a superclass before it can successfully compile the @interface for its subclass. The
compiler needs the layout (types, sizes, and ordering) of the instance variables of the superclass. Recall that when you add instance variables in a subclass, they get tacked onto the
end of the superclass's instance variables. The compiler then uses that information to figure
out where in memory to find instance variables, starting with the hidden self pointer that
comes with each method call. The compiler needs to see the entire contents of the class to
correctly calculate the location of the instance variables.

Next on the operating table is Slant6. Create the *Slant6.m* and *Slant6.h* files in Xcode, and
then cut Slant6's @interface out of *CarParts-Split*.m. If you've done your carving and glu-
ing properly, *Slant6.h* should look like this now:

```
#import "Engine.h"

@interface Slant6 : Engine
@end // Slant6
```

The file only imports *Engine.h* and not <Cocoa/Cocoa.h>. Why? We know that *Engine.h*
already imports <Cocoa/Cocoa.h>, so we don't have to do it ourselves here. However, it's OK
if you want to put #import <Cocoa/Cocoa.h> in this file, because #import is smart enough
not to include any file more than once.

Slant6.m is just a cut-and-paste of the @implementation section from *CarParts-Split*.m, with
the customary #import of the *Slant6.h* header file:

```
#import "Slant6.h"

@implementation Slant6

- (NSString *) description
{
  return (@"I am a slant-6. VROOOM!");
} // description

@end // Slant6
```

Do the same steps to move AllWeatherRadial to its own pair of files. No doubt you've got
the hang of this by now. Here's a look at *AllWeatherRadial.h*:

```
#import "Tire.h"
```

```
@interface AllWeatherRadial : Tire
@end // AllWeatherRadial
```

And here's *AllWeatherRadial.m*:

```
#import "AllWeatherRadial.h"

@implementation AllWeatherRadial

- (NSString *) description
{
  return (@"I am a tire for rain or shine");
} // description

@end // AllWeatherRadial
```

Poor *CarParts-Split.m* is just a shell of its former self. It's now a bunch of #imports and one lonely function, like so:

```
#import <Foundation/Foundation.h>

#import "Tire.h"
#import "Engine.h"
#import "Car.h"
#import "Slant6.h"
#import "AllWeatherRadial.h"


int main (int argc, const char * argv[])
{
  Car *car = [Car new];

  int i;
  for (i = 0; i < 4; i++) {
    Tire *tire = [AllWeatherRadial new];

    [car setTire: tire
          atIndex: i];
  }

  Engine *engine = [Slant6 new];
  [car setEngine: engine];

  [car print];

  return (0);

} // main
```

If we build and run the project now, we'll get exactly the same output as before we started spreading stuff around into various files.

Summary

In this chapter, you learned the essential skill of using multiple files to organize your source code. Typically, each class gets two files: a header file that contains the `@interface` for the class and a dot-m file that holds the `@implementation`. Users of the class then import (using `#import`) the header file to gain access to the class's features.

Along the way we encountered cross-file dependencies, in which a header file or source file needs information from another header file. A tangled web of imports can increase your compile times and can cause unnecessary recompilations. Judicious use of the `@class` directive, in which you tell the compiler "trust that you'll see a class by this name eventually," can reduce compile time by cutting down on the number of header files you have to import.

 Next up is a tour of some interesting Xcode features. See you there.

Chapter 7

More About Xcode

*M*ac programmers spend most of their time writing code inside Xcode. Xcode is a nice tool with a lot of wonderful features, not all of which are obvious. When you're going to be living inside a powerful tool for a long time, you'll want to learn as much about it as you can. In this chapter, we'll introduce you to some Xcode editor tips and tricks that are useful when you're writing and navigating your code and locating information you need. We'll also touch on some ways Xcode can help you debug your code.

Xcode is a huge application, and it is extremely customizable, sometimes ridiculously so. (Did we mention that it's huge?) Entire books can be (and have been) written about just Xcode, so we'll stick to the highlights to get you productive quickly. We recommend using the Xcode defaults when you're starting out. When something bugs you, though, you can probably find a setting that can be tweaked to your liking.

When faced with a big tool like Xcode, a good strategy is to skim through the documentation until just about the point when your eyes glaze over. Use Xcode for a while, and then skim the documents again. Each time you read, more will make sense. Lather, rinse, repeat, and you'll have terrific hair.

We'll be talking about Xcode 3.1, the current version at the time of this writing. Apple loves adding new things and moving old things around between Xcode versions, so if you're using Xcode 42.0, the screen shots are probably out of date. Now, on to the tips!

Changing the Company Name

One thing you may have noticed when you create a new Objective-C source file is the comment block that Xcode generates for you:

```
//
//  TapDance.h
//  Groovilicous
//
//  Created by markd on 7/25/08.
//  Copyright 2008 __MyCompanyName__. All rights reserved.
//
```

Xcode includes the file name and the project name, as well as the creation user and time, which is because this information lets you know at a glance which file you're looking at and who was responsible for its creation, as well as giving you a clue as to its general vintage. The default company name, though, is unfortunate. Last time I checked, __MyCompanyName__ wasn't hiring Mac programmers, only TPS report creators.

For inexplicable reasons, Xcode 3.1 does not include any user interface for changing the __MyCompanyName__ placeholder. You need to drop down into Terminal to change it. Because you're going to be creating a lot of new source files, let's go ahead and change the company name to something more reasonable. It can be your own name, your company's name, or something totally made up.

First, open the *Utilities* folder in the Finder. You can use ⌘⇧U to navigate directly to it. Look for the Terminal application and run it. In Terminal, enter the following command exactly as it's printed, all on one line, except use your company name instead of "Length-O-Words.com".

```
defaults write com.apple.Xcode PBXCustomTemplateMacroDefinitions➡
    '{"ORGANIZATIONNAME" = "Length-O-Words.com";}'
```

After you type that on one line, press enter. If it works, you won't see any output reply. Luckily, you have to run this command only once. Quit and restart Xcode, and now the generated file comments for new files look much better:

```
//
//  HulaDance.h
//  Untitled3
//
//  Created by markd on 7/25/08.
//  Copyright 2008 Length-O-Words.com. All rights reserved.
//
```

And we promise that you won't see any more of Terminal for the rest of this chapter.

Using Editor Tips and Tricks

Xcode provides you with a couple of basic ways of organizing the project and source code editors. The way we've shown so far is the default interface, which is mostly an all-in-one window for your minute-by-minute project and coding tasks. Some auxiliary windows are also hanging around, like the run log shown in Figure 7-1. A single editing pane is used for all source files, and the contents of the editor change based on which source file is selected in the left-hand *Groups & Files* pane.

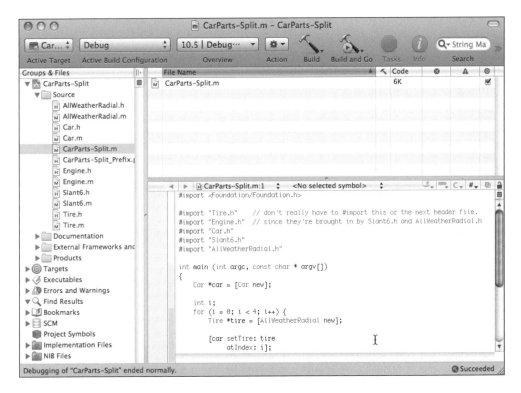

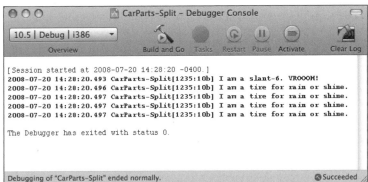

Figure 7-1. *Xcode's default user interface: soure code and debugger*

Xcode also has a mode in which each of your source files open in its own window as you edit it. If you have a lot of screen real estate and don't mind dealing with many windows, then that may be the work style for you. Here, we're going to assume you'll be using the code editor embedded in the *Project* window, because it makes taking screen shots a whole lot easier.

On the left side of the window is the *Groups & Files* list, which shows you all the moving parts of your project: your source files, the frameworks you link to, and the *Targets* that describe how to actually build your individual programs. You'll also find some utilities like the bookmarks in your project (we'll cover bookmarks in a little bit), access to source code control repositories (handy if you're collaborating with other programmers), all your project symbols, and some smart folders.

At the top of the window, underneath the toolbar, is a browser, which shows you selected files from *Groups & Files*. You can use the search box to narrow down the list of files shown. Figure 7-2 shows a search for the letter *n* after we selected the *Source* folder.

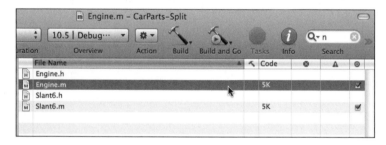

Figure 7-2. *Narrowing down the list of files*

The browser shows each of the matching source files with "n" in its name. You can click files in the browser to put them into the editor. Because larger projects may have over a hundred source files, the browser is a handy way to navigate around if you have lots of files. We'll talk a bit more about navigating through your source files later in this chapter.

When you're working on code, you'll want to hide the browser so that you get more vertical screen real estate. One of the default tool bar icons on the far right side of the window (not shown in these screen shots) is called *Editor*; it toggles the browser on and off. ⌘⇧E is a quick shortcut for this toggle.

Even when you're using the single-window mode, having a source file or two in its own window can be useful, especially if you're comparing two different files. Double-clicking a source file in the *Groups & Files* pane opens the file in a new window. You can have the same file open in two windows, but be warned that sometimes the two windows can get out of sync until you click each of them.

Writing Your Code with a Little Help from Xcode

Many programmers write code all day. Many programmers write code all night, too. For all of those programmers, Xcode has some features that make writing code easier and more fun.

Indentation (Pretty Printing)

You've probably noticed that all the code in this book is nicely indented, with bodies of if statements and for loops shifted over so they're indented farther than surrounding code. Objective-C does not require you to indent your code, but doing so is a good idea because it makes seeing the structure of your code easier at a glance. Xcode automatically indents your code as you type it.

Sometimes, heavy editing can leave the code in a messy state. Xcode can help here, too. Control-click (or right-click) to see the editor's contextual menu, and then choose *Re-indent selection*. Xcode will go through the selection, tidying everything up. There's no built-in hot-key for this, but you can add one in Xcode's preferences *Key Bindings* pane.

⌘[and ⌘] shift the selected code left or right, which is handy if you just put an if statement around some code.

Let's say you have this in the editor:

```
Engine *engine = [Slant6 new];
[car setEngine: engine];
```

Later, you decide you only want to create a new engine if the user set a preference:

```
if (userWantsANewEngine) {
Engine *engine = [Slant6 new];
[car setEngine: engine];
}
```

You can select the two middle lines of code and press ⌘] to shift them over.

You can infinitely tweak Xcode's indentation engine. You might prefer spaces to tabs. You might like your braces to be put on a new line instead of having them up on the same line with the if statement. Whatever you want to do, chances are you can tailor Xcode to abide by your One True Code formatting style. Here's a handy tip: if you want to quickly and easily start a heated Internet discussion among programmers, begin talking about code formatting preferences.

Code Completion (Code Sense)

You may have noticed that Xcode sometimes offers suggestions while you're typing code. This is Xcode's Code Sense feature, often just called **code completion**. As you're writing your program, Xcode builds an index of a whole lot of stuff, including names of variables and methods in your projects and the frameworks you include. It knows about local variable names and their types. It probably even knows if you've been naughty or nice. As you're typing, Xcode is constantly comparing what you're typing with its index of symbols. If there's a match, Xcode will offer a suggestion, as shown in Figure 7-3.

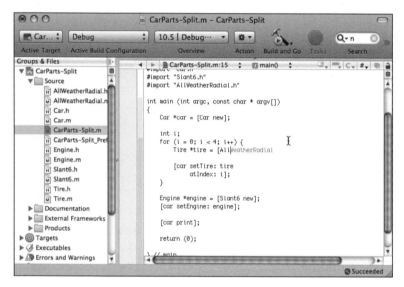

Figure 7-3. *Xcode code completion*

Here, we've started typing *[All*, and Xcode thinks we might be wanting to send a message to the AllWeatherRadial class. Xcode happened to guess correctly, so we can press tab to accept *AllWeatherRadial* as the completion.

But you say, "Aww, that's too easy! We only have one class that starts with 'All'!". That's true, but Xcode will offer the completion menu even if there are many possibilities, and, in any case, you can press the escape key to have Xcode open a menu with all possible completions, as shown in Figure 7-4.

You can see there are quite a few possibilities that start with "all". Xcode realizes that the current project contains a class that starts with "all" and assumes that's the logical first choice. The colored boxes next to the name indicate what the symbol is: *E* for an enumerated symbol, *f* for a function, *#* for a #define, *m* for a method, *C* for a class, and so on.

If you don't want to bring up the menu, you can use control-period to cycle through the options or shift-control-period to cycle backward. Don't worry if you don't catch all the shortcuts as we go along. There's a handy cheat sheet at the end of this chapter.

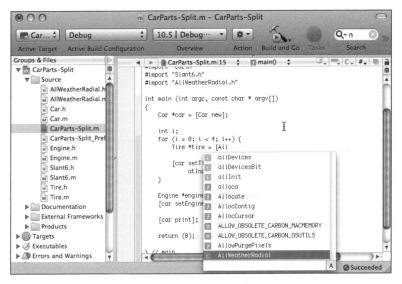

Figure 7-4. *Possible completions for "all"*

You can use the completion menu as a quick API reference for a class. Consider `NSDictionary`, which has a method that lets you specify a list of arguments representing the keys and objects used to build a dictionary. Is it `+dictionaryWithKeysAndObjects`, or is it `+dictionaryWith➥ObjectsAndKeys`? Who can remember? One easy way to find out is to start a method call to `[NSDictionary`, type a space to indicate you've finished typing the class name, and press escape. Xcode will realize that you're going to be putting the name of a method there and will display all the methods that `NSDictionary` responds to, and sure enough, there's `dictionary➥WithObjectsAndKeys`, shown near the top of the menu in Figure 7-5.

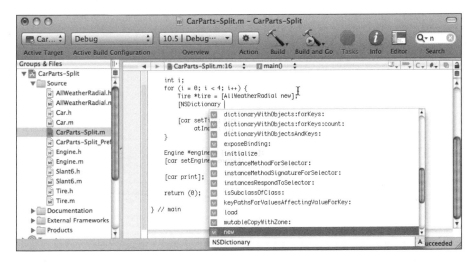

Figure 7-5. *Exploring a class with Code Sense*

Sometimes, when you use code completion, you'll get strange little boxes in among your completion, as illustrated in Figure 7-6. What's going on there?

```
Engine *engine = [Slant6 new];
[car setTire: (Tire *)tire atIndex: (int)index)
```

Figure 7-6. *Code completion placeholders*

Notice that Xcode is suggesting -setTire:atIndex:, which takes two parameters. Xcode's Code Sense goes farther than just filling out names. The two parameters shown there are actually placeholders. If you press tab again, the method will complete to setTire, as shown in Figure 7-7.

```
Engine *engine = [Slant6 new];
[car setTire: (Tire *)tire atIndex: (int)index
```

Figure 7-7. *Selecting a placeholder*

The first placeholder is highlighted. Type anything to replace it with a real argument. You can click the second placeholder and replace it too. You don't even have to take your hands off the keyboard. You can move to the next placeholder by typing control-forward slash.

Kissing Parentheses

As you type your code, you might sometimes notice the screen flash a little when you type certain characters, such as),], or }. When this happens, Xcode is showing you what the closing symbol matches, as shown in Figure 7-8.

```
for (i = 0; i < 4; i++) {
    Tire *tire = [AllWeatherRadial new];
    [car setTire: tire atIndex: i]|
}
```

Figure 7-8. *Kissing the parentheses*

This feature is sometimes called "kissing the parentheses" and can be really handy when you're closing up a complex set of delimiters. Make sure that every closing character you type matches with the opening character you expect. If you cross the streams, like trying to type] when should really type), Xcode will beep at you and not show the kissy-kissy stuff.

You can also double-click one of those delimiters, and Xcode will select all the code between it and its mate.

Mass Edits

Sometimes, you have a code change that you want to make in a couple of places, but you don't want to do every edit individually. Making a lot of similar edits manually is fraught with peril, since humans aren't typically very good at boring repetitive work. Luckily for us, computers thrive on boring and repetitive work.

The first Xcode feature to help us here doesn't actually manipulate code but installs a safety net. Chose **File ➤ Make Snapshot** (or its handy shortcut, command-control-S) and Xcode will remember the state of your project. You're now free to edit source files and fold, spindle, and mutilate your stuff all you want. If you realize you've made a terrible mistake, you can use the snapshots window, which you can access from **File ➤ Snapshots**, to recover from a previous snapshot. It's a good idea to take a snapshot before doing anything too adventurous.

NOTE

The snapshots are actually stored in a disk image that lives in *~/Library/Application Support/Developer/ Shared/SnapshotRepository.sparseimage*. Sometimes, this disk image can become corrupted (from too much hard living?), and Xcode will give you a mysterious "Snapshot Failed: A project snapshot cannot be created" error. If you get this error, try deleting the sparse image and rebooting.

Of course, Xcode has search-and-replace functionality. There is an **Edit ➤ Find** submenu with several handy choices. **Find in Project** lets you do search and replace across the files in your project. Figure 7-9 shows the projectwide search and replace window.

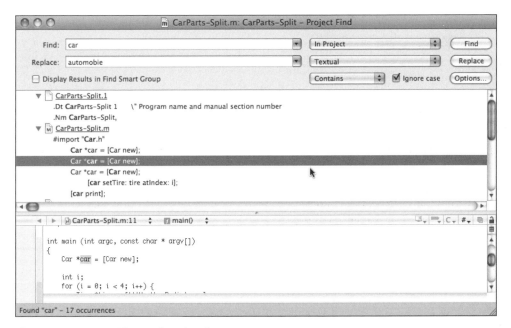

Figure 7-9. *Projectwide search and replace*

Let's say we're thinking of changing "car" to "automobile." After filling in the blanks and clicking *Find*, you can see that there are references to the Car class and car local variable. You could uncheck the *Ignore case* checkbox and just change the local variables inside of main. You can click *Replace All* to make the change globally.

Search and replace functionality is a blunt instrument for doing this kind of surgery, however. It does too much if you're just trying to rename a variable in a function (because it might clobber stuff in the whole file), and it doesn't do enough if you're trying to rename a class. Specifically, it doesn't rename the source file.

Xcode has two features to fill those gaps. The first has the svelte moniker of "Edit all in Scope." You can choose a symbol, like a local variable or a parameter, and select **Edit ➤ Edit all in Scope**. Then, as you type, all the occurrences of that symbol are instantly updated. Not only is it a fast way to make a lot of changes, it looks really cool while you're doing it.

Figure 7-10 shows "car" being edited in scope. Notice that all of the car local variables have a box around them. Once you start typing *Automobile*, all of the boxes will change, like in Figure 7-11.

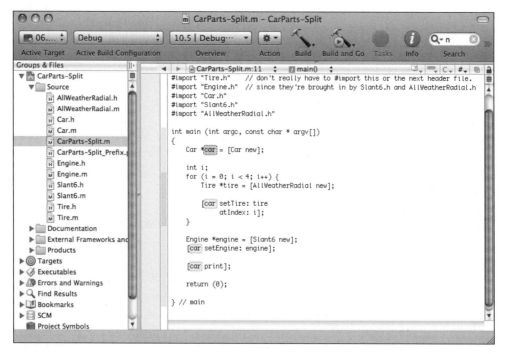

Figure 7-10. *Starting to edit all in scope; changing the car to an automobile*

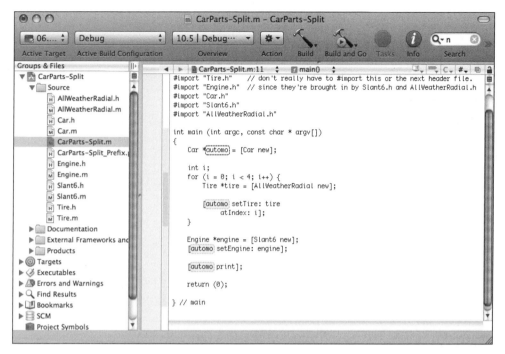

Figure 7-11. *Editing all in scope*

When you're done, just click elsewhere in the source editing window, and you'll get out of **Edit all in Scope** mode.

Sometimes, you'll go to make a change like this and find the **Edit all in Scope** menu item disabled. This feature is tied closely to the syntax coloring in Xcode, so if you have that feature turned off or have twiddled with it a lot, **Edit all in Scope** may refuse to work. To fix it, go back to the preferences and twiddle with syntax coloring again until it works—there's a bit of voodoo involved.

Recall our use of the term "refactoring" in previous chapters? It's not just a word we made up to sound really smart. Xcode has some refactoring tools built in. One of the refactoring helpers lets you easily rename a class. Not only does it rename the class but it does fancy things like renaming the source files to match. And if you have a GUI program, it even digs into the nib files and changes things there. (Don't worry if that last sentence is total gibberish to you right now. It's a really cool feature, and we'll explain more about nib files in Chapter 14.)

Let's try changing all of our Car classes to Automobile ones. Open *Car.h* in the editor, and put your insertion point in the word Car. Choose **Edit ➤ Refactor**. You'll see a dialog like the one shown in Figure 7-12, where we've entered *Automobile* as the replacement for *Car*.

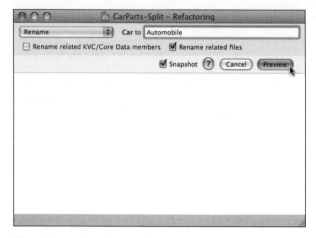

Figure 7-12. *Starting to refactor*

You'll want to make sure the *Snapshot* checkbox is checked, just as a safety net. Xcode figures out what it will do after you click *Preview* and presents it to you as shown in Figure 7-13.

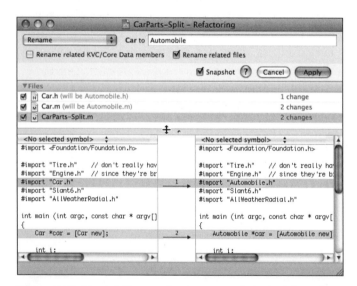

Figure 7-13. *Xcode telling us what it wants to do in the refactoring*

You can see that Xcode will rename *Car.h* and *Car.m* to the corresponding *Automobile*-style names. You can click a source file to see what changes Xcode will make in the file merge viewer at the bottom of the window. Looking there, you'll see that Xcode has changed *Car* to *Automobile* in the #import, as well as the class name in the proper places.

Sadly, refactoring does not rename things in comments, so end-of-class comments, file header comments generated by Xcode, or any documentation comments you may have written will need to be fixed manually. You can search and replace to make this a bit easier.

Navigating Around in Your Code

Most source files have a familiar life cycle. They're created new and get a lot of code added to them quickly to make them do their magic. Next, they go into a mode where additions and modifications are about fifty-fifty and then into a maintenance mode, in which you have to read a lot of the file before you add new code or make changes. Finally, after a class has matured, you end up browsing its code to figure out how the class works before using it elsewhere in your program. This section explores various ways of navigating around your code as it lives its life.

emacs is Not a Mac

An ancient text editor called emacs, invented in the 1970s, is available on modern Macs. Some throwbacks (including Mark Dalrymple) use it on a daily basis. We won't talk about emacs much here, except to describe some of its key bindings—and we'll even tell you what that means.

The phrase "emacs key bindings" describes keystrokes that let you move the text cursor without taking your hand off the main part of the keyboard. Just as many folks prefer arrow keys over reaching for the mouse, emacs users prefer these cursor movement keys instead of reaching for the arrow keys. And here's the punch line: amazingly enough, these same movement keys work in any Cocoa text field, including not just Xcode but also TextEdit, Safari's URL bar and text fields, Pages and Keynote text areas, and many more. Here they are:

- *control-F*: Move **f**orward, to the right (same as the right arrow).

- *control-B*: Move **b**ackwards, to the left (same as the left arrow).

- *control-P*: Move to the **p**revious line (same as the up arrow).

- *control-N*: Move to the **n**ext line (same as the down arrow).

- *control-A*: Move to the beginning of a line (same as the as command-left arrow).

- *control-E*: Move to the **e**nd of a line (same as the as command-right arrow).

- *control-T*: **T**ranspose (swap) the characters on either side of the cursor.

- *control-D*: **D**elete the character to the right of the cursor.

- *control-K*: **K**ill (delete) the rest of the line. This is handy if you want to redo the end of a line of code.

- *control-L*: Center the insertion point in the window. This is great if you cursor or want to quickly scroll the window so the insertion point is fr

If you get these keystrokes into your head and under your fingers, you can m movements and editing operations much faster—not just in Xcode.

Search Your Feelings, Luke

At the upper-right corner of the Xcode project window is a search box. Xcode filters the contents of the browser based on what you type there. To use the search box, select something in the *Groups & Files* list, such as your *Source* folder. The browser shows all your source files. Type something, like *Car*, and you would see the list filtered down to as shown in Figure 7-14.

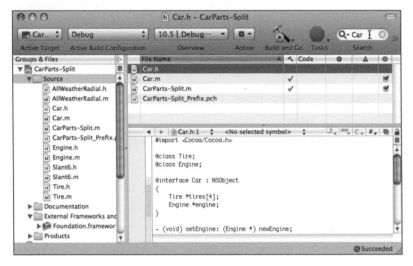

Figure 7-14. *Filtering the cars*

You can also look into frameworks you're using. Select *Foundation Framework* in the *External Frameworks and Libraries* folder, and you'll see a list of header files provided by the framework. You can trim this down by putting text into the search box, such as typing *array* and getting both of the array-related Foundation headers, as shown in Figure 7-15.

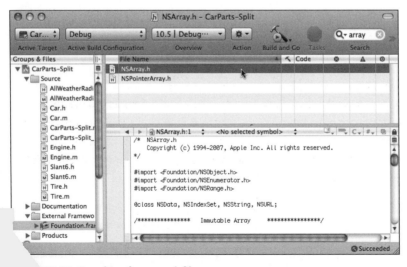

7-15. *Searching framework files*

Open Sesame Seed!

You're looking at one of your source files, and you see #import at the top. Wouldn't it be great if you could open that header file quickly without having to do a lot of mousing around? You can! Just select the file name (you can even leave off the .h), hold down the Option key, and choose **File ➤ Open Quickly**. You can use the shortcut ⌘⌥⇧D. Xcode opens the header file for you.

If you don't have any text selected, choosing **Open Quickly** opens a dialog box, which is another way of finding a file to look at, with the shortcut ⌘⇧D. It's a very simple window containing just a search field and a table, but it is a very quick way to do searches across the contents of your project. Type *tire* in the search box to look for things tire-related, as shown in Figure 7-16. You can also put in other terms, like *NSArray* to see the NSArray header files.

Figure 7-16. *The Open Quickly dialog*

If all you want is to see the counterpart to a file—*Blah.h* if you're looking at *Blah.m*, or vice versa—you can do that by pressing ⌘⌥↑ (command-option-up arrow).

Bookmarks

Xcode lets you place bookmarks in your code. You may have some interesting places in your code, like a line you want to fix later, or you might want to mark the definition of a very important class. To create a bookmark, put your insertion point in a source file, or select a region of text. Then choose **Edit ➤ Add to Bookmarks**, or use the default shortcut of ⌘D (same as in Safari) and when prompted, type the name of the bookmark.

You will see your bookmarks in the *Bookmarks* section in the *Groups & Files* pane, as shown in Figure 7-17.

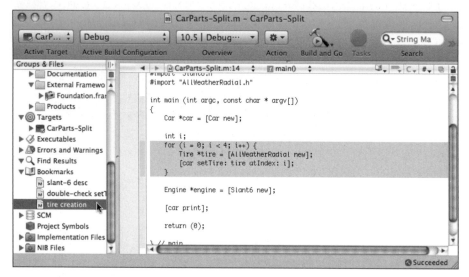

Figure 7-17. *Xcode's bookmarks*

Focus Your Energy

You may have noticed the two empty columns immediately to the left of your source code. The wider column to the left is known as the **gutter**, and we'll have our minds there later when we discuss debugging. The narrower one is known as the **focus ribbon**, and as its name implies, it allows you to focus your attention on different parts of your code.

Notice the shades of gray in the focus ribbon: the more deeply nested a bit of code is, the darker the gray next to it in the ribbon. This color-coding gives you a hint of the complexity of your code at a glance. You can hover over different gray regions of the focus bar to high-light the corresponding hunk of code, as in Figure 7-18.

You can click in the focus ribbon to collapse chunks of code. Say you're convinced that the if statement and the for loop shown in Figure 7-18 are correct and you don't want to look at them anymore, so you can concentrate (focus your attention, as it were) on the rest of the code in the function. Click to the left of the if statement, and its body will collapse as shown in Figure 7-19.

You can see now that the body of the if statement has been replaced by a box with an ellipsis in it. Double-click the box to expand the code back the way it was, or click the disclosure triangle in the focus ribbon. The code isn't gone; it's just hidden, so your file should compile and work fine even like this. **Code folding** is another name for this kind of feature. Check out the **View ➤ Code Folding** menu for a lot of additional options.

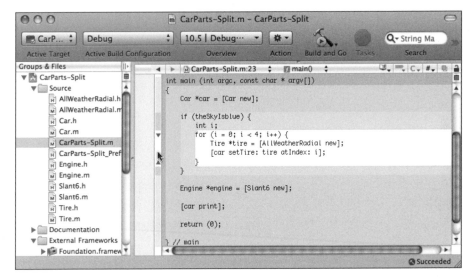

Figure 7-18. *Highlighting code with the focus ribbon*

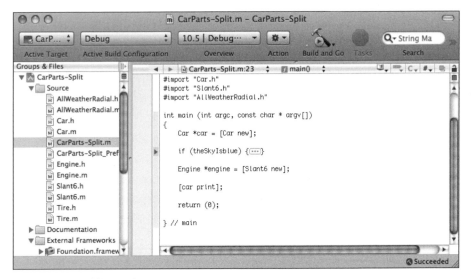

Figure 7-19. *Folding code*

The Navigation Bar Is Open

At the top of the code editor is a little ribbon of controls, shown in Figure 7-20, known as the **navigation bar**. Many of its controls are there to let you quickly bounce around your source files in the project.

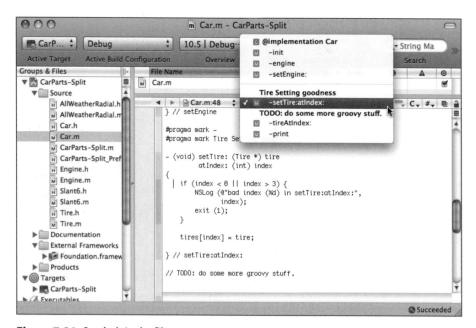

Figure 7-20. *The navigation bar*

From left to right, you have backward and forward buttons that cycle you through the history of files you've had open during this editing session. They work like Safari's back and forward arrows. Next to those buttons is a pop-up menu that shows the current file (*Car.m*) and line number in the file where the insertion point is located (*48*). Click this menu to see your file history, and choose a file to open in the editor if you so desire.

Next is the function menu. It shows that the insertion point is currently in the method -setTire:atIndex:, and that's what's in the menu. Click the menu to see all the interesting symbols, as shown in Figure 7-21.

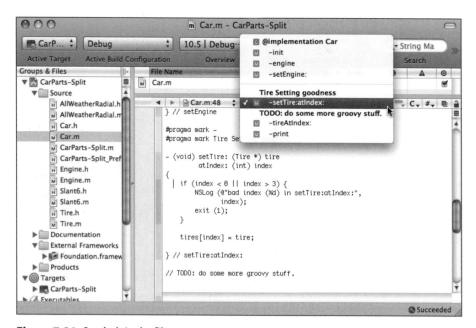

Figure 7-21. *Symbols in the file*

-setTire:atIndex: is highlighted, because that's where the cursor is. You can see the other methods above and below it, sorted by the order in a file. Option-click the function menu sort it alphabetically. You'll also notice a couple of extra things in there, like *Tire Setting goodness* and a *TODO*. Where did those come from?

You can stick stuff into this menu in a couple of ways. One way is to use #pragma mark stuff to put the string *stuff* into the menu. This is handy for adding human-readable anchors for other humans to see and use. #pragma mark - (minus sign) puts a separator line into the menu. Xcode also looks in comments that begin with words like MARK: (behaves the same as #pragma mark), TODO:, FIXME:, !!!:, and ???:, and puts that text into the function menu, too. These are all programmer signals for "better come back and look at this before you inflict this program on an unsuspecting public."

NOTE

"Pragma" comes from a Greek word meaning "action." #pragma is a way to pass on information or instructions to compilers and code editors that are outside of the usual lines of Objective-C code. Pragmas are usually ignored, but they may have meaning to tools used in software development. If a tool does not understand a pragma, the tool should nod, smile, and ignore it, without generating a warning or an error.

The next control, the one that looks like a little book, shows any bookmarks that have been set in the current file. You'll notice this icon is the same as the *Bookmarks* icon in the *Groups & Files* pane.

The next control has all the breakpoints in the file. We'll talk about breakpoints more in the "Debugging" section later in this chapter.

The **C** menu lets you navigate up and down the class hierarchy. If you have *Engine.m* displaying in the code editor and you bring up the class menu, you'll see something like Figure 7-22.

Figure 7-22. *The navigation bar class menu*

Engine is the highlighted item in Figure 7-22. You can see that Xcode knows Slant6 is a subclass and NSObject is the superclass. Selecting Slant6 opens *Slant6.m*. Selecting NSObject brings up *NSObject.h* from the Foundation headers. We don't have access to *NSObject.m*, because that belongs to Apple, so Xcode does the next best thing and brings up the header. If you choose NSObject, which opens the *NSObject.h* header file, and then open the class menu again, you'll see all the subclasses of NSObject. There are lots of them! As you can see, this menu is very handy for navigating around your code's inheritance tree.

The next menu, labeled with a #, is the included files menu; the included files menu shown in Figure 7-23 will appear if you're looking at *Slant6.h*.

This shows that *Slant6.h* #imports (or #includes) *Engine.h*. Xcode also knows that two other files, *CarParts-Split.m* and *Slant6.m*, include this *Slant6.h*. This menu is another way to quickly move around the dependencies of your project.

Figure 7-23.
The included files menu

The overlapping squares icon opens the counterpart for this file, just like the shortcut ⌘⌥↑.

The last icon on the row, the lock, lets you make a file read only. If you're just browsing a file, you can mark it as read only so you don't accidentally introduce any changes, in case (for example) the cat jumps up and walks on the keyboard.

Right below the lock, at the top of the scrollbar, is the split button. Click it to split the source window in half, allowing you to see two places of your file at once, as in Figure 7-24. You can resize each with the split bar.

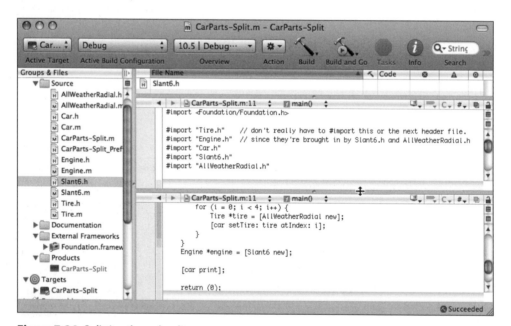

Figure 7-24. *Splitting the code editor*

Each editing pane gets its own navigation bar, which you can use to point each pane at a different file. Option-clicking the split box makes the split vertical instead of horizontal. You can continue this to an extreme, as shown in the ridiculous Figure 7-25. You can get rid of a pane by clicking the rectangle button underneath the split button.

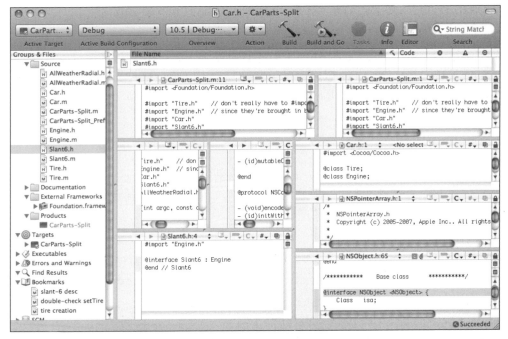

Figure 7-25. *Splitting the code editor too many times*

Getting Information

Bouncing around your code and the Cocoa header files is all fine and dandy, but sometimes you need to get some information from outside your own code. Luckily, Xcode comes with a treasure trove of documentation and reference material (what is a trove, anyway?).

Research Assistance, Please

The little floating *Research Assistant* window updates itself based on what you're interacting with in Xcode. Open the Research Assistant by choosing **Help ➤ Show Research Assistant**.

For instance, say you have your insertion point inside of the word *NSString*. The Research Assistant will look like Figure 7-26.

There's a huge amount of information available. The first two items bring up the `NSString` class reference documentation in the documentation window. The *NSString.h* item brings up the header file in the editor.

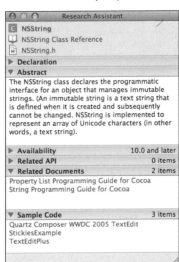

Figure 7-26. *The Research Assistant*

The *Abstract* pane describes the class. If you had your cursor in the middle of a method call, the *Abstract* would describe the method, along with related calls. There are pointers to higher level documentation and some sample code that use a NSString a lot.

The Research Assistant is incredibly useful when you are looking at the different build settings you can tweak. Just select the build setting in the project information panel and see the explanation in the Research Assistant.

Is There a Documentor in the House?

If you want to go directly to Apple's official documentation for an API, a very fast way to do that is to option–double-click a symbol; this is simply a shortcut for doing a documentation search for that symbol.

Say you had a line of code like [someString UTF8String], which converts someString (an NSString) into a C-style string expressed in Unicode. If you option–double-click *UTF8String*, the documentation browser opens and searches for *UTF8String*, as shown in Figure 7-27.

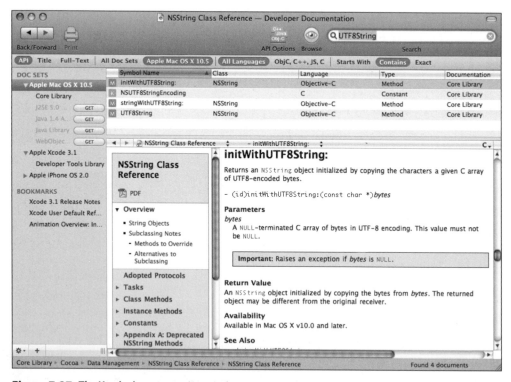

Figure 7-27. *The Xcode documentation window*

That's a mighty busy window, and it packs in a lot of information. In the upper-right corner is a search box, which comes prepopulated with *UTF8String*. The ribbon of buttons underneath the toolbar lets you refine which documentation sets are searched. You can look at all documentation or documentation for just Mac OS X or the iPhone. Or you can limit your search by language, so if you're only editing JavaScript, you don't need to wade through C++ information.

Below the button ribbon is a pane on the left that contains documentation sets and a set of bookmarks. You can add bookmarks to specific chunks of documentation by using the trusty ⌘D shortcut. These bookmarks are distinct from the project bookmarks you might have placed in your code. Documentation bookmarks are global to Xcode and are not limited to a specific project.

On the right side of the window at the top is a browser showing all the search matches. In Figure 7-27, it shows three methods and a constant. The most interesting is the last one, *UTF8*, which is the call we're actually making here.

Below that is a browser that shows the documents. It's kind of a small area for reading documentation, but it's easy to open the documentation into another Xcode window or even into a web browser. To open the documents in another window, control-click (or right-click) on the documentation area to open a menu.

Debugging

Bugs happen. It's a fact of life that errors creep into your programs, especially when you're just starting out with a new language and a new platform. When faced with problems, take a deep breath; take a sip of you favorite beverage; and systematically try to figure out what's gone wrong. This process of figuring out program errors is called **debugging**.

Ooongawa!

The easiest kind of debugging is brute force, **caveman debugging**, in which you put in print statements (like NSLog) to show the flow of control of your program, along with some data values. You've probably been doing this all along without knowing its name. You may run into some folks who look down on caveman debugging, but it can be an effective tool, especially if you're just learning a new system. So ignore those naysayers.

Xcode's Debugger

In addition to everything else, Xcode includes a debugger. A **debugger** is a program that sits between your program and the operating system and can interrupt your program, making it stop in its tracks and allowing you to poke around the program's data and even change things. When you're done looking around, you can resume execution to see what happens. You can also single step through code, running line by line to see precisely what effect the code is having on your data.

There are a couple of places in Xcode where you can use the debugger. The first is right in your text editor, clicking in the gutter to set breakpoints. A **breakpoint** is a place where the debugger should stop your program and let you see what's going on.

Xcode provides a mini debugger, which is a floating window with some basic controls that let you do simple debugging tasks without all of Xcode getting in your way.

Xcode also has a debugger window that provides a lot of information at a glance, and a debugging console where you can type commands directly to the debugger.

NOTE

The debugger used by Xcode is GDB, part of the GNU project. GDB is available on a zillion different platforms, and you can run it from the command line if you want. GDB is very well documented, although it is a bit opaque, and there are several GDB tutorials available on the web.

We'll discuss debugging inside the Xcode text editor. You should definitely play around with the other debugging modes if you want to learn more.

Subtle Symbolism

When you're planning on debugging a program, you need to make sure you're using a *Debug* build configuration. You can check this in the **Active Build Configuration** pop-up menu in the Xcode toolbar. The *Debug* configuration tells the compiler to emit extra debugging symbols, which the debugger uses to figure out what's where in your program.

Also, make sure you run with the debugger. There are a couple of ways to run your programs from within Xcode. Selecting **Run ➤ Run**, or pressing ⌘R, will run your program without using the debugger. To use the debugger, choose either **Run ➤ Go (Debug)**, or **Run ➤ Debug**, or use the shortcut ⌘Y.

Let's Debug!

Getting started with the debugger is a bit easier with a GUI program than with the command-line programs we've been using so far. A GUI program is used to sitting around waiting for the user to do something, so using it gives us lots of time to find the debugger buttons, interrupt the program, and start poking around it. Our command-line programs, on the other hand, come and go so fast you can't do much debugging on them. So let's start by setting a breakpoint in main. We'll be using *06.01 CarParts-split* from the last chapter.

Open *CarParts-Split*.m, and click in the gutter, which, as you saw earlier, is the wide bar to the left of the focus ribbon. You should get a blue arrow thingy (yes, that's a technical term) indicating your new breakpoint, as shown in Figure 7-28.

You can delete a breakpoint by dragging it out of the gutter, and you can disable it by clicking it. Opening its contextual menu will show a bunch of choices. Be sure to check out some of the built-in breakpoints. For example, you can get Xcode to talk to you! Yeah, I know it's a common myth that programmers are loners, but sometimes you do need to hear a voice that's different from the voices in your head.

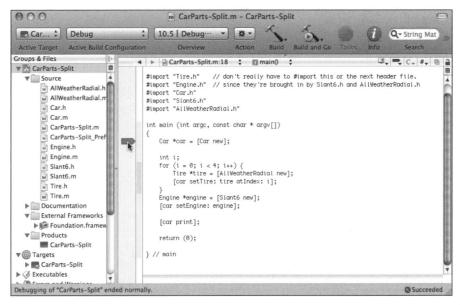

Figure 7-28. *Setting a breakpoint*

Now, select **Run ➤ Debug** to run your program. Your program should stop at the breakpoint, as shown in Figure 7-29. Notice the red arrow pointing at a line of code. This is like the sign on the mall map that says, "You are here."

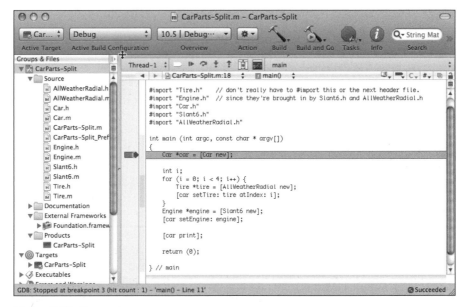

Figure 7-29. *You are here.*

The status line at the bottom of the Xcode window says *GDB: Stopped at breakpoint . . .* You'll see that you've grown a new control strip above the navigation bar, shown in Figure 7-30.

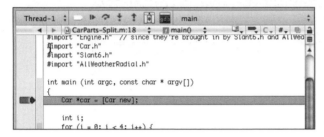

Figure 7-30. *Debugger controls*

Starting from the left, the first pop-up lets you select which thread you want to look at. You won't need to bother with threaded programming for a while, so you can ignore this for now.

NOTE

> **Threaded programming** is programming with multiple streams of execution happening at the same time, and it is very difficult to do correctly. Threaded programming often creates bugs that are incredibly difficult to chase down. If anyone tells you threaded programming is easy, they're either deluded or trying to sell you something.

The next control looks like a breakpoint, and it toggles all breakpoints on or off. You might decide, "Hey, I think I fixed everything." Rather than deleting all your breakpoints, you can just turn them off and let the program run. When you discover another bug, you can turn them back on and get back to debugging.

The next four controls deal with what happens next, as far as program control goes. The first looks like the play button from a CD player. (Recall those? If not, maybe ask your parents.) This is the continue button; you could also us the shortcut ⌘⌥P. After you click it, the program runs until it hits a breakpoint, finishes, or crashes.

The next control, which looks like a dot with someone jumping over it, is the step over button (you could also press ⌘⌥O). This one executes one line of code and then returns control back to you. If you click the step over button three times, the "you are here" arrow will move to the -setTire:atIndex call, as shown in Figure 7-31.

The next button, the arrow pointing down into a dot, is the step into button (you can also press ⇧⌘I). If you have the source code for the function or method you're currently sitting on, Xcode will step into that function, bring up its code, and set the "you are here" arrow at the beginning of it, as shown in Figure 7-32.

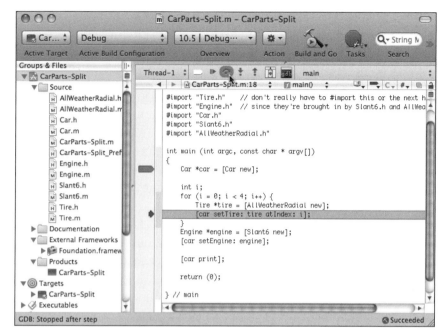

Figure 7-31. *After single stepping*

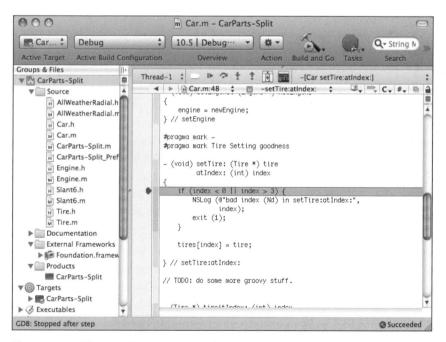

Figure 7-32. *After stepping into a method*

The last button is step out (press ⌘⇧T), which will let the current function finish and then return control to you on the next line of the calling function. If you're following along, don't use this one just yet. We'll be looking at some data values in this method in a little bit.

Finishing up the tour, the next button (a box with a spray can in it) brings up the Xcode debug window, and the button after that brings up the GDB console, where you can type stuff into the debugger directly.

The final control is a pop-up menu that shows the **call stack**, which is the current set of active functions. If A calls B, and B calls C, C is considered to be at the top of the stack, with B and A below it. If you open the call stack menu now, it will have `-[Car setTire:atIndex:]`, followed by `main`. That means that `main` called `-setTire:atIndex:`. With more complex programs, this call stack, also called a **stack trace**, can have dozens of entries in it. Sometimes, the best fact learned during a debugging session is, "How the heck did *this* code get called?" By looking at the call stack, you can see who called whom to get to the current state (of confusion).

Taking a Look-See

Now that you're stopped, what should you do next? Usually, when you set a breakpoint or single-step to a particular part of your program, you're interested in the **program state**—the values of variables.

Xcode has **datatips**, similar to the tooltips that tell you what a button does you hover over it. In the Xcode editor, you can hover over a variable, or a method argument, and Xcode pops up a little window that shows the value, as shown in Figure 7-33.

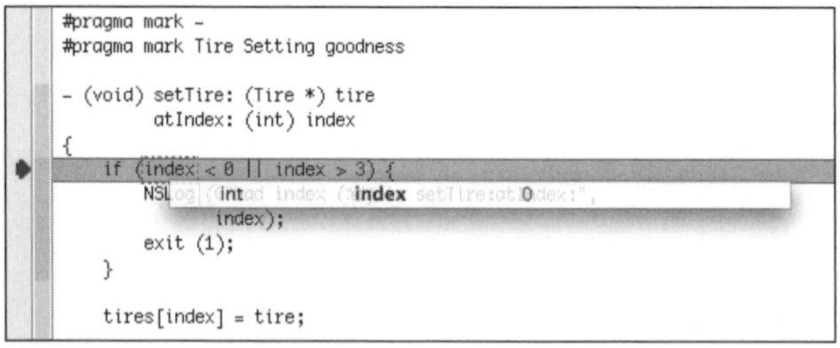

```
#pragma mark -
#pragma mark Tire Setting goodness

- (void) setTire: (Tire *) tire
         atIndex: (int) index
{
    if (index < 0 || index > 3) {
        NSLog (int index (index setTire:at 0 dex:",
                index);
        exit (1);
    }

    tires[index] = tire;
```

Figure 7-33. *Xcode datatip*

Figure 7-33 has us hovering over `index`. The datatip pops up and shows us the value is zero, as we expect. You can change the value by clicking the zero and typing in a new value. For example, you can type *37*, and then do a couple of step over commands to see the program exit from the out-of-bounds index.

While you're still in the loop, hover over `tires`, and you'll get an array. Scoot the mouse down, and hover over the arrow until it expands, showing you all four tires. Next, move down and over the first tire, and Xcode will show the guts of the tire to you. There are no instance variables in our tires, so there's not much to see. But if the class had instance variables, they would be displayed and editable. You can see the result of all this hovering and mousing in Figure 7-34.

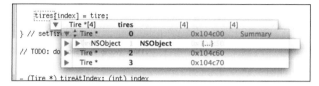

Figure 7-34. *Digging into the program's data*

And that's the whirlwind tour of the Xcode debugger. This information, plus huge amounts of your time, should be enough to let you debug any problems you come across. Happy debugging!

Cheat Sheet

We mentioned a lot of keyboard shortcuts in this chapter. As promised, we've collected them all in one easy place—Table 7-1. Feel free to tear out this page before you give the book to someone else, unless you think that would be rude.

Table 7-1. *Xcode Keyboard Shortcuts*

Keystroke	Description
⌘⇧E	Expand the editor
⌘[	Shift the code block to the left
⌘]	Shift the code block to the right
Tab	Accept a completion
Esc	Show the completion menu
Control-. (period)	Cycle through the completions
Shift-control-. (period)	Cycle backward through the completions
Control-/	Move to the next completion placeholder
Command-control-S	Make a snapshot
Control-F	Move the cursor forward
Control-B	Move the cursor backward
Control-P	Move the cursor to the previous line
Control-N	Move the cursor to the next line
Control-A	Move the cursor to the beginning of the line
Control-E	Move the cursor to the end of the line

(continued)

Table 7-1. (continued)

Keystroke	Description
Control-**T**	Transpose the characters adjacent to the cursor
Control-**D**	Delete the character to the right of the cursor
Control-**K**	Delete the line
Control-**L**	Center the cursor in the text editor
⌘⇧D	Show the Open Quickly window
⌘⌥⇧D	Open the file named by the selected text
⌘⌥↑	Open the counterpart file
⌘D	Add a bookmark
Option—double-click	Search in documentation
⌘Y	Run the program with the debugger
⌘⌥P	Continue (in the debugger)
⌘⌥O	Step over
⌘⌥I	Step into
⌘⌥T	Step out

Summary

This chapter was pretty information-dense, and we really didn't talk about Objective-C all that much. What's the deal? Just like woodworkers needs to know more than just wood (for example, they need to know all that stuff about tools), an Objective-C programmer needs to know more than just the language. Being able to quickly write, navigate, and debug your code in Xcode means that you spend less time wrestling with the environment and spend more time doing the fun stuff.

Next up is a meaty introduction to some of the classes in Cocoa. That should be fun!

Chapter 8

A Quick Tour of the Foundation Kit

*Y*ou've already seen that Objective-C is a pretty nifty language, and we haven't even finished exploring all the features it has to offer. For now, we're going to take a quick side trip and have a look at Cocoa's Foundation framework. Although strictly part of Cocoa and not built in to Objective-C, the Foundation framework is so important that we thought it worth exploring in this book.

As you saw in Chapter 2, Cocoa is actually composed of two different frameworks: Foundation and Application Kit. The Application Kit has all the user interface objects and high-level classes. You'll get a taste of the AppKit (as the cool kids call it) in Chapter 14.

Cocoa's Foundation framework has a bunch of useful low-level, data-oriented classes and types. We'll be visiting a number of these, such as NSString, NSArray, NSEnumerator, and NSNumber. Foundation has more than a hundred classes, all of which you can explore by looking at the documentation installed with Xcode. These documents live at */Developer/ADC Reference Library/documentation/ index.html*.

Before we continue, here's a note about the projects for this chapter and for the rest of this book. We'll still be making Foundation tool projects, but we'll leave in the boilerplate code, which follows (slightly reformatted to fit on this page):

```
#import <Foundation/Foundation.h>

int main (int argc, const char * argv[]) {
  NSAutoreleasePool * pool
     = [[NSAutoreleasePool alloc] init];
```

```
  // insert code here...
    NSLog(@"Hello, World!");

  [pool drain];
  return 0;
}
```

Take a look through this code. `main()` starts by creating (via `alloc`) and initializing (via `init`) an NSAutoreleasePool. The pool is drained at the end. This is a sneak preview of Cocoa memory management, which we'll discuss in the next chapter. For now, please just nod, smile, and leave the NSAutoreleasePool stuff in there. If you take it out, you won't hurt yourself, but you'll get some very strange messages when you run your programs.

Some Useful Types

Before digging into real live Cocoa classes, let's take a look at some `structs` that Cocoa provides for our benefit.

Home on the Range

The first structure is NSRange:

```
typedef struct _NSRange {
    unsigned int location;
    unsigned int length;
} NSRange;
```

This structure is used to represent a range of things, usually a range of characters in a string or a range of items in an array. The `location` field holds the starting position of the range, and `length` is the number of elements in the range. For the string "Objective-C is a cool language", the word "cool" can be described by the range that starts at `location` 17 and has `length` 4. `location` can have the value NSNotFound to indicate that the range doesn't refer to anything, probably because it's uninitialized.

You can make a new NSRange in three different ways. First, you can assign the field values directly:

```
NSRange range;
range.location = 17;
range.length = 4;
```

Second, you can use the C aggregate structure assignment mechanism (doesn't that sound impressive?):

```
NSRange range = { 17, 4 };
```

Finally, Cocoa provides a convenience function called NSMakeRange():

```
NSRange range = NSMakeRange (17, 4);
```

The nice thing about NSMakeRange() is that you can use it anywhere you can use a function, such as in a method call as an argument:

```
 [anObject flarbulateWithRange: NSMakeRange (13, 15)];
```

Geometric Types

You'll often see types that deal with geometry, such as NSPoint and NSSize. NSPoint represents an (x, y) point in the Cartesian plane:

```
typedef struct _NSPoint {
    float x;
    float y;
} NSPoint;
```

. NSSize holds a width and a height:

```
typedef struct _NSSize {
    float width;
    float height;
} NSSize;
```

In the Shapes family of programs, we could have used an NSPoint and an NSSize instead of our custom rectangle struct, but we wanted to keep things as simple as possible at the time. Cocoa provides a rectangle type, which is a composition of a point and a size:

```
typedef struct _NSRect {
    NSPoint origin;
    NSSize size;
} NSRect;
```

Cocoa gives us convenience functions for making these bad boys too: NSMakePoint(), NSMakeSize(), and NSMakeRect().

Stringing Us Along

The first real live class on our tour is NSString, Cocoa's string handling class. A string is just a sequence of human-readable characters. Since computers tend to interact with humans on a regular basis, having a way to store and manipulate human-readable text is a fine idea. You've met NSStrings before, with the special NSString literal, indicated by an at sign before a double-quoted string, as in @"Hi!". These literal strings are as much NSStrings as the ones you create programmatically.

If you've ever done any string processing in C, such as the stuff covered in *Learn C on the Mac* by Dave Mark (Apress 2009), you know it's pretty painful. C implements strings as simple arrays of characters that mark their end with a trailing zero-byte. Cocoa's NSString has a bunch of built-in methods that make string handling much easier.

Build That String

You've seen functions like printf() and NSLog() that take a format string and some arguments and emit formatted output. NSString's stringWithFormat: method creates a new NSString just like that, with a format and arguments:

```
+ (id) stringWithFormat: (NSString *) format, ...;
```

And you make a new string like this:

```
NSString *height;
height = [NSString stringWithFormat:
    @"Your height is %d feet, %d inches", 5, 11];
```

The resulting string is "Your height is 5 feet, 11 inches".

Class Methods

A couple of interesting things are going on in stringWithFormat:'s declaration. The first is the ellipses (...) at the end, which tells you (and the compiler) that this method will take any number of additional arguments, specified in a comma-separated list, just like printf() and NSLog().

Another wacky and even more important fact about stringWithFormat: is the very special leading character in the declaration: a plus sign. What's up with that? When the Objective-C runtime builds a class, it creates a **class object** that represents the class. The class object contains pointers to the superclass, class name, and to the list of the class's methods. The class object also contains a long that specifies the size, in bytes, for newly created instance objects of that class.

When you declare a method with the plus sign, you've marked the method as a **class method**. This method belongs to the class object (as opposed to an instance object of the class) and is typically used to create new instances. Class methods used to create new objects are called **factory methods**.

stringWithFormat: is a factory method. It creates a new object for you based on the arguments you give it. Using stringWithFormat: to make a new string is a whole lot easier than starting off with an empty string and building all the individual components.

Class methods can also be used to access global data. AppKit's NSColor class has some class methods named after various colors, such as redColor and blueColor. To get hold of a blue color to draw with, you write something like this:

```
NSColor *haveTheBlues = [NSColor blueColor];
```

The vast majority of methods you create will be instance methods and will be declared with a leading minus sign (-). These methods will operate on a specific object instance, such as getting a Circle's color or a Tire's air pressure. If the method performs a more general-purpose function, such as creating an instance object or accessing some global class data, you'll likely declare the method as a class method using the leading plus sign (+).

Size Matters

Another handy NSString method (an instance method) is length, which returns the number of characters in the string:

```
- (unsigned int) length;
```

You'd use it like this:

```
unsigned int length = [height length];
```

or in expressions like so:

```
if ([height length] > 35) {
    NSLog (@"wow, you're really tall!");
}
```

Comparative Politics

Comparison is a frequent operation with strings. Sometimes you want to see if two strings are equal (for example, is username equal to 'markd'?). Other times, you want to see how two strings would be ordered against each other, so you can sort a list of names. NSString provides several comparison functions to help you out.

isEqualToString: compares the receiver (the object that the message is being sent to) with a string that's passed in as an argument. isEqualToString: returns a BOOL (YES or NO) indicating if the two strings have the same contents. It's declared like this:

```
- (BOOL) isEqualToString: (NSString *) aString;
```

And this is how you use it:

```
NSString *thing1 = @"hello 5";
NSString *thing2;
thing2 = [NSString stringWithFormat: @"hello %d", 5];

if ([thing1 isEqualToString: thing2]) {
    NSLog (@"They are the same!");
}
```

To compare strings, use the compare: method, which is declared as follows:

```
- (NSComparisonResult) compare: (NSString *) string;
```

compare: does a character-by-character comparison of the receiving object against the passed-in string. It returns an NSComparisonResult (which is just an enum) that shows the result of the comparison:

```
typedef enum _NSComparisonResult {
    NSOrderedAscending = -1,
    NSOrderedSame,
    NSOrderedDescending
} NSComparisonResult;
```

COMPARING STRINGS: DO IT RIGHT

When comparing strings for equality, you want to use `isEqualToString:` rather than just comparing their pointer values, for instance:

```
if ([thing1 isEqualToString: thing2]) {
    NSLog (@"The strings are the same!");
}
```

is different from

```
if (thing1 == thing2) {
    NSLog (@"They are the same object!");
}
```

That's because the `==` operator works on only the values of the `thing1` and `thing2` *pointers*, not what they point to. Because `thing1` and `thing2` are different strings, the second comparison will think they're different.

Sometimes you do want to check for identity between two objects: is `thing1` exactly the same object as `thing2`? That's the time to use the `==` operator. If you want to check for equivalence (that is, do these two strings represent the same thing?), use `isEqualToString:`.

If you've ever used the C functions `qsort()` or `bsearch()`, this might look familiar. If the result from `compare:` is `NSOrderedAscending`, the left-hand value is smaller than the right-hand one—that is, the target of `compare` sorts earlier in the alphabet than the string that's been passed in. For instance, `[@"aardvark" compare: @"zygote"]` would return `NSOrderedAscending:`.

Similarly, `[@"zoinks" compare: @"jinkies"]` would return `NSOrderedDescending`. And, as you'd expect, `[@"fnord" compare: @"fnord"]` would return `NSOrderedSame`.

Insensitivity Training

`compare:` does a case-sensitive comparison. In other words, `@"Bork"` and `@"bork"`, when compared, won't return `NSOrderedSame`. There's another method, `compare:options:`, that gives you more control:

```
- (NSComparisonResult) compare: (NSString *) string
                       options: (unsigned) mask;
```

The options parameter is a bit mask. You can use the bitwise-OR operator (|) to add option flags together. Some common options follow:

- NSCaseInsensitiveSearch: Uppercase and lowercase characters are considered the same.

- NSLiteralSearch: Perform an exact comparison, including case.

- NSNumericSearch: Numbers in strings are compared as numbers, rather than their character values. Without this, "100" would sort before "99," which strikes most non-programmers as rather bizarre, or even wrong.

For example, if you want to perform a comparison ignoring case but ordering numbers correctly, you would do this:

```
if ([thing1 compare: thing2
          options: NSCaseInsensitiveSearch
                  | NSNumericSearch]
      == NSOrderedSame) {
    NSLog (@"They match!");
}
```

Is It Inside?

Sometimes you want to see if a string has another string inside it. For example, you might want to know if a file name has ".mov" at the end so you can open it in QuickTime Player, or you could check whether it starts with "draft" to see if it's a draft version of a document. Here are two methods that help: the first checks whether a string starts with another string, and the second determines if a string ends with another string:

```
- (BOOL) hasPrefix: (NSString *) aString;
- (BOOL) hasSuffix: (NSString *) aString;
```

And you'd use these methods as follows:

```
NSString *filename = @"draft-chapter.pages";

if ([fileName hasPrefix: @"draft") {
    // this is a draft
}
if ([fileName hasSuffix: @".mov") {
    // this is a movie
}
```

So draft-chapters.pages would be recognized as a draft version (because it starts with "draft"), but would not be recognized as a movie (it has ".pages" at the end rather than ".mov").

If you want to see if a string is somewhere inside another string, use `rangeOfString:`

```
- (NSRange) rangeOfString: (NSString *) aString;
```

When you send `rangeOfString:` to an `NSString` object, you pass it the string to look for. It then returns an `NSRange` struct to show you where the matching part of the string is and how large the match is. So the following example

```
NSRange range;
range = [fileName rangeOfString: @"chapter"];
```

comes back with `range.start` at 6, and `range.length` set to 7. If the argument isn't found in the receiver, `range.start` will be equal to `NSNotFound`.

Mutability

`NSString`s are **immutable**. That doesn't mean you can't keep them quiet; it refers to the fact that once they're created, you can't change them. You can do all sorts of stuff with them, like make new strings with them, find characters in them, and compare them to other strings, but you can't change them by taking off characters or by adding new ones.

Cocoa provides a subclass of `NSString` called `NSMutableString`. Use that if you want to slice and dice a string in place.

NOTE

> Programmers coming from Java should feel at home with this distinction. `NSString` behaves like the java `String` class, and `NSMutableString` is like Java's `StringBuffer` class.

You can create a new `NSMutableString` by using the class method `stringWithCapacity:`, which is declared like so:

```
+ (id) stringWithCapacity: (unsigned) capacity;
```

The capacity is just a suggestion to `NSMutableString`, like when you tell your teenager what time to be home. The string is not limited to the capacity you supply—it's just an optimization. For example, if you know you're building a string that's 40 megabytes in size, `NSMutableString` can preallocate a chunk of memory to hold it, making subsequent operations much faster. Create a new mutable string like this:

```
NSMutableString *string;
string = [NSMutableString stringWithCapacity: 42];
```

Once you have a mutable string, you can do all sorts of wacky tricks with it. A common operation is to append a new string, using appendString: or appendFormat:, like this:

```
- (void) appendString: (NSString *) aString;
- (void) appendFormat: (NSString *) format, ...;
```

appendString takes its aString parameter and copies it to the end of the receiving object. appendFormat works like stringWithFormat:, but instead of creating a new string object, it appends the formatted string to the end of the receiving string, for example:

```
NSMutableString *string;
string = [NSMutableString stringWithCapacity: 50];
[string appendString: @"Hello there "];
[string appendFormat: @"human %d!", 39];
```

At the end of this code, string will have the friendly value "Hello there human 39!".

You can remove characters from the string with the deleteCharactersInRange: method:

```
- (void) deleteCharactersInRange: (NSRange) range;
```

You'll often use deleteCharactersInRange: coupled with rangeOfString:. Remember that NSMutableString is a subclass of NSString. Through the miracle of object-oriented programming, you also can use all the features of NSString with NSMutableStrings, including rangeOfString:, the comparison methods, and everything else. For example, let's say you list all your friends, but then you decide you don't like Jack any more and you want to remove him from the list:

First, make the list of friends:

```
NSMutableString *friends;
friends = [NSMutableString stringWithCapacity: 50];
[friends appendString: @"James BethLynn Jack Evan"];
```

Next, find the range of characters where Jack lives:

```
NSRange jackRange;
jackRange = [friends rangeOfString: @"Jack"];
jackRange.length++; // eat the space that follows
```

In this case, the range starts at 15 and has a length of 5. Now, we can remove Jack from our Christmas card list:

```
  [friends deleteCharactersInRange: jackRange];
```

This leaves the string as "James BethLynn Evan".

Mutable strings are very handy for implementing description methods. You can use appendString and appendFormat to create a nice description for your object.

We get a couple of behaviors for free because NSMutableString is a subclass of NSString. The first freebie is that anywhere an NSString is used, we can substitute an NSMutableString. Any methods that take an NSString will also take an NSMutableString. The user of the string really doesn't care if it's mutable or not.

The other free behavior comes from the fact that inheritance works just as well with class methods as it does with instance methods. So, the handy stringWithFormat: class method in NSString works for making new NSMutableStrings. You can easily populate a mutable string from a format:

```
NSMutableString *string;
string = [NSMutableString stringWithFormat: @"jo%dy", 2];
```

string starts out with the value "jo2y", but you can perform other operations, such as deleting characters from a given range or inserting characters at a particular position. Check out the documentation for NSString and NSMutableString to learn full details on the dozens of methods available in these classes.

Collection Agency

Individual objects floating around is nifty, but frequently you'll want to get things organized. Cocoa provides a number of collection classes such as NSArray and NSDictionary whose instances exist just to hold onto other objects.

NSArray

You've used arrays in C. In fact, earlier in this very book, we used an array to hold four tires for a car. You might remember that we ran into some difficulties with that code. For instance, we had to check to make sure the index into the array was valid: it couldn't go below 0 or beyond the end of the array. Another problem: the array length of 4 was hard-coded into the Car class, meaning we couldn't have a car with more than four tires. Sure, that doesn't seem like much of a limitation, but you never know if the Flying Rocket Cars of the Future that we've all been promised will need more than four tires for a smooth landing.

NSArray is a Cocoa class that holds an ordered list of objects. You can put any kind of objects in an NSArray: NSString, Car, Shape, Tire, or whatever else you want.

Once you have an NSArray of objects, you can work with it in various ways, such as by having an object's instance variable point to the array, passing the array as an argument to a method or function, getting a count of the number of objects stored inside it, grabbing an object at a particular index, finding an object in the array, looping over the contents, or a zillion other magic tricks.

NSArray has two limitations. First, it will hold only Objective-C objects. You can't have primitive C types, like int, float, enum, struct, or random pointers in an NSArray. Also, you can't store nil (the zero or NULL value for objects) in an NSArray. There are ways of working around these limitations, as you'll see in a little while.

You can create a new NSArray by using the class method arrayWithObjects:. You give it a comma-separated list of objects, with nil at the end to signal the end of the list (which, by the way, is one of the reasons you can't store nil in an array):

```
NSArray *array;
array = [NSArray arrayWithObjects:
                 @"one", @"two", @"three", nil];
```

This makes a three-element array composed of literal NSString objects. Once you have an array, you can get a count of the number of objects it contains:

```
- (unsigned) count;
```

And you can fetch an object at a particular index:

```
- (id) objectAtIndex: (unsigned int) index;
```

You can combine these two to print out the contents of the array:

```
int i;
for (i = 0; i < [array count]; i++) {
    NSLog (@"index %d has %@.",
           i, [array objectAtIndex: i]);
}
```

The output would look like this:

```
index 0 has one.
index 1 has two.
index 2 has three.
```

If you refer to an index that's greater than the number of objects in the array, Cocoa prints a complaint at runtime. For example, run this code:

```
[array objectAtIndex: 208000];
```

You'll see this:

```
*** Terminating app due to uncaught exception 'NSRangeException',
reason: '*** -[NSCFArray objectAtIndex:]: index (208000) beyond bounds (3)'
```

So there.

Because you'll probably see messages like this from time to time in your Cocoa programming career, let's spend a moment taking a closer look. After giving you the smack down by saying that it terminated your program, the message mentions this was because of an "uncaught exception." An **exception** is Cocoa's way of saying "I don't know how to deal with this." There are ways to catch exceptions in code and handle them yourself, but you don't need to do that when you're just starting out. This particular exception is an NSRangeException, which means there's something wrong with a range parameter being passed to a method. The method in particular is NSCFArray objectAtIndex:. NSCFArray looks a lot like NSArray, which is a hint about what's going wrong.

NOTE

> When you see the characters "CF" in Cocoa, you're looking at something related to Apple's Core Foundation framework. Core Foundation is like Cocoa but implemented in C, and much of it is open source if you want to download it and poke around. Many Core Foundation objects and Cocoa objects are **toll-free bridged**, meaning they can be used interchangeably. The NSCFArray you're seeing here is Apple's implementation of NSArray but using CFArray to do the heavy lifting.

The last bits of information in the exception message are the most interesting. This part of the message says we're asking for something at index 208000 in an array, but oops, the array only has three items—missed it by *that much*. Using this information, you can trace back to the offending code and find the error.

Tracking down the cause of an exception can be frustrating. All you get is this message in the *Run* window. With a GUI program, the program keeps running. There's a way to get Xcode to break into the debugger when an exception happens, which is a bit better. To make this happen, choose **Run ➤ Show ➤ Breakpoints**. You'll get a window that shows all the current breakpoints (these are the places the Xcode debugger will stop your program so you can poke around its innards), breakpoints specific to the current project, and breakpoints that are applied globally, as shown in Figure 8-1.

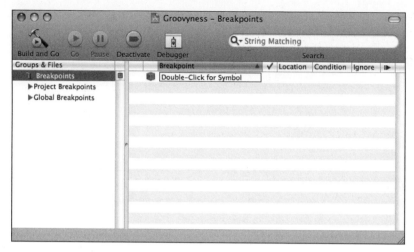

Figure 8-1. *Xcode's breakpoints window*

We'll add two breakpoints that will make tracking down these exceptions easier. First, we'll set a breakpoint on -[NSException raise]. Select *Global Breakpoints*. Double-click the *Double-Click for Symbol* box; type *-[NSException raise]*, and press return. Your breakpoint window should look like the one shown in Figure 8-2.

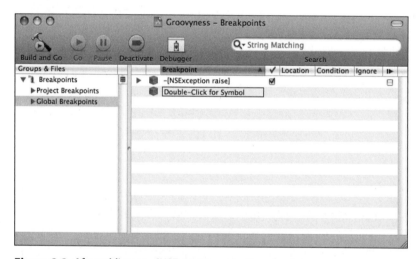

Figure 8-2. *After adding an –[NSException raise] breakpoint*

Also, add a global breakpoint for objc_exception_throw. Now, when you run the program and an exception is thrown, the debugger will stop and point to the offending line, as shown in Figure 8-3. You might need to click in the stack trace pane (it's the top-left pane of Figure 8-3) to move the focus to the appropriate source file. In this example, we clicked the main function in that list to see our code.

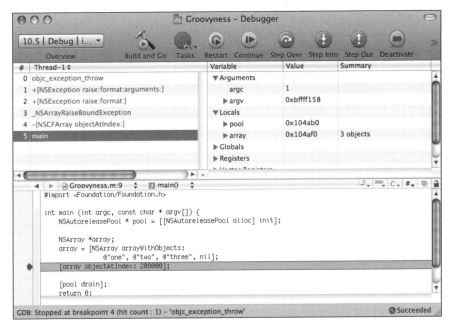

Figure 8-3. *The XCode debugger pointing to the offending line*

You might not be happy that Cocoa complains so vehemently if your program merely transgresses the bounds of an array. But trust us: you'll come to realize it's actually a *great thing*, because it allows you to catch errors that otherwise might go undetected.

Like NSString, NSArray has a lot of features. For example, you can tell an array to give you the location of a particular object, make a new array based on a range of elements in the current array, join all the elements into a string with a given separator (that one is handy for making comma-separated lists), or make a new array that's a sorted version of the array you already have.

DOING THE SPLITS

If you've used scripting languages like Perl or Python, you're probably used to splitting a string into an array and joining an array's elements into a single string. You can do that with NSArray too.

To split an NSArray, use -componentsSeparatedByString:, like this:

```
NSString *string = @"oop:ack:bork:greeble:ponies";
NSArray *chunks = [string componentsSeparatedByString: @":"];
```

And to join an NSArray and create a string of its contents, use componentsJoinedByString::

```
string = [chunks componentsJoinedByString: @" :-) "];
```

The preceding line would produce an NSString with the contents "oop :-) ack :-) bork :-) greeble :-) ponies".

Mutable Arrays

NSArray creates immutable objects, just as NSString does. Once you create an array with a certain number of objects, that's it for that array: you can't add or remove any members. The objects contained in the array are free to change, of course (like a Car getting a new set of Tires after it fails a safety inspection), but the array object itself will stay the same forever.

To complement NSArray, NSMutableArray exists so that we can add and remove objects whenever we want. It uses a class method, arrayWithCapacity, to make a new mutable array:

```
+ (id) arrayWithCapacity: (unsigned) numItems;
```

Like NSMutableString's stringWithCapacity:, the array's capacity is just a hint about its eventual size. The capacity value exists so that Cocoa can perform some optimizations on the code. Cocoa doesn't prepopulate the array with objects, and it doesn't use the capacity value to limit the array. You create a new mutable array like this:

```
NSMutableArray *array;
array = [NSMutableArray arrayWithCapacity: 17];
```

Add objects to the end of the array by using addObject:.

```
- (void) addObject: (id) anObject;
```

You can add four tires to an array with a loop like this:

```
for (i = 0; i < 4; i++) {
    Tire *tire = [Tire new];
    [array addObject: tire];
}
```

You can remove an object at a particular index. For example, if you don't like the second tire, you can use removeObjectAtIndex: to get rid of it. Here's how the method is defined:

```
- (void) removeObjectAtIndex: (unsigned) index;
```

You use it like this:

```
[array removeObjectAtIndex: 1];
```

Note that the second tire lives at index 1. NSArray objects are zero-indexed, like C arrays.

There are now three tires left. No hole is created in the array after you remove an object. The objects in the array that follow the removed object all get shifted down to fill the gap.

There are a bunch of cool things you can do with other methods of mutable arrays, like inserting an object at a particular index, replacing an object, sorting the array, plus all the goodies that NSArray provides as an ancestor.

Enumeration Nation

Performing an operation on each element of the array is a common NSArray operation. For example, you might tell all the shapes in the array to change their color to green, if you really liked green that much. Or you might want every tire in the car to go flat on the driver, for realism in constructing your Pittsburgh-area driving simulator. You can write a loop to index from 0 to [array count] and get the object at the index, or you can use an NSEnumerator, which is Cocoa's way of describing this kind of iteration over a collection. To use NSEnumerator, you ask the array for the enumerator using objectEnumerator:

```
- (NSEnumerator *) objectEnumerator;
```

You use the method like this:

```
NSEnumerator *enumerator;
enumerator = [array objectEnumerator];
```

There's also a reverseObjectEnumerator method if you want to walk the collection from back to front. !looC

After you get an enumerator, you crank up a while loop that asks the enumerator for its nextObject every time through the loop:

```
- (id) nextObject;
```

When nextObject returns nil, the loop is done. This is another reason why you can't store nil values in the array: there's no way to tell whether a nil result was a value stored in the array or the nil that signals the end of the loop.

The whole loop then looks like this:

```
NSEnumerator *enumerator;
enumerator = [array objectEnumerator];

id thingie;
while (thingie = [enumerator nextObject]) {
    NSLog (@"I found %@", thingie);
}
```

There's one gotcha if you're enumerating over a mutable array: you can't change the container, such as by adding or removing objects. If you do, the enumerator will become confused and you'll get undefined results. "Undefined results" can mean anything from "Hey, it seems to have worked!" to "Oops, it crashed my program."

Fast Enumeration

In Mac OS X 10.5 (Leopard), Apple introduced a number of small tweaks to Objective-C as it boosted the language version to 2.0. The first of these tweaks we'll examine is called **fast enumeration**, and it uses syntax familiar to users of scripting languages. Here's what it looks like:

```
for (NSString *string in array) {
    NSLog (@"I found %@", string);
}
```

The body of the loop will spin for each element in the array, with the variable string holding each array value. It's much more concise than the enumerator syntax and much faster.

Like all the new Objective-C 2.0 features, this is not available on Tiger (Mac OS X 10.4). If you or your users need to run your programs on Tiger, you can't use this new syntax. Bummer.

OK, so now we have three ways to iterate through an array: by index, with NSEnumerator, and now with fast enumeration. Which one do you use?

If you're only going to be running on Leopard or later OS versions, use fast enumeration. It's more succinct and much faster.

If you need to support Tiger, go the NSEnumerator way. Xcode includes a refactoring to convert code to Objective-C 2.0 and will automatically convert NSEnumerator loops into fast enumeration.

Only use -objectAtIndex if you really need to access things by index, like if you're skipping around the array (for example, accessing every third object in it) or if you are iterating through multiple arrays at the same time.

NSDictionary

No doubt you've heard of dictionaries. Maybe you even use one occasionally. In programming, a **dictionary** is a collection of keywords and their definitions. Cocoa has a collection class called NSDictionary that performs these duties. An NSDictionary stores a value (which can be any kind of object) under a given key (usually an NSString). You can then use that key to look up the corresponding value. So, for example, if you have an NSDictionary that stores all the contact information for a person, you can ask that dictionary "Give me the value for the key home-address." Or say, "Give me the value for the key email-address."

NOTE

> Why not just have an array and look at the values inside it? A dictionary (which is also known as a **hash table** or an **associative array**) uses a storage mechanism that's optimized for key lookups. Rather than scanning an entire array looking for an item, the dictionary can immediately put its electronic hands on the data it's after. For frequent lookups and for large data sets, a dictionary can be hundreds of times faster than an array. That's, like, really fast.

As you can probably guess, NSDictionary, like NSString and NSArray, is an immutable object. However, the NSMutableDictionary class that lets you add and remove stuff at will. To make a new NSDictionary, you supply all the objects and keys that live in the dictionary at creation time. The easiest way to get started with a dictionary is to use the class method dictionaryWithObjectsAndKeys:.

```
+ (id) dictionaryWithObjectsAndKeys:
          (id) firstObject, ...;
```

This method takes an alternating sequence of objects and keys, terminated by a nil value (as you can probably guess, you can't store a nil value in an NSDictionary). Let's say we want to make a dictionary to hold the tires of our car using human-readable labels rather than arbitrary indexes in an array. You can create such a dictionary like this:

```
Tire *t1 = [Tire new];
Tire *t2 = [Tire new];
Tire *t3 = [Tire new];
Tire *t4 = [Tire new];

NSDictionary *tires;

tires = [NSDictionary dictionaryWithObjectsAndKeys:
          t1, @"front-left", t2, @"front-right",
          t3, @"back-left", t4, @"back-right", nil];
```

To access a value in the dictionary, use the objectForKey: method, giving it the key you previously stored the value under:

```
- (id) objectForKey: (id) aKey;
```

So, to find the back-right tire, you can do this:

```
Tire *tire = [tires objectForKey: @"back-right"];
```

If there's no back-right tire in the dictionary (if it's a funky three-wheeler), objectForKey: returns nil.

To make a new NSMutableDictionary, send the dictionary message to the NSMutable➡ Dictionary class. You can also create a new mutable dictionary and give Cocoa a hint of its eventual size by using dictionaryWithCapacity: (have you started to notice that Cocoa has a very regular naming system?).

```
+ (id) dictionaryWithCapacity: (unsigned int) numItems;
```

As we mentioned earlier with NSMutableString and NSMutableArray, the capacity is just a hint, not a limit to the size of the dictionary,

You can add things to the dictionary by using setObject:forKey:.

```
- (void) setObject: (id) anObject  forKey: (id) aKey;
```

Here's another way to make the dictionary that holds the tires:

```
NSMutableDictionary *tires;
tires = [NSMutableDictionary dictionary];

[tires setObject: t1  forKey: @"front-left"];
[tires setObject: t2  forKey: @"front-right"];
[tires setObject: t3  forKey: @"back-left"];
[tires setObject: t4  forKey: @"back-right"];
```

If you use setObject:forKey: on a key that's already there, it replaces the old value with the new one. If you want to take a key out of a mutable dictionary, use the removeObjectForKey: method:

```
- (void) removeObjectForKey: (id) aKey;
```

So, if we want to model one of our tires falling off, we can just remove it:

```
 [tires removeObjectForKey: @"back-left"];
```

Use but Don't Extend

Because you're inventive, you might be tempted to create subclasses of NSString, NSArray, or NSDictionary. Resist the urge. In some languages, you do end up subclassing string and array classes to get work done. But in Cocoa, many classes are actually implemented as **class clusters**, which are a bunch of implementation-specific classes hidden behind a common interface. When you make an NSString object, you might actually end up getting an NSLiteralString, NSCFString, NSSimpleCString, NSBallOfString, or any number of undocumented implementation-detail objects. As an example of how this works, recall that earlier in this chapter, when we indexed past the array bounds and got an exception message, the class in the listing was actually NSCFArray. Go back and take a look.

As a user of NSString or NSArray, you don't have to care which class is being used under the hood. But trying to subclass a class cluster is an exercise in pain and frustration. Instead of subclassing, you can usually solve such programming problems by composing an NSString or NSArray into one of your classes or by using categories (described in Chapter 12).

Family Values

NSArrays and NSDictionaries hold only objects. They can't directly contain any primitive types, like int, float, or struct. But you can use objects that embed a primitive value. For example, stick an int into an object, and you can then put that object into an NSArray or NSDictionary.

NSNumber

Cocoa provides a class called NSNumber that **wraps** (that is, implements as objects) the primitive numeric types. You can create a new NSNumber using these class methods:

```
+ (NSNumber *) numberWithChar: (char) value;
+ (NSNumber *) numberWithInt: (int) value;
+ (NSNumber *) numberWithFloat: (float) value;
+ (NSNumber *) numberWithBool: (BOOL) value;
```

There are many more of these creation methods, including unsigned versions and varieties for long and long long integers, but these are the most common ones. After you create an NSNumber, you can then put it into a dictionary or an array:

```
NSNumber *number;
number = [NSNumber numberWithInt: 42];
[array addObject: number];
[dictionary setObject: number  forKey: @"Bork"];
```

Once you have a primitive type wrapped in an NSNumber, you can get it back out by using one of these instance methods:

```
- (char) charValue;
- (int) intValue;
- (float) floatValue;
- (BOOL) boolValue;
- (NSString *) stringValue;
```

It's perfectly OK to mix and match the creation methods and the extraction methods. For example, it's all right to create an NSNumber with numberWithFloat: and get the value back with intValue. NSNumber will do the proper conversions for you.

NOTE

The wrapping of a primitive type in an object is often called **boxing**, and taking the primitive type out is **unboxing**. Some languages have an **autoboxing** feature that will automatically converts a primitive to its corresponding wrapped type and back. Objective-C does not support autoboxing.

NSValue

NSNumber is actually a subclass of NSValue, which wraps arbitrary values. You can use NSValue to put structures into NSArrays and NSDictionaries. Create a new NSValue using this class method:

```
+ (NSValue *) valueWithBytes: (const void *) value
            objCType: (const char *) type;
```

You pass the address of the value you want to wrap (such as an NSSize or your own struct). Usually, you take the address (using the & operator in C) of the variable you want to save. You also supply a string describing the type, usually by reporting the types and sizes of the entries in the struct. You don't actually have to write code to build this string yourself. There's a compiler directive called @encode that takes a type name and generates the proper magic for you. So, to put an NSRect into an NSArray, you do something like this:

```
NSRect rect = NSMakeRect (1, 2, 30, 40);

NSValue *value;
value = [NSValue valueWithBytes: &rect
                objCType: @encode(NSRect)];

[array addObject: value];
```

You can extract the value using getValue:

```
- (void) getValue: (void *) value;
```

When you call getValue:, you pass the address of a variable that you want to hold the value:

```
value = [array objectAtIndex: 0];
[value getValue: &rect];
```

NOTE

In the `getValue:` example, you can see the use of `get` in the name of the method to indicate that we're providing a pointer as the place to store the value the method generates.

Convenience methods are provided for putting common Cocoa `structs` into `NSValues`, and we have conveniently listed them here:

```
+ (NSValue *) valueWithPoint: (NSPoint) point;
+ (NSValue *) valueWithSize: (NSSize) size;
+ (NSValue *) valueWithRect: (NSRect) rect;

- (NSPoint) pointValue;
- (NSSize) sizeValue;
- (NSRect) rectValue;
```

To store and retrieve an NSRect in an NSArray, you do this:

```
value = [NSValue valueWithRect: rect];
[array addObject: value];
....
NSRect anotherRect = [value rectValue];
```

NSNull

We've told you that you can't put `nil` into a collection, because `nil` has special meaning to `NSArray` and `NSDictionary`. But sometimes you really need to store a value that means "there's nothing here at all." For example, let's say you have a dictionary that holds a person's contact information, and under the key @"home fax machine", you store the user's home fax number. If that key holds a phone number value, you know that person has a fax machine. But if there's no value in the dictionary, does it mean that person has no home fax machine or that you don't know if they have one or not? By using `NSNull`, you can eliminate the ambiguity. You can decide that a value of `NSNull` for the key @"home fax machine" means the person definitely does not have a fax machine, and no value for the key means that you don't know if the person has one or not.

`NSNull` is probably the simplest of all Cocoa classes. It has but a single method:

```
+ (NSNull *) null;
```

And you add it to a collection like this:

```
[contact setObject: [NSNull null]
        forKey: @"home fax machine"];
```

You access it as follows:

```
id homefax;
homefax = [contact objectForKey: @"home fax machine"];

if (homefax == [NSNull null]) {
    // ... no fax machine.  rats.
}
```

[NSNull null] always returns the same value, so you can use == to compare it with other values.

Example: Looking for Files

OK, enough with the theoretical blah blah, with details on NSBlahBlah. Here's an actual working program that uses some of the classes found in this chapter. FileWalker (found in the *08-01 FileWalker project* folder) will paw through your home directory looking for *.jpg* files and print a list of what it finds. It's not terribly exciting, we admit, but it actually does something.

FileWalker uses NSString, NSArray, NSEnumerator, and two other Foundation classes to interact with the file system.

Our example also uses NSFileManager. The NSFileManager class lets you do stuff with the file system, like create directories, remove files, move files around, and get information about files. In this example, we're going to ask NSFileManager to make an NSDirectoryEnumerator for us, which we'll use to chug through a hierarchy of files.

This entire program resides in the main() function, because we're not making any of our own classes. Here is main() in its entirety:

```
int main (int argc, const char *argv[])
{
    NSAutoreleasePool *pool;
    pool = [[NSAutoreleasePool alloc] init];

    NSFileManager *manager;
    manager = [NSFileManager defaultManager];

    NSString *home;
    home = [@"~" stringByExpandingTildeInPath];

    NSDirectoryEnumerator *direnum;
    direnum = [manager enumeratorAtPath: home];

    NSMutableArray *files;
```

```
    files = [NSMutableArray arrayWithCapacity: 42];

    NSString *filename;
    while (filename = [direnum nextObject]) {
        if ([[filename pathExtension]
                        isEqualTo: @"jpg"]) {
            [files addObject: filename];
        }
    }

    NSEnumerator *fileenum;
    fileenum = [files objectEnumerator];

    while (filename = [fileenum nextObject]) {
        NSLog (@"%@", filename);
    }

    [pool drain];
    return (0);

} // main
```

Now, let's deconstruct this program bit by bit. At the top is the autorelease pool boilerplate code (Chapter 9 covers this in detail, as you'll see):

```
    NSAutoreleasePool *pool;
    pool = [[NSAutoreleasePool alloc] init];
```

Our next step is to get hold of an NSFileManager to play with. NSFileManager has a class method named defaultManager that gives us an NSFileManager object of our very own:

```
    NSFileManager *manager;
    manager = [NSFileManager defaultManager];
```

This is a common idiom in Cocoa. There are a number of classes that have a **singleton architecture**: only one of them is needed. You really need only one file manager, or one font manager, or one graphics context. These classes provide a class method to give you access to a single, shared object, which you then use to get your work done.

In this case, we need a directory iterator. But before we can ask the file manager for a directory iterator, we must figure out where in the file system to start looking at files. Starting from the top level of your hard drive could take a long time, so let's just look in your home directory.

How do we specify this directory? We could start with an absolute path, like */Users/markd/*, but that has the limitation that it only works if your home directory is named *markd*. Luckily, Unix (and Mac OS X) has a shorthand character for the home directory, which is ~ (also known as the *tilde*). Yes, there really is a use for that character even when you're not typing in *Español*). ~/Documents is the *Documents* directory, and *~/junk/oopack.txt* would be found at */Users/markd/junk/oopack.txt* on Mark's machine. NSString has a method that will take the tilde and expand it. That method is used in the next two lines of code:

```
NSString *home;
home = [@"~" stringByExpandingTildeInPath];
```

stringByExpandingTildeInPath will replace ~ with the current user's home directory. On Mark's machine, home would be */Users/markd*. Next, we feed this path string to the file manager:

```
NSDirectoryEnumerator *direnum;
direnum = [manager enumeratorAtPath: home];
```

enumeratorAtPath: returns an NSDirectoryEnumerator, which is a subclass of NSEnumerator. Each time you call nextObject on this enumerator object, it returns another path to a file in that directory. This method goes down into subdirectories too. By the time the iteration loop ends, you have the path for every single file in your home directory. There are some extra features provided by NSDirectoryEnumerator, such as getting a dictionary of attributes for every file, but we won't use those here.

Because we're looking for *.jpg* files (that is, path names that end in ".jpg"), and we're going to print their names, we need a place to store those names. We could just NSLog() them as we come across them in the enumeration, but in the future, we might want to do some operation on all the files at a different spot in the program. An NSMutableArray is a dandy choice here. We'll make a mutable array and add matching paths to it:

```
NSMutableArray *files;
 files = [NSMutableArray arrayWithCapacity: 42];
```

We have no idea how many *.jpg* files will actually be found, so we just picked 42 because— well, you know why. And because the capacity isn't a limitation on the size of the array, we'll be fine in any case.

Finally, we get to the real meat of the program. Everything else has been set up, and now it's time for the loop:

```
NSString *filename;
while (filename = [direnum nextObject]) {
```

The directory enumerator returns an NSString with the path to the file it's pointing to. And, just like NSEnumerator, it will return nil when it's done, which will stop the loop when there's nothing else to do.

NSString provides a number of convenience utilities for dealing with pathnames and file-names. For example, the pathExtension method gives you the extension for the file (minus the dot that precedes it). So, calling pathExtension on a file named *oopack.txt* would return @"txt" and the pathExtension for *VikkiCat.jpg* would be @"jpg".

We use nested method calls to grab the path extension, and send that string the message isEqualTo:. If that call returns YES, the filename is added to the array of files, like so:

```
if ([[filename pathExtension] isEqualTo: @"jpg"]) {
    [files addObject: filename];
}
```

After the directory loop ends, the files array is enumerated and its contents are printed using NSLog():

```
    NSEnumerator *fileenum;
    fileenum = [files objectEnumerator];

    while (filename = [fileenum nextObject]) {
        NSLog (@"%@", filename);
    }
```

Next, we do some housekeeping, with more autorelease pool boilerplate code, and, finally, we tell main() to return 0 to indicate a successful exit:

```
    [pool drain];
    return (0);

} // main
```

Here's the start of a sample run on Mark's machine:

```
cocoaheads/DSCN0798.jpg
cocoaheads/DSCN0804.jpg
cow.jpg
Development/Borkware/BorkSort/cant-open-file.jpg
Development/Borkware/BSL/BWLog/accident.jpg
```

It works! It might take a while to show results though, because it may have to dig through many thousands of images to do its thing.

Behind the Sign That Says "Beware of the Leopard"

FileWalker uses the classic style of iteration. The project *08.02 FileWalkerPro* shows how to do this stuff with fast enumeration. One nifty feature of the fast enumeration syntax is that you can feed it an already existing NSEnumerator or subclass. And it just so happens that NSDirectoryEnumerator is a subclass of NSEnumerator, so we can happily send the results of –enumeratorAtPath: to fast enumeration:

```
int main (int argc, const char * argv[]) {
    NSAutoreleasePool * pool = [[NSAutoreleasePool alloc] init];

    NSFileManager *manager;
    manager = [NSFileManager defaultManager];

    NSString *home;
    home = [@"~" stringByExpandingTildeInPath];

    NSMutableArray *files;
    files = [NSMutableArray arrayWithCapacity: 42];

    for (NSString *filename
            in [manager enumeratorAtPath: home]) {
        if ([[filename pathExtension]
                    isEqualTo: @"jpg"]) {
            [files addObject: filename];
        }
    }
    for (NSString *filename in files) {
        NSLog (@"%@", filename);
    }
}
```

As you can see, this version is simpler than the previous one: we've jettisoned two enumerator variables and the supporting code for them.

Summary

We've covered a lot of stuff in this chapter! We introduced three new language features: class methods, which are methods that are handled by the class itself instead of a particular instance; the @encode() directive used for methods that need a description of a C type to do their work; and fast enumeration.

We looked at a number of useful Cocoa classes, including NSString, NSArray, and NSDictionary. NSString holds human-readable text, while NSArray and NSDictionary hold collections of objects. These objects are immutable: they can't change after you create them. Cocoa provides mutable versions of these classes, which let you change their contents at will.

Despite all our efforts (and despite the length of this chapter), we've just barely scratched the surface of the hundreds of different classes in Cocoa. You can have fun and get smarter by digging around and learning about more of these classes.

Finally, we used the classes we learned about to spin through our home directory looking for groovy pictures.

In the next chapter, we dive into the mysteries of memory management, and you'll learn how you can clean up after yourself if you make any messes.

Chapter 9

Memory Management

*n*ext on our plate is memory management using Objective-C and Cocoa (yum!). Memory management is a part of a more general problem in programming called **resource management**. Every computer system has finite resources for your program to use. These include memory, open files, network connections, and so on. If you use a resource, such as by opening a file, you need to clean up after yourself (in this case, by closing the file). If you keep on opening files but never close them, you'll eventually run out of file capacity. Think about your public library. If everyone borrowed books but never returned them, eventually the library would close because it would have no more books, and everybody would be sad. Nobody wants that.

Of course, when your program ends, the operating system reclaims the resources it used. But as long as your program is running, it uses resources, and if you don't practice cleanliness, some resource will eventually be used up, and your program will probably crash.

Not every program uses files or network connections, but every program uses memory. Memory-related errors are the bane of every programmer who uses a C-style language. Our friends in the Java and scripting worlds have it easy: memory management happens automatically for them, like having their parents clean up their rooms. We, on the other hand, have to make sure to allocate memory when we need it and free that memory when we're done. If we allocate without freeing, we'll **leak memory**: our program's memory consumption will grow and grow until we run out of memory and then the program will crash. We need to be equally careful not to use any memory after we free it. We might be using stale data, which can cause all sorts of errors, or something else might have moved into that memory, and then we end up corrupting the new stuff.

NOTE

Memory management is a hard problem. Cocoa's solution is rather elegant but does take some time to wrap your mind around. Even programmers with decades of experience have problems when first encountering this material, so don't worry if it leaves your head spinning for awhile.

If you know that your programs will only be run on Leopard or later, you can take advantage of Objective-C 2.0's garbage collection, which we'll discuss at the end of this chapter. We won't feel sad if you skip to the end, really. If you want to run on older versions of Mac OS X or you're doing iPhone development, you will want to read the whole chapter.

Object Life Cycle

Just like the birds and the bees out here in the real world, objects inside a program have a life cycle. They're born (via an `alloc` or a new); they live (receive messages and do stuff), make friends (via composition and arguments to methods), and eventually die (get freed) when their lives are over. When that happens, their raw materials (memory) are recycled and used for the next generation.

Reference Counting

Now, it's pretty obvious when an object is born, and we've talked a lot about how to use an object, but how do we know when an object's useful life is over? Cocoa uses a technique known as **reference counting**, also sometimes called **retain counting**. Every object has an integer associated with it, known as its **reference count** or **retain count**. When some chunk of code is interested in an object, the code increases the object's retain count, saying, "I am interested in this object." When that code is done with the object, it decreases the retain count, indicating that it has lost interest in that object. When the retain count goes to 0, nobody cares about the object anymore (poor object!), so it is destroyed and its memory is returned to the system for reuse.

When an object is created via `alloc` or new, or via a copy message (which makes a copy of the receiving object), the object's retain count is set to 1. To increase its retain count, send the object a `retain` message. To decrease its retain count, send the object a `release` message.

When an object is about to be destroyed because its retain count has reached 0, Objective-C will automatically send the object a `dealloc` message. You can override `dealloc` in your objects. Do this to release any related resources you might have allocated. Don't ever call `dealloc` directly. You can rely on Objective-C to invoke your `dealloc` method when it's time to kill your object. To find out the current retain count, send the `retainCount` message. Here are the signatures for `retain`, `release` and `retainCount`:

```
- (id) retain;
- (void) release;
- (unsigned) retainCount;
```

Retain returns an id. That way, you can chain a retain call with other message sends, incrementing its retain count and then asking it to do some work. For instance, `[[car retain] setTire: tire atIndex: 2];` asks car to bump up its retain count and perform the setTire action.

The first project in this chapter is RetainCount1, located in the *09.01 RetainCount-1* project folder. This program creates an object (RetainTracker) that calls `NSLog()` when it's initialized and when it gets deallocated:

```
@interface RetainTracker : NSObject
@end // RetainTracker


@implementation RetainTracker

- (id) init
{
  if (self = [super init]) {
    NSLog (@"init: Retain count of %d.",
           [self retainCount]);
  }

  return (self);

} // init


- (void) dealloc
{
  NSLog (@"dealloc called. Bye Bye.");
  [super dealloc];

} // dealloc

@end // RetainTracker
```

The `init` method follows the standard Cocoa idiom for object initialization, which we'll explore in the next chapter. As we mentioned earlier, the `dealloc` message is sent (and, as a result, the `dealloc` method called) automatically when an object's retain count reaches 0. Our versions of `init` and `dealloc` use `NSLog()` to write out a message saying that they were called.

`main()` is where a new RetainTracker object is created, and the two methods defined by that class get called indirectly. When a new RetainTracker is created, retain and release messages are sent to increase and decrease the retain count, while we watch the fun, courtesy of NSLog():

```
int main (int argc, const char *argv[])
{
  RetainTracker *tracker = [RetainTracker new];
  // count: 1

  [tracker retain]; // count: 2
  NSLog (@"%d", [tracker retainCount]);

  [tracker retain]; // count: 3
  NSLog (@"%d", [tracker retainCount]);

  [tracker release]; // count: 2
  NSLog (@"%d", [tracker retainCount]);

  [tracker release]; // count: 1
  NSLog (@"%d", [tracker retainCount]);

  [tracker retain]; // count 2
  NSLog (@"%d", [tracker retainCount]);

  [tracker release]; // count 1
  NSLog (@"%d", [tracker retainCount]);

  [tracker release]; // count: 0, dealloc it

  return (0);

} // main
```

In real life, of course, you wouldn't be doing multiple retains and releases in a single function like this. Over its lifetime, an object might see patterns of retains and releases like this from a bunch of different places in your program over time. Running the program lets us see the retain counts:

```
init: Retain count of 1.
2
3
2
1
2
1
dealloc called. Bye Bye.
```

So, if you alloc, new, or copy an object, you just need to release it to make it go away and let the memory get reclaimed.

Object Ownership

"So," you're thinking, "didn't you say this was hard? What's the big deal? You create an object, use it, release it, and memory management is happy. That doesn't sound terribly complicated." It gets more complex when you factor in the concept of **object ownership**. When something is said to "own an object," that something is responsible for making sure the object gets cleaned up.

An object with instance variables that point to other objects is said to own those other objects. For example, in CarParts, a car owns the engine and tires that it points to. Similarly, a function that creates an object is said to own that object. In CarParts, main() creates a new car object, so main() is said to own the car.

A complication arises when more than one entity owns a particular object, which is why the retain count can be larger than 1. In the case of the RetainCount1 program, main() owned the RetainTracker object, so main() is responsible for cleaning up the object.

Recall the engine setter method for Car:

```
- (void) setEngine: (Engine *) newEngine;
```

and how it was called from main():

```
Engine *engine = [Engine new];
[car setEngine: engine];
```

Who owns the engine now? Does main() own it or does Car? Who is responsible for making sure the Engine gets a release message when it is no longer useful? It can't be main(), because Car is using the engine. It can't be Car, because main() might be using the engine later.

The trick is to have Car retain the engine, increasing its retain count to 2. That makes sense, since two entities, Car and main(), are now using the engine. Car should retain the engine inside setEngine:, and main() should release the engine. Then Car releases the engine when it's done (in its dealloc method), and the engine's resources will be reclaimed.

Retaining and Releasing in Accessors

A first crack at writing a memory management–savvy version of setEngine might look like this:

```
- (void) setEngine: (Engine *) newEngine
{
```

```
    engine = [newEngine retain];

    // BAD CODE: do not steal. See fixed version below.
} // setEngine
```

Unfortunately, that's not quite enough. Imagine this sequence of calls in main():

```
Engine *engine1 = [Engine new]; // count: 1
[car setEngine: engine1]; // count: 2
[engine1 release]; // count: 1

Engine *engine2 = [Engine new]; // count: 1
[car setEngine: engine2]; // count: 2
```

Oops! We have a problem with engine1 now: its retain count is still 1. main() has already released its reference to engine1, but Car never did. We have now leaked engine1, and leaky engines are never a good thing. That first engine object will sit around idling (sorry, we'll stop with the puns for awhile) and consuming a chunk of memory.

Here's another attempt at writing setEngine:.

```
- (void) setEngine: (Engine *) newEngine
{
  [engine release];
  engine = [newEngine retain];

  // More BAD CODE: do not steal. Fixed version below.
} // setEngine
```

That fixes the case of the leaked engine1 that you saw previously. But it breaks when newEngine and the old engine are the same object. Ponder this case:

```
Engine *engine = [Engine new]; // count: 1
Car *car1 = [Car new];
Car *car2 = [Car new];

[car1 setEngine: engine]; // count: 2
[engine release]; // count 1

[car2 setEngine: [car1 engine]]; // oops!
```

Why is this a problem? Here's what's happening. [car1 engine] returns a pointer to engine, which has a retain count of 1. The first line of setEngine is [engine release], which makes the retain count 0, and the object gets deallocated. Now, both newEngine and the engine instance variable are pointing to freed memory, which is bad. Here's a better way to write setEngine:

```
- (void) setEngine: (Engine *) newEngine
{
  [newEngine retain];
  [engine release];
  engine = newEngine;

} // setEngine
```

If you retain the new engine first, and newEngine is the same object as engine, the retain count will be increased and immediately decreased. But the count won't go to 0, and the engine won't be destroyed unexpectedly, which would be bad. In your accessors, if you retain the new object before you release the old object, you'll be safe.

NOTE

There are different schools of thought on how proper accessors should be written, and arguments and flame wars erupt on various mailing lists on a semiregular basis. The technique shown in the "Retaining and Releasing in Accessors" section works well and is (somewhat) easy to understand, but don't be surprised if you see different accessor management techniques when you look at other people's code.

Autorelease

Memory management can be a tough problem, as you've seen so far when we encountered some of the subtleties of writing setter methods. And now it's time to examine yet another wrinkle. You know that objects need to be released when you're finished with them. In some cases, knowing when you're done with an object is not so easy. Consider the case of a description method, which returns an NSString that describes an object:

```
- (NSString *) description
{
  NSString *description;

  description = [[NSString alloc]
    initWithFormat: @"I am %d years old", 4];

  return (description);

} // description
```

Here, we're making a new string instance with alloc, which gives it a retain count of 1, and then we return it. Who is responsible for cleaning up this string object?

It can't be the description method. If you release the description string before returning it, the retain count goes to 0, and the object will be obliterated immediately.

The code that uses the description could hang onto the string in a variable and then release it when finished, but that makes using the descriptions extremely inconvenient. What should be just one line of code turns into three:

```
NSString *desc = [someObject description];
NSLog (@"%@", desc);
[desc release];
```

There has got to be a better way. And luckily, there is!

Everyone into the Pool!

Cocoa has the concept of the **autorelease pool**. You've probably seen NSAutoreleasePool in the boilerplate code generated by Xcode. Now it's time to see what it's all about.

The name provides a good clue. It's a *pool* (collection) of stuff, presumably objects, that *auto*matically get *released*.

NSObject provides a method called autorelease:

```
- (id) autorelease;
```

This method schedules a release message to be sent at some time in the future. The return value is the object that receives the message; retain uses this same technique, which makes chaining calls together easy. What actually happens when you send autorelease to an object is that the object is added to an NSAutoreleasePool. When that pool is destroyed, all the objects in the pool are sent a release message.

NOTE

There's no magic in the autorelease concept. You could write your own autorelease pool by using an NSMutableArray to hold the objects and send all those objects a release message in the dealloc method. But there's no need for reinvention—Apple has done the hard work for you.

So we can now write a description method that does a good job with memory management:

```
- (NSString *) description
{
  NSString *description;
  description = [[NSString alloc]
    initWithFormat: @"I am %d years old", 4];

  return ([description autorelease]);

} // description
```

So you can write code like this:

```
NSLog (@"%@", [someObject description]);
```

Now, memory management works just right, because the `description` method creates a new string, autoreleases it, and returns it for the `NSLog()` to use. Because that description string was autoreleased, it's been put into the currently active autorelease pool, and, sometime later, after the code doing the `NSLog()` has finished running, the pool will be destroyed.

The Eve of Our Destruction

When does the autorelease pool get destroyed so that it can send a release message to all of the objects it contains? For that matter, when does a pool get created in the first place? In the Foundation tools we've been using, the creation and destruction of the pool has been explicit:

```
NSAutoreleasePool *pool;
pool = [[NSAutoreleasePool alloc] init];
...
[pool release];
```

When you create an autorelease pool, it automatically becomes the active pool. When you release that pool, its retain count goes to 0, so it then gets deallocated. During the deallocation, it releases all the objects it has.

When you're using the AppKit, Cocoa automatically creates and destroys an autorelease pool for you on a regular basis. It does so after the program handles the current event (such as a mouse click or key press). You're free to use as many autoreleased objects as you like, and the pool will clean them up for you automatically whenever the user does something.

> **NOTE**
>
> You may have seen in Xcode's autogenerated code an alternate way of destroying an autorelease pool's objects: the `-drain` method. This method empties out the pool without destroying it. `-drain` is only available in Mac OS X 10.4 (Tiger) and later. In our own code (not generated by Xcode), we'll be using `-release`, since that will work on versions of the OS back to the beginning of time.

Pools in Action

RetainTracker2 shows the autorelease pool doing its thing. It's found in the *09-02 RetainTracker-2* project folder. This program uses the same `RetainTracker` class we built in RetainTracker1, which `NSLog()`s when a `RetainTracker` object is initialized and when it's released.

RetainTracker2's `main()` looks like this:

```
int main (int argc, const char *argv[])
{
  NSAutoreleasePool *pool;
  pool = [[NSAutoreleasePool alloc] init];

  RetainTracker *tracker;
  tracker = [RetainTracker new]; // count: 1

  [tracker retain]; // count: 2
  [tracker autorelease]; // count: still 2
  [tracker release]; // count: 1

  NSLog (@"releasing pool");
  [pool release];
  // gets nuked, sends release to tracker

  return (0);

} // main
```

To start, we create the autorelease pool:

```
NSAutoreleasePool *pool;
pool = [[NSAutoreleasePool alloc] init];
```

Now, any time we send the autorelease message to an object, it jumps into this pool:

```
RetainTracker *tracker;
tracker = [RetainTracker new]; // count: 1
```

Here, a new tracker is created. Because it's being made with a new message, it has a retain count of 1:

```
 [tracker retain]; // count: 2
```

Next, it gets retained, just for fun and demonstration purposes. The object's retain count goes to 2:

```
 [tracker autorelease]; // count: still 2
```

Then the object gets autoreleased. Its retain count is unchanged: it's still 2. The important thing to note is that the pool that was created earlier now has a reference to this object. When pool goes away, the tracker object will be sent a release message.

```
 [tracker release]; // count: 1
```

Next, we release it to counteract the retain that we did earlier. The object's retain count is still greater than 0, so it's still alive:

```
NSLog (@"releasing pool");
[pool release];
// gets nuked, sends release to tracker
```

Now, we release the pool. An `NSAutoreleasePool` is an ordinary object, subject to the same rules of memory management as any other. Because we made the pool with an `alloc`, it has a retain count of 1. The release decreases its retain count to 0, so the pool will be destroyed and its `dealloc` method called.

Finally, `main` returns 0 to indicate that everything was successful:

```
  return (0);

} // main
```

Can you guess what the output is going to look like? Which will come first, the `NSLog()` before we release the pool or the `NSLog` from `RetainTracker`'s `dealloc` method?

Here's the output from a run of RetainTracker2:

```
init: Retain count of 1.
releasing pool
dealloc called. Bye Bye.
```

As you probably guessed, the `NSLog()` before releasing the pool happens prior to the `NSLog()` from `RetainTracker`.

The Rules of Cocoa Memory Management

Now you've seen it all: `retain`, `release`, and `autorelease`. Cocoa has a number of memory management conventions. They're pretty simple rules, and they're applied consistently throughout the toolkit.

NOTE

Forgetting these rules is a common mistake, as is trying to make them too complicated. If you find yourself scattering `retain`s and `release`s around aimlessly, hoping to fix some bug, you don't understand the rules. That means it's time to slow down, take a deep breath, maybe go get a snack, and read them again.

Here are the rules:

- When you create an object using new, alloc, or copy, the object has a retain count of 1. You are responsible for sending the object a release or autorelease message when you're done with it. That way, it gets cleaned up when its useful life is over.

- When you get hold of an object via any other mechanism, assume it has a retain count of 1 and that it has already been autoreleased. You don't need to do any further work to make sure it gets cleaned up. If you're going to hang on to the object for any length of time, retain it and make sure to release it when you're done.

- If you retain an object, you need to (eventually) release or autorelease it. Balance these retains and releases.

That's it—just three rules.

You'll be safe if you remember the mantra, "If I get it from new, alloc, or copy, I have to release or autorelease it."

Whenever you get hold of an object, you must be aware of two things: how you got it, and how long you plan on hanging on to it (see Table 9-1).

Table 9-1. *Memory Management Rules*

Obtained Via . . .	Transient	Hang On
alloc/new/copy	Release when done	Release in dealloc
Any other way	Don't need to do anything	Retain when acquired, release in dealloc

Transient Objects

Let's take a look at some common memory-management life cycle scenarios. In the first, you're using an object, temporarily, in the course of some code, but you're not going to be keeping it around for very long. If you get the object from new, alloc, or copy, you need to arrange its demise, usually with a release:

```
NSMutableArray *array;
array = [[NSMutableArray alloc] init]; // count: 1
// use the array
[array release]; // count: 0
```

If you get the object from any other mechanism, such as arrayWithCapacity:, you don't have to worry about destroying it:

```
NSMutableArray *array;
array = [NSMutabelArray arrayWithCapacity: 17];
// count: 1, autoreleased
// use the array
```

arrayWithCapacity: is not alloc, new, or copy, so you can assume that the object being returned has a retain count of 1 and has already been autoreleased. When the autorelease pool goes away, array is sent the release message, its retain count goes to 0, and its memory is recycled.

Here's some code that uses an NSColor:

```
NSColor *color;
color = [NSColor blueColor];
// use the color
```

blueColor is not alloc, new, or copy, so you can assume it has a retain count of 1 and is autoreleased. blueColor returns a global **singleton** object—a single object that's shared by every program that needs it—and won't actually ever get destroyed, but you don't need to worry about those implementation details. All you need to know is that you do *not* need to explicitly release the color.

Hanging on to Objects

Frequently, you'll want to keep an object around for more than a couple of lines of code. Typically, you'll put these objects into instance variables of other objects, add them to a collection like NSArray or NSDictionary, or more rarely, keep them as global variables.

If you're getting an object from init, new, or copy, you don't need to do anything special. The object's retain count will be 1, so it will stick around. Just be sure to release the object in the dealloc method of the owner-object that's hanging on to it:

```
- (void) doStuff
{
  // flonkArray is an instance variable
  flonkArray = [NSMutableArray new]; // count: 1
} // doStuff


- (void) dealloc
{
  [flonkArray release]; // count: 0
  [super dealloc];
} // dealloc
```

If you get an object from something other than alloc, new, or copy, you need to remember to retain it. When you're writing a GUI application, think in event loops. You want to retain autoreleased objects that will survive for longer than the current event loop.

So what's an event loop? A typical graphical application spends a lot of time waiting on the user to do something. The program sits twiddling its thumbs until the very slow human at the controls decides to click the mouse or press a key. When one of these events does happen, the program wakes up and gets to work doing whatever is necessary to respond to the event. After the event is handled, the application goes back to sleep waiting for the next event. To keep your program's memory footprint low, Cocoa creates an autorelease pool before it starts handling the event and destroys the pool after the event is handled. This keeps the amount of accumulated temporary objects to a minimum.

The previous methods would be written as follows when using autoreleased objects:

```
- (void) doStuff
{
  // flonkArray is an instance variable
  flonkArray
    = [NSMutableArray arrayWithCapacity: 17];
  // count: 1, autoreleased
  [flonkArray retain]; // count: 2, 1 autorelease

} // doStuff


- (void) dealloc
{
  [flonkArray release]; // count: 0
  [super dealloc];
} // dealloc
```

At the end of the current event loop (if it's a GUI program) or when the autorelease pool gets destroyed, flonkArray will be sent a release message, which will lower its retain count from 2 to 1. Because the count is greater than 0, the object lives on. We still need to release the object in our dealloc so that it gets cleaned up. If we didn't have the retain in doStuff, flonkArray would get destroyed unexpectedly.

Remember that the autorelease pool is purged at well-defined times: when it's explicitly destroyed in your own code or at the end of the event loop when using the AppKit. You don't have to worry about a demon that goes around destroying autorelease pools at random. You also don't have to retain each and every object you use, because the pool won't go away in the middle of a function.

KEEPING THE POOL CLEAN

Sometimes autorelease pools don't get cleaned out as often as you would like. Here's a common question that comes up on Cocoa mailing lists: "I'm autoreleasing all the objects I use, but my program's memory is growing to absolutely huge levels." That problem is usually caused by something like this:

```
int i;
for (i = 0; i < 1000000; i++) {
  id object = [someArray objectAtIndex: i];
  NSString *desc = [object description];
  // and do something with the description
}
```

This program is running a loop that generates an autoreleased object (or two or ten) every time through a whole bunch of iterations. Remember that the autorelease pool is only purged at well-defined times, and the middle of this loop is not one of those times. Inside this loop, a million description strings are being created, and all of them are put into the current autorelease pool, so we have a million strings sitting around. Once the pool gets destroyed, the million strings will finally go away, but it won't happen before then.

The way to work around this is to create your own autorelease pool inside the loop. This way, every thousand times through the loop, you can nuke the pool and make a new one (as follows, with new code in bold):

```
NSAutoreleasePool *pool;
pool = [[NSAutoreleasePool alloc] init];
int i;
for (i = 0; i < 1000000; i++) {
  id object = [someArray objectAtIndex: i];
  NSString *desc = [object descrption];
  // and do something with the description
  if (i % 1000 == 0) {
    [pool release];
    pool = [[NSAutoreleasePool alloc] init];
  }
}
[pool release]
```

Every thousand times through the loop, the new pool is destroyed and a newer one is created. Now, no more than a thousand description strings will be in existence at one time, and the program can breathe easier. Autorelease pool allocation and destruction are pretty cheap operations, so you could even make a new pool in every iteration of the loop.

Autorelease pools are kept as a stack: if you make a new autorelease pool, it gets added to the top of the stack. An `autorelease` message puts the receiver into the topmost pool. If you put an object into a pool, and then make a new pool and destroy it, the autoreleased object will still be around, because the pool holding that object is still in existence.

Take Out Those Papers and the Trash

Objective-C 2.0 introduces automatic memory management, also called garbage collection. Programmers used to languages like Java or Python are well acquainted with the concept of garbage collection. You just create and use objects and then, shockingly, forget about them. The system automatically figures out what's still being used and what can be recycled. Turning on garbage collection is very easy, but it's an opt-in feature. Just go to the *Build* tab of the project information window, and choose *Required [-fobjc-gc-only]*, as shown in Figure 9-1.

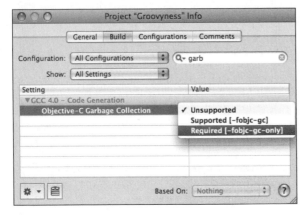

Figure 9-1. *Enabling garbage collection*

> ## NOTE
>
> `-fobjc-gc` is for code that supports both garbage collection and retain/release, such as library code that can be used in both environments.

When you enable garbage collection, the usual memory management calls all turn into no-op instructions; that's a fancy way of saying they don't do anything.

The Objective-C garbage collector is a generational garbage collector. Newly created objects are much more likely to turn into garbage than objects that have been hanging around for awhile. At regular times, the garbage collector starts looking at your variables and objects and follows the pointers between them. Any object it discovers without anything pointing to it is garbage, which is fit to be thrown away. The worst thing you can do is keep a pointer to an object that you're done with. So if you point to an object in an instance variable (recall composition), be sure to assign `nil` to your instance variable, which removes your reference to this object and lets the garbage collector know it can be purged.

Like the autorelease pool, garbage collection is triggered at the end of an event loop. You can also trigger garbage collection yourself if you're not in a GUI program, but that's beyond the scope of what we want to talk about here.

With garbage collection, you don't need to worry too much about memory management. There are some subtle nuances when using memory received from the `malloc` function or with Core Foundation objects, but they're obscure enough that we won't be covering them. For now, you can just create objects and not worry about releasing them. We'll be discussing garbage collection as we go along.

Note that you can't use garbage collection if you're writing iPhone software. In fact, in iPhone programming, Apple recommends you avoid using `autorelease` in your own code and that you also avoid convenience functions that give you autoreleased objects.

Summary

In this chapter, you learned about Cocoa's memory management methods: `retain`, `release`, and `autorelease`.

Each object maintains a retain count. Objects start their lives with a retain count of 1. When the object is retained, the retain count increases by 1, and when the object is released, the retain count is decreased by 1. When the retain count reaches 0, the object is destroyed. The object's `dealloc` message is called first, and then its memory is recycled, ready for use by other objects.

When an object receives the `autorelease` message, its retain count doesn't change immediately; instead, the object is placed into an `NSAutoreleasePool`. When this pool is destroyed, all the objects in the pool are sent a `release` message. Any objects that have been autoreleased will then have their retain counts decremented by 1. If the count goes to 0, the object is destroyed. When you use the AppKit, an autorelease pool will be created and destroyed for you at well-defined times, such as when the current user event has been handled. Otherwise, you are responsible for creating your own autorelease pool. The template for Foundation tools includes code for this.

Cocoa has three rules about objects and their retain counts:

- If you get the object from a `new`, `alloc`, or `copy` operation, the object has a retain count of 1.

- If you get the object any other way, assume it has a retain count of 1 and that it has been autoreleased.

- If you retain an object, you must balance every `retain` with a `release`.

Coming up next, we'll talk about `init` methods: how to make your objects hit the ground running.

Chapter 10

Object Initialization

So far, we've created new objects in two different ways. The first way is [SomeClass new], and the second is [[SomeClass alloc] init]. These two techniques are equivalent, but the common Cocoa convention is to use alloc and init rather than new. Typically, Cocoa programmers use new as training wheels until they have enough background to be comfortable with alloc and init. It's time for your training wheels to come off.

Allocating Objects

Allocation is the process by which a new object is born. It's the happy time when a chunk of memory is obtained from the operating system and designated as the location that will hold the object's instance variables. Sending the alloc message to a class causes that class to allocate a chunk of memory large enough to hold all its instance variables. alloc also conveniently initializes all the memory to 0. That way, you don't have the problem of uninitialized memory causing all sorts of random bugs that afflicts many languages. All your BOOLs start out as NO; all your ints are 0; all your floats become 0.0; all your pointers are nil; and all your base are belong to us (sorry, couldn't resist).

A newly allocated object isn't ready to be used right away: you need to initialize it before you can work with it. Some languages, including C++ and Java, perform object allocation and initialization in a single operation using a constructor. Objective-C splits the two operations into explicit allocation and initialization stages. A common beginner's error is to use only the alloc operation, like this:

```
Car *car = [Car alloc];
```

This might work, but without the initialization, you can get some strange behavior (also known as "bugs") later on. The rest of this chapter is all about the vital concept of initialization.

Initializing Objects

The counterpart to allocation is initialization. **Initialization** takes a chunk of memory and gets it ready to become a productive member of society. init methods—that is, methods that do initialization—almost always return the object they're initializing. You can (and should) chain your allocs and initializations like this:

```
Car *car = [[Car alloc] init];
```

and not like this:

```
Car *car = [Car alloc];
[car init];
```

This chaining technique is important because an initialization method might return an object that's not the same as the one that was allocated. If you think that's pretty odd, you're right. But it can happen.

Why might a programmer want an init method to return a different object? If you recall the discussion on class clusters at the end of Chapter 8, you saw that classes like NSString and NSArray are really just false fronts for a whole lot of specialized classes. An init method can take arguments, so the method code gets a chance to look at the arguments and decide that another class of object would be more appropriate. For example, let's say a new string is being made from a very long string, or maybe from a string of Arabic characters. Based on this knowledge, the string initializer might decide to create an object of a different class, one better suited to the needs of the desired string, and return that instead of the original object.

Writing Initialization Methods

Earlier, we asked you to endure some nod-and-smile moments when we presented initialization methods, mainly because they looked a little weird. Here's the init method from an earlier version of CarParts:

```
- (id) init
{
  if (self = [super init]) {
    engine = [Engine new];

    tires[0] = [Tire new];
    tires[1] = [Tire new];
    tires[2] = [Tire new];
    tires[3] = [Tire new];
```

```
    }

    return (self);

} // init
```

The main weirdness hits you on the very first line:

```
if (self = [super init]) {
```

This code implies that `self` might change. Change `self` in the middle of a method? Are we crazy? Well, maybe, but not this time. The first bit of code that runs in that statement is `[super init]`. That code lets the superclass do its initialization work. For classes that inherit from `NSObject`, calling on the superclass lets `NSObject` do any processing it needs to do so that objects can respond to messages and deal with retain counts. For classes that inherit from another class, this is their chance to do their own version of clean-slate initialization.

We just said that `init` methods like this one can return totally different objects. Remember that instance variables are found at a memory location that's a fixed distance from the hidden `self` parameter. If a new object is returned from an `init` method, we need to update `self` so that any subsequent instance variable references affect the right places in memory. That's why we need the `self = [super init]` assignment. Keep in mind that this assignment affects the value of `self` only for this method. It doesn't change anything outside the method's scope.

An `init` method can return `nil` if there's a problem initializing an object. For example, you might be using an `init` method that takes a URL and initializes an image object using an image file from a web site. If the network is down, or a redesign of the web site has moved the picture, you won't get a useful image object. The `init` method would then return `nil`, indicating the object couldn't be initialized. The test `if (self = [super init])` won't run the body code if `nil` is returned from `[super init]`. Combining the assignment with a check for a nonzero value like this is a classic C idiom that lives on in Objective-C.

The code to get the object up and running is in the braces of the `if` statement's body. In the original Car `init` method, the body of the `if` statement creates an engine and four tires. From the memory management perspective, this code does the right thing, because objects returned via new start out with their reference counts set to 1.

Finally, the last line of the method is

```
return (self);
```

An `init` method returns the object that was just initialized. Since we assigned the return value of [super init] to self, that's what we should return.

Some programmers don't like the combined assignment and test for a nonzero value. Instead, they write their `init` methods like this:

```
self = [super init];
if (self) {
    ....
}
return (self);
```

And that's fine. The key is that you assign back to `self`, especially if you're accessing any instance variables. No matter which way you do it, be aware that combining the assignment and test is a common technique, and you'll see it a lot in other people's code.

The `self = [super init]` style is the source of some controversy. One faction says you should always do this, just in case the superclass changes something in the initialization. The other camp says that this object changing is so rare and obscure that you need not bother—just use a plain `[super init]`. Those in this camp point out that if even if the `init` changes the object, that new object probably doesn't take any new instance variables you have added.

This is a truly thorny problem in the abstract, but in the real world, it doesn't happen very often. We recommend always using the `if (self = [super init])` technique just to be safe and to catch the "`init` returning `nil`" behavior of some `init` methods. But if you choose to use a plain `[super init]`, that's fine too. Just be prepared to do a little debugging if you happen to catch one of the obscure corner cases.

What to Do When You're Initializing

What should you put in your `init` methods? This is the place to do your clean-slate initialization work. You assign values to instance variables and create the other objects that your object needs to do its work. When you write your `init` methods, you must decide how much work you want to do there. The CarParts programs showed two different approaches over the course of its evolution.

The first way used the `init` method to create the engine and all four tires. This made the Car immediately useful out of the box: call `alloc` and `init`, and take the car out for a test drive. We changed the next version to create nothing at all in the `init` method. We just left empty spaces for the engine and tires. The code that created the object would then have to create an engine and tires and set them using accessor methods.

Which way is right for you? The decision comes down to flexibility over performance, as do many tradeoffs in programming. The original Car `init` method is very convenient. If the intended use of the Car class is to create a basic car and then use it, that's the right design.

On the other hand, if the car will often be customized with different kinds of tires and engines, as in a racing game, we'll be creating the engine and tires just to have them thrown away. Such a waste! Objects would be created and then destroyed without ever being used.

> NOTE
>
> Even if you don't provide calls to customize your object's attributes, you can still wait to create them until a caller asks for them. This is a technique known as **lazy evaluation**, and it can give you a performance boost if you're creating complex objects in your –init that might not actually be used.

Isn't That Convenient?

Some objects have more than one method that starts with the word init. In fact, it's important to remember that init methods are nothing special. They're just ordinary methods that follow a naming convention.

Many classes have **convenience initializers**. These are init methods that do some extra work, saving you the trouble of doing it yourself. To give you an idea of what we're talking about, here's a sampling of some of NSString's init methods:

```
- (id) init;
```

This basic method initializes a new, empty string. For immutable NSStrings, this method isn't terribly useful. But you can allocate and initialize a new NSMutableString and start throwing characters into it. You'd use it like this:

```
NSString *emptyString = [[NSString alloc] init];
```

That code gives you an empty string.

```
- (id) initWithFormat: (NSString *) format, ...;
```

This version initializes a new string to the result of a formatting operation, just like we did with NSLog() and with the stringWithFormat: class method you saw in Chapter 7. Here's an example that gives the flavor of using this init method:

```
string = [[NSString alloc]
        initWithFormat: @"%d or %d", 25, 624];
```

This gives you a string with the value of "25 or 624".

```
- (id) initWithContentsOfFile: (NSString *) path;
```

The `initWithContentsOfFile:` method opens the text file at the given path, reads everything there, and initializes a string with the contents. The following line of code reads the file `/tmp/words.txt`:

```
string = [[NSString alloc]
    initWithContentsOfFile: @"/tmp/words.txt"];
```

That's some pretty powerful stuff. This would take a whole bunch of code in C (you would have to open the file, read blocks of data, append to a string, make sure the trailing zero-byte is in the right place, and close the file). For us Objective-C devotees, it becomes a single line of code. Nice.

More Parts Is Parts

Let's revisit CarParts, last seen in Chapter 6 when we broke out each class into its own source file. This time, we'll add some initialization goodness to the `Tire` class and clean up Car's memory management along the way. For those of you following along at home, the project directory that has the finished program for this chapter is *10.01 CarPartsInit*, or *10.01 CarPartsInit-GC* for a garbage-collected version.

init for Tires

Tires in the real world are more interesting creatures than the ones we've simulated in CarParts so far. In your real tires, you have to keep track of the tire pressure (don't want it to get too low) and the tread depth (once it goes below a couple of millimeters, the tires aren't safe anymore). Let's extend `Tire` to keep track of the pressure and tread depth. Here's the class declaration that adds two instance variables and the corresponding accessor methods:

```
#import <Cocoa/Cocoa.h>

@interface Tire : NSObject
{
    float pressure;
    float treadDepth;
}

- (void) setPressure: (float) pressure;
- (float) pressure;

- (void) setTreadDepth: (float) treadDepth;
- (float) treadDepth;

@end // Tire
```

And here's the implementation of Tire, which is pretty straightforward:

```objc
#import "Tire.h"

@implementation Tire

- (id) init
{
  if (self = [super init]) {
    pressure = 34.0;
    treadDepth = 20.0;
  }

  return (self);

} // init


- (void) setPressure: (float) p
{
  pressure = p;
} // setPressure


- (float) pressure
{
  return (pressure);
} // pressure


- (void) setTreadDepth: (float) td
{
  treadDepth = td;
} // setTreadDepth


- (float) treadDepth
{
  return (treadDepth);
} // treadDepth


- (NSString *) description
{
  NSString *desc;
  desc = [NSString stringWithFormat:
      @"Tire: Pressure: %.1f TreadDepth: %.1f",
          pressure, treadDepth];
```

```
    return (desc);

} // description

@end // Tire
```

The accessor methods provide a way for users of the tire to change the pressure and the tread depth. Let's take a quick look at the init method:

```
- (id) init
{
    if (self = [super init]) {
        pressure = 34.0;
        treadDepth = 20.0;
    }

    return (self);

} // init
```

There should be no surprises here. The superclass (NSObject, in this case) is told to initialize itself, and the return value from that call is assigned to self. Then, the instance variables are assigned to useful default values. Let's make a brand new tire like this:

```
Tire *tire = [[Tire alloc] init];
```

The tire's pressure will be 34 psi, and its tread depth will be 20 mm.

We should change the description method, too:

```
- (NSString *) description
{
    NSString *desc;
    desc = [NSString stringWithFormat:
        @"Tire: Pressure: %.1f TreadDepth: %.1f",
            pressure, treadDepth];
    return (desc);

} // description
```

The description method now uses NSString's stringWithFormat: class method to make a string that includes the tire pressure and tread depth. Does this method follow our rules of good memory management behavior? Yes, it does. Because the object was not created by an alloc, copy, or new, it has a retain count of 1 and we can consider it to be autoreleased. So, this string will get cleaned up when the autorelease pool is destroyed.

Updating main()

Here is the `main.m` file, which is a hair more complicated than it was before:

```
#import "Engine.h"
#import "Car.h"
#import "Slant6.h"
#import "AllWeatherRadial.h"


int main (int argc, const char * argv[])
{
  NSAutoreleasePool *pool;
  pool = [[NSAutoreleasePool alloc] init];

  Car *car = [[Car alloc] init];

  int i;
  for (i = 0; i < 4; i++) {
    Tire *tire;
    tire = [[Tire alloc] init];

    [tire setPressure: 23 + i];
    [tire setTreadDepth: 33 - i];

    [car setTire: tire
         atIndex: i];

    [tire release];
  }

  Engine *engine = [[Slant6 alloc] init];
  [car setEngine: engine];

  [car print];
  [car release];

  [pool release];

  return (0);

} // main
```

Let's pull `main()` apart, piece by piece. We start by making an autorelease pool for auto-released objects to swim around in while they await the pool's destruction:

```
NSAutoreleasePool *pool;
pool = [[NSAutoreleasePool alloc] init];
```

Then, we create a new car using `alloc` and `init`:

```
Car *car = [[Car alloc] init];
```

After that, a loop spins around four times (from 0 to 3). This is where the new tires are made:

```
int i;
for (i = 0; i < 4; i++) {
```

Each time through the loop, a new tire is created and initialized:

```
    Tire *tire;
    tire = [[Tire alloc] init];
```

Each tire starts out with its pressure and tread depth set in Tire's `init` method. But we're going to customize the values, just for fun. Because no two tires are identical in the real world, we're going to tweak the pressure and tread depths using the accessor methods:

```
    [tire setPressure: 23 + i];
    [tire setTreadDepth: 33 - i];
```

Next, we'll give the tire to the car:

```
    [car setTire: tire
         atIndex: i];
```

Now that we're done with the tire, we release it:

```
    [tire release];
```

This code assumes that Car is doing the right memory management thing, arranging to retain the object. Note that the Car as shown in Chapter 6 doesn't follow our memory management guidelines—we were so young and naive then—but we'll show you how to fix that in a little while.

After the tires are assembled, a new engine is created, just as before, and the engine is placed in the car:

```
    Engine *engine = [[Slant6 alloc] init];
    [car setEngine: engine];
    [engine release];
```

As with the tires, the engine is released, because we're done using it. It's up to the Car to make sure the engine gets deallocated.

Finally, the Car is told to print itself out, and the Car is released because we're done with it:

```
    [car print];
    [car release];
```

Now the autorelease pool gets released, which causes its retain count to go to 0, deallocates the pool, and sends the `release` message to every object in the pool. When this happens, the `NSStrings` generated by the `Tire` description method get cleaned up:

```
[pool release];
```

And then `main` ends, at last. But before we can run the program, we need to fix up the Car class so that it handles its memory management correctly. But first, here's what main would look like in a garbage-collected world:

```
int main (int argc, const char * argv[])
{
  Car *car = [[Car alloc] init];

  int i;
  for (i = 0; i < 4; i++) {
    Tire *tire;
    tire = [[Tire alloc] init];

    [tire setPressure: 23 + i];
    [tire setTreadDepth: 33 - i];

    [car setTire: tire
         atIndex: i];
  }

  Engine *engine = [[Slant6 alloc] init];
  [car setEngine: engine];

  [car print];

  return (0);

} // main
```

As you can see, it's a fair bit shorter and simpler without the extra memory management calls.

Cleaning Up the Car

Instead of using a regular C array in Car, let's use an `NSMutableArray`. Why? Because that will give us bounds checking for free. To do this, we'll change the `@interface` section of the Car class to use a mutable array (the changed line of code is in bold):

```
#import <Cocoa/Cocoa.h>

@class Tire;
@class Engine;
```

```
@interface Car : NSObject
{
    NSMutableArray *tires;
    Engine *engine;
}

- (void) setEngine: (Engine *) newEngine;

- (Engine *) engine;

- (void) setTire: (Tire *) tire
         atIndex: (int) index;

- (Tire *) tireAtIndex: (int) index;

- (void) print;

@end // Car
```

We've upgraded pretty much every method of Car to follow the memory management rules. Let's start with init:

```
- (id) init
{
    if (self = [super init]) {

        tires = [[NSMutableArray alloc] init];

        int i;
        for (i = 0; i < 4; i++) {
            [tires addObject: [NSNull null]];
        }
    }

    return (self);

} // init
```

You've seen self = [super init] a bajillion times already; you've practically memorized it. As you know by now, it just makes sure that the superclass gets the object up and running.

Next, we create an NSMutableArray. There's a handy NSMutableArray method called replaceObjectAtIndex:withObject: that's perfect for implementing setTire:atIndex:. To use replaceObjectAtIndex:withObject:, we need to have an object at the given index so it can be replaced. A fresh NSMutableArray doesn't have any contents, so we need some object as a placeholder. NSNull is great for that kind of thing. So, we put four NSNull objects (which you first saw in Chapter 8) into the array. In general, you don't have to prepack your NSMutableArrays with NSNulls, but in this case, doing so makes things a little easier later on.

At the end of init, we return self, because that's the object we just finished initializing.

Next come the accessor methods for the engine. These are setEngine: and engine. setEngine: uses the "retain the object passed in and release the current object" technique that we showed earlier:

```
- (void) setEngine: (Engine *) newEngine
{
    [newEngine retain];
    [engine release];

    engine = newEngine;

} // setEngine
```

And the engine accessor method simply returns the current engine:

```
- (Engine *) engine
{
    return (engine);
} // engine
```

Now let's do the tire accessors. First comes the setter:

```
- (void) setTire: (Tire *) tire
    atIndex: (int) index
{
    [tires replaceObjectAtIndex: index
        withObject: tire];

} // setTire:atIndex:
```

This method uses replaceObjectAtIndex:withObject: to remove the existing object from the collection and replace it with the new object. We don't have to do any explicit memory management with the tire, because NSMutableArray will automatically retain the new tire and release the object that lives at the index, whether it's an NSNull placeholder or a previously stored tire object. NSMutableArray will release all of its objects when it gets destroyed, so the tire will get cleaned up.

The tireAtIndex: getter uses the objectAtIndex: method provided by NSArray to get the tire from the array:

```
- (Tire *) tireAtIndex: (int) index
{
    Tire *tire;
```

```
    tire = [tires objectAtIndex: index];

    return (tire);

} // tireAtIndex:
```

RAPID RETURN

It's perfectly legal to make the following method a one-liner by directly returning the result value of objectAtIndex:

```
- (Tire *) tireAtIndex: (int) index
{
    return ([tires objectAtIndex: index]);
} // tireAtIndex:
```

The extra variable in the original makes the code a little easier to read (at least, to us) and setting a breakpoint easier, so we can see which object is being returned. This technique also makes it easier for the caveman debuggers to stick an NSLog() between the objectAtIndex: call and the end of the method when we return the tire object.

We still need to make sure the car cleans up after the objects it's hanging onto—specifically, the engine and the tires array. The dealloc method is the place to do this:

```
- (void) dealloc
{
    [tires release];
    [engine release];

    [super dealloc];

} // dealloc
```

That's enough to make sure all memory is reclaimed when this car gets sent to the junkyard. Be sure to call the superclass's dealloc method! Leaving that out is a common mistake.

Finally, there's the print method for the car, which prints out the tires and the engine:

```
- (void) print
{
    int i;
    for (i = 0; i < 4; i++) {
        NSLog (@"%@", [self tireAtIndex: i]);
    }
```

```
    NSLog (@"%@", engine);

} // print
```

The print method loops through the tires and logs each one. It's interesting that the loop uses the tireAtIndex: method rather than poking at the array itself. If you want to touch the array directly, you're welcome to do so. However, if you use the accessors, even in the implementation of a class, you'll insulate that code from any changes. For example, if the tire storage mechanism changes again in the future (say, back to a C-style array), you won't have to change the print method.

Now (finally!), we can run CarPartsInit. The results look like this:

```
Tire: Pressure: 23.0 TreadDepth: 33.0
Tire: Pressure: 24.0 TreadDepth: 32.0
Tire: Pressure: 25.0 TreadDepth: 31.0
Tire: Pressure: 26.0 TreadDepth: 30.0
I am a slant-6. VROOOM!
```

Car Cleaning, GC Style

OK, so what about garbage collection? What does this class look like in that world? setEngine gets simpler.

```
- (void) setEngine: (Engine *) newEngine
{
    engine = newEngine;

} // setEngine
```

We change the engine instance variable. When Cocoa's garbage collection machinery runs, it realizes nobody else is pointing to the old engine, so the garbage collector makes that engine go away. On the other hand, because we have an instance variable pointing to the newEngine, it won't be collected; the garbage collector knows somebody is using it.

The dealloc method goes away completely: there is no use for dealloc in the GC world. If you need to do some work when an object goes away, you can override -finalize, which is called when the object is finally collected, but there are some subtleties associated with finalize. But for the kind of programming you'll be doing in Cocoa, you won't need to worry about finalize.

Making a Convenience Initializer

No code is created perfect. You can always make improvements. Think back to the `main()` function and how we created the tires:

```
tire = [[Tire alloc] init];
[tire setPressure: 23 + i];
[tire setTreadDepth: 33 - i];
```

That's four message sends and three lines of code. Doing that in one operation would be nice. Let's make a convenience initializer that takes both the pressure and tread depth at the same time. Here's `Tire` with a convenience initializer added (in bold):

```
@interface Tire : NSObject
{
    float pressure;
    float treadDepth;
}
- (id) initWithPressure: (float) pressure
          treadDepth: (float) treadDepth;

- (void) setPressure: (float) pressure;
- (float) pressure;

- (void) setTreadDepth: (float) treadDepth;
- (float) treadDepth;

@end // Tire
```

The implementation of that method is pretty plain, with no new surprises:

```
- (id) initWithPressure: (float) p
        treadDepth: (float) td
{
    if (self = [super init]) {
        pressure = p;
        treadDepth = td;
    }

    return (self);

} // initWithPressure:treadDepth:
```

Now, allocating and initializing a tire is a single-step operation:

```
Tire *tire;
tire = [[Tire alloc]
            initWithPressure: 23 + i
            treadDepth: 33 - i];
```

The Designated Initializer

Unfortunately, not all is well in initialization land. A couple of subtleties crop up when we start adding convenience initializers. Let's add two more convenience initializers to Tire:

```
@interface Tire : NSObject
{
  float pressure;
  float treadDepth;
}

- (id) initWithPressure: (float) pressure;
- (id) initWithTreadDepth: (float) treadDepth;

- (id) initWithPressure: (float) pressure
        treadDepth: (float) treadDepth;

- (void) setPressure: (float) pressure;
- (float) pressure;

- (void) setTreadDepth: (float) treadDepth;
- (float) treadDepth;

@end // Tire
```

The two new initializers, initWithPressure: and initWithTreadDepth:, are for folks who know they want a tire with either a particular pressure or a particular tread depth but don't care about the value of the other attribute and are happy to accept the default. Here's a first attempt at an initialization (which we'll be fixing later):

```
- (id) initWithPressure: (float) p
{
  if (self = [super init]) {
    pressure = p;
    treadDepth = 20.0;
  }

  return (self);

} // initWithPressure


- (id) initWithTreadDepth: (float) td
{
  if (self = [super init]) {
    pressure = 34.0;
    treadDepth = td;
```

```
    }

    return (self);

} // initWithTreadDepth
```

We now have four init methods: init, initWithPressure:, initWithTreadDepth:, and initWithPressure:treadDepth:. Each of these knows the default pressure (34), the tread depth (20), or both. That works out OK, and the code is correct.

The problems come when we start subclassing Tire.

The Subclassing Problem

We already have a subclass of Tire named AllWeatherRadial. Now, suppose that AllWeatherRadial wants to add two new instance variables, rainHandling and snowHandling, which are floating point values that indicate how the tire handles on wet and on snowy roads. We need to make sure these get set to reasonable values when a new AllWeatherRadial is made.

So, here is the new interface for AllWeatherRadial, with the new instance variables and accessors:

```
@interface AllWeatherRadial : Tire
{
    float rainHandling;
    float snowHandling;
}

- (void) setRainHandling: (float) rainHandling;
- (float) rainHandling;

- (void) setSnowHandling: (float) snowHandling;
- (float) snowHandling;

@end // AllWeatherRadial
```

And the accessor methods are *trés* boring:

```
- (void) setRainHandling: (float) rh
{
    rainHandling = rh;
} // setRainHandling


- (float) rainHandling
```

```
{
  return (rainHandling);
} // rainHandling


- (void) setSnowHandling: (float) sh
{
  snowHandling = sh;
} // setSnowHandling


- (float) snowHandling
{
  return (snowHandling);
} // snowHandling
```

We updated the description method to show the various tire parameters:

```
- (NSString *) description
{
  NSString *desc;
  desc = [[NSString alloc] initWithFormat:
    @"AllWeatherRadial: %.1f / %.1f / %.1f / %.1f",
        [self pressure], [self treadDepth],
        [self rainHandling],
        [self snowHandling]];

  return (desc);

} // description
```

Here's the for loop in main(), which creates new AllWeatherRadials with their default
values:

```
  int i;
  for (i = 0; i < 4; i++) {
    AllWeatherRadial *tire;

    tire = [[AllWeatherRadial alloc] init];

    [car setTire: tire
        atIndex: i];

    [tire release];
  }
```

When we run the program, though, there's a problem:

```
AllWeatherRadial: 34.0 / 20.0 / 0.0 / 0.0
AllWeatherRadial: 34.0 / 20.0 / 0.0 / 0.0
AllWeatherRadial: 34.0 / 20.0 / 0.0 / 0.0
AllWeatherRadial: 34.0 / 20.0 / 0.0 / 0.0
I am a slant-6. VROOOM!
```

The AllWeatherRadial attributes didn't get set to reasonable default values. What happened? We need to set the values in an init method, so we'll have to override init. But Tire also has initWithPressure:, initWithTreadDepth:, and initWithPressure:treadDepth:. Do we have to override all of those? And even if we do, what happens if Tire adds a new initializer? It would be bad if a change in Tire breaks AllWeatherRadial.

Luckily, the folks who brewed up Cocoa anticipated this problem. They came up with the concept of the **designated initializer**. One init method in a class is the designated initializer. All the initializer methods of the class use the designated initializer to do the initialization work. Subclasses use their superclass's designated initializer for their superclass initialization. The init method that takes the most arguments usually ends up being the designated initializer. If you're using someone else's code, be sure to check the documentation to see which method is the designated initializer.

Fixing Tire's Initializers

First, we need to decide which of Tire's initializers should be dubbed the designated initializer. initWithPressure:treadDepth: is a good choice. It has the most arguments, and it's the most flexible of the initializers.

To fulfill the promise of the designated initializer, all other initializers should be implemented in terms of initWithPressure:treadDepth:. It looks something like this:

```
- (id) init
{
  if (self = [self initWithPressure: 34
                    treadDepth: 20]) {
  }

  return (self);

} // init
```

```
- (id) initWithPressure: (float) p
{
  if (self = [self initWithPressure: p
                    treadDepth: 20.0]) {
  }

  return (self);

} // initWithPressure


- (id) initWithTreadDepth: (float) td
{
  if (self = [self initWithPressure: 34.0
                    treadDepth: td]) {
  }

  return (self);

} // initWithTreadDepth
```

NOTE

You don't really need the empty bodies for the `if` statements, as in `initWithPressure:treadDepth:`. We like to do that so that all the `init` methods have a consistent look.

Adding the AllWeatherRadial Initializer

Now, it's time to add an initializer to `AllWeatherRadial`. The only method we need to add is an override of the designated initializer:

```
- (id) initWithPressure: (float) p
      treadDepth: (float) td
{
  if (self = [super initWithPressure: p
                    treadDepth: td]) {
    rainHandling = 23.7;
    snowHandling = 42.5;
  }

  return (self);

} // initWithPressure:treadDepth
```

Now, when we run the program, the proper defaults are set:

```
AllWeatherRadial: 34.0 / 20.0 / 23.7 / 42.5
AllWeatherRadial: 34.0 / 20.0 / 23.7 / 42.5
AllWeatherRadial: 34.0 / 20.0 / 23.7 / 42.5
AllWeatherRadial: 34.0 / 20.0 / 23.7 / 42.5
I am a slant-6. VROOM!
```

VROOM, indeed!

Initializer Rules

You're not required to create an initializer method for your class. If you don't have any state you need to set up or the default behavior of alloc in clearing everything out to zero is good enough, you might choose not to bother with an init.

If you do write an initializer, be sure you call the superclass's designed initializer in your own designated initializer.

If you have more than one initializer, pick one to be the designated initializer. That method will be the one that calls the superclass's designated initializer. Implement all of your other initializers in terms of your designated initializer, as we did previously.

Summary

In this chapter, you learned all about object allocation and initialization. In Cocoa, these are two separate operations: alloc, a class method that comes from NSObject, allocates a chunk of memory and clears it to zero. init methods, which are instance methods, get an object up and running.

A class can have more than one init method. These init methods are usually convenience methods that make getting the object configured the way you want easier. You'll choose one of these init methods to be the designated initializer. All other init methods are coded in terms of the designated initializer.

In your own init methods, you need to call either your own designated initializer or the superclass's designated initializer. Be sure to assign the value of the superclass's initialzer to self and return that value from your init method. It's possible for a superclass to decide to return an entirely different object.

Coming next are properties, a quick and easy way to make your accessor methods.

Chapter 11

Properties

*r*emember back in the mists at the dawn of time when we wrote accessor methods for our instance variables? We wrote a lot of boilerplate code, creating both a `-setBlah` method to set the object's `blah` attribute (obviously) and a `-blah` method to retrieve it. If the attribute is an object, we needed to retain the new one and release the old one. There are utilities out there that will turn your class definition into method declarations and definitions that you can paste into your files. But still, writing accessor methods is a lot of mind-numbing work that can better be applied to doing the cool stuff that's unique to your program.

In Objective-C 2.0, Apple introduced **properties**, a combination of new compiler directives and a new attribute accessor syntax. The new properties feature greatly reduces the amount of mindless code you have to write. Throughout this chapter, we'll be modifying *10.01 CarParts-Init* to use properties. The final code for this chapter can be found in the *11.01 CarProperties* project.

Remember that Objective-C 2.0 features can only be used on Mac OS X 10.5 (Leopard) or later. Properties are used heavily in newer parts of Cocoa (especially the snazzy Core Animation features) and are also used a lot in iPhone development, so they're worth getting familiar with.

Shrinking Property Values

First off, we're going to convert one of the simpler classes, AllWeatherRadial, to use properties. To make the discussion a little more interesting, we'll add a couple of calls in main to
change some values on the AllWeatherRadials we create. We're simulating someone buy-
ing four tires on sale from different stores, so all four have different handling characteristics.

Here is main again, with the new lines in bold:

```
int main (int argc, const char * argv[])
{
  NSAutoreleasePool *pool;
  pool = [[NSAutoreleasePool alloc] init];

  Car *car = [[Car alloc] init];

  int i;
  for (i = 0; i < 4; i++) {
    AllWeatherRadial *tire;

    tire = [[AllWeatherRadial alloc] init];
    [tire setRainHandling: 20 + i];
    [tire setSnowHandling: 28 + i];
    NSLog(@"the tire's handling is %.f %.f",
          [tire rainHandling],
          [tire snowHandling]);

    [car setTire: tire
         atIndex: i];

    [tire release];
  }

  Engine *engine = [[Slant6 alloc] init];
  [car setEngine: engine];

  [car print];
  [car release];

  [pool release];

  return (0);

} // main
```

If you run the program now, you'll get this output, showing our newly changed tire handling
values:

```
tire 0's handling is 20 28
tire 1's handling is 21 29
tire 2's handling is 22 30
tire 3's handling is 23 31
AllWeatherRadial: 34.0 / 20.0 / 20.0 / 28.0
AllWeatherRadial: 34.0 / 20.0 / 21.0 / 29.0
AllWeatherRadial: 34.0 / 20.0 / 22.0 / 30.0
AllWeatherRadial: 34.0 / 20.0 / 23.0 / 31.0
I am a slant-6. VROOOM!
```

Shrinking the Interface

Now let's look at AllWeatherRadial's class interface:

```
#import <Foundation/Foundation.h>
#import "Tire.h"

@interface AllWeatherRadial : Tire {
  float rainHandling;
  float snowHandling;
}

- (void) setRainHandling: (float) rainHanding;
- (float) rainHandling;

- (void) setSnowHandling: (float) snowHandling;
- (float) snowHandling;

@end // AllWeatherRadial
```

This should be old hat for you. Let's clean it up, property-style:

```
#import <Foundation/Foundation.h>
#import "Tire.h"

@interface AllWeatherRadial : Tire {
  float rainHandling;
  float snowHandling;
}

@property float rainHandling;
@property float snowHandling;

@end // AllWeatherRadial
```

A bit simpler, isn't it? No need for the four method definitions. Notice that we've grown two keywords preceded by at signs. Recall that the at sign is a signal for "Objective-C weirdness coming your way"! @property is a new compiler feature that says that a new object attribute is being declared.

@property float rainHandling; says that objects of the class AllWeatherRadial have an attribute, of type float, called rainHandling. It also says that you can set the property by calling -setRainHanding: and that you can access the attribute by calling -rainHandling. You can run the program now, and it behaves just as it did before. All @property is doing is automatically declaring the setter and getter methods for the attribute. The attribute doesn't actually have to match the name of the instance variable, but it will in most cases. We'll talk about this a bit later. There are also some additional knobs you can turn on the properties; we'll talk about them later too, so please hang on.

Shrinking the Implementation

Now, let's look at the AllWeatherRadial implementation again:

```
#import "AllWeatherRadial.h"

@implementation AllWeatherRadial

- (id) initWithPressure: (float) p
            treadDepth: (float) td
{
  if (self = [super initWithPressure: p
                    treadDepth: td]) {
    rainHandling = 23.7;
    snowHandling = 42.5;
  }

  return (self);

} // initWithPressure:treadDepth


- (void) setRainHandling: (float) rh
{
    rainHandling = rh;
} // setRainHandling


- (float) rainHandling
{
    return (rainHandling);
} // rainHandling


- (void) setSnowHandling: (float) sh
```

```
{
    snowHandling = sh;
} // setSnowHandling


- (float) snowHandling
{
    return (snowHandling);
} // snowHandling


- (NSString *) description
{
  NSString *desc;
  desc = [[NSString alloc] initWithFormat:
    @"AllWeatherRadial: %.1f / %.1f / %.1f / %.1f",
            [self pressure], [self treadDepth],
            [self rainHandling],
            [self snowHandling]];

    return (desc);

} // description

@end // AllWeatherRadial
```

In the previous chapter, we discussed the init method, the designated initializer, all the setter and getter methods, and the description. We're now going to ruthlessly eliminate of all
the setter and getter methods and replace them with two lines of code:

```
#import "AllWeatherRadial.h"

@implementation AllWeatherRadial

@synthesize rainHandling;
@synthesize snowHandling;

- (id) initWithPressure: (float) p
            treadDepth: (float) td
{
  if (self = [super initWithPressure: p
                    treadDepth: td]) {
    rainHandling = 23.7;
    snowHandling = 42.5;
  }

  return (self);
```

```
} // initWithPressure:treadDepth


- (NSString *) description
{
  NSString *desc;
  desc = [[NSString alloc] initWithFormat:
    @"AllWeatherRadial: %.1f / %.1f / %.1f / %.1f",
              [self pressure], [self treadDepth],
              [self rainHandling],
              [self snowHandling]];

  return (desc);

} // description

@end // AllWeatherRadial
```

@synthesize is a new compiler feature that says "create the accessors for this attribute." For the line of code @synthesize rainHandling;, the compiler emits the compiled code for -setRainHandling: and -rainHandling.

NOTE

You may be familiar with **code generation**: Cocoa accessor-writing utilities and UI builders on other platforms generate source code, which is then compiled. But @synthesize is not code generation. You won't ever see the code that implements -setRainHandling: and -rainHandling, but these methods will exist and will be callable. This gives Apple the flexibility of changing the way accessors are generated in Objective-C, possibly leading to safer implementations or better performance.

If you run the program now, you'll get the same results as we got before the changes.

Dots Incredible

Objective-C 2.0 properties introduce a new bit of syntactic sugar that makes accessing object attributes easier. These new features also make Objective-C a bit more approachable for folks who are used to languages like C++ and Java.

Recall the two new lines we added to main to change the tire's handling values:

```
[tire setRainHandling: 20 + i];
[tire setSnowHandling: 28 + i];
```

We can replace that code with this:

```
tire.rainHandling = 20 + i;
tire.snowHandling = 28 + i;
```

If you run the program again, you'll see the same results. We use NSLog to report the handling values of the tires:

```
NSLog(@"tire %d's handling is %.f %.f", i,
      [tire rainHandling],
      [tire snowHandling]);
```

We can now replace that code with this:

```
NSLog(@"tire %d's handling is %.f %.f", i,
      tire.rainHandling,
      tire.snowHandling);
```

The "dot notation" looks a lot like structure access in C and object access in Java—on purpose. When you see a dot on the left-hand side of an equal sign, the setter for that attribute name (-setRainHandling: and -setSnowHandling:) will be called. Otherwise, if you see a dot next to an object variable, the getter for that attribute name (-rainHandling and -snowHandling) is called.

NOTE

Dot notation is just shorthand for calling accessor methods. No additional magic is happening under the hood. In Chapter 15, we'll talk about key-value coding, which actually uses some hard-core runtime magic. There is no connection between the property dot notation and the cool stuff key-value coding does behind the scenes.

If you're using properties, and you get strange error messages about accessing something that is not a struct, make sure you've included all the necessary header files for the classes you're using.

That's pretty much it for the new stuff that properties introduce. Of course, we have some additional cases to discuss for the proper handling of object attributes and for avoiding the exposure of both setters and getters. Let's talk about those next.

Objecting to Properties

So far we've looked at properties for scalar types—float in particular, but the same techniques apply for int, char, BOOL, and struct. For example, you can have an NSRect property if you want.

Objects bring some added complications. Recall that we retain and release objects as they flow through our accessors. For some object values, particularly string values, you want to always -copy them. Yet for other object values, like delegates (which we'll talk about in the next chapter), you don't want to retain them at all.

NOTE

> Whoa, wait a minute. What's with that copying and not retaining?
>
> You want to make copies of string arguments. A common error is to get a string from the user interface, like a text field, and use that as something's name. The strings you get from text fields are typically mutable strings and will change when the user types something new. Making a copy of the string prevents the value from changing unexpectedly.
>
> Now, what about not retaining objects? There is a special case, called a **retain cycle**, in which reference counting breaks down. If you have an owner/owned relationship, as between Car and Engine, you want the car to retain (own) the engine but not the other way around. The engine should not retain the car it has been installed in. If the car retains the engine, and the engine retains the car, then neither reference count will go to zero, and neither will ever be cleaned up. Car's dealloc won't get called until the engine releases the car in its dealloc, and the engine's dealloc won't get called until car's dealloc releases the Engine. They just sit there, staring at each other, waiting for the other to blink. The general rule is that the owner object retains the ownee object, and not the other way around.
>
> Lucky garbage collection users don't need to worry about this case.

Let's add a new feature to Car so that we can play with some new property syntax. That's gonna be exciting! We'll give the car a name. We'll start out old school and use traditional accessor methods. First is Car.h, with the new goodies in bold:

```
#import <Cocoa/Cocoa.h>

@class Tire;
@class Engine;

@interface Car : NSObject {
    NSString *name;
    NSMutableArray *tires;
    Engine *engine;
}
```

```
- (void)setName: (NSString *) newName;
- (NSString *) name;

- (void) setEngine: (Engine *) newEngine;
- (Engine *) engine;


- (void) setTire: (Tire *) tire
          atIndex: (int) index;
- (Tire *) tireAtIndex: (int) index;

- (void) print;

@end // Car
```

Now we add the implementation of the accessors (notice that we're copying the name), along with choosing a default name for the car and displaying it in the description:

```
#import "Car.h"

@implementation Car

- (id) init
{
  if (self = [super init]) {

    name = @"Car";
    tires = [[NSMutableArray alloc] init];

    int i;
    for (i = 0; i < 4; i++) {
      [tires addObject: [NSNull null]];
    }
  }

  return (self);

} // init


- (void) dealloc
{
    [name release];
    [tires release];
    [engine release];

    [super dealloc];
```

```objc
} // dealloc


- (void)setName: (NSString *)newName {
    [name release];
    name = [newName copy];
} // setName


- (NSString *)name {
    return (name);
} // name


- (Engine *) engine
{
    return (engine);
} // engine


- (void) setEngine: (Engine *) newEngine
{
    [newEngine retain];
    [engine release];

    engine = newEngine;

} // setEngine


- (void) setTire: (Tire *) tire
        atIndex: (int) index
{
    [tires replaceObjectAtIndex: index
          withObject: tire];

} // setTire:atIndex:


- (Tire *) tireAtIndex: (int) index
{
    Tire *tire;
    tire = [tires objectAtIndex: index];

    return (tire);
```

```
} // tireAtIndex:


- (void) print
{
    NSLog (@"%@ has:", name);
    int i;
    for (i = 0; i < 4; i++) {
        NSLog (@"%@", [self tireAtIndex: i]);
    }

    NSLog (@"%@", engine);

} // print

@end // Car
```

And we'll set the name in main:

```
    Car *car = [[Car alloc] init];
    [car setName: @"Herbie"];
```

Run the program, and you'll see the car's name at the beginning of the output. OK, let's start adding properties to Car. Here is *Car.h* in all its glory:

```
#import <Cocoa/Cocoa.h>

@class Tire;
@class Engine;

@interface Car : NSObject {
    NSString *name;
    NSMutableArray *tires;
    Engine *engine;
}

@property (copy) NSString *name;
@property (retain) Engine *engine;

- (void) setTire: (Tire *) tire
        atIndex: (int) index;
- (Tire *) tireAtIndex: (int) index;

- (void) print;

@end // Car
```

You'll notice the declarations of the simple accessors are gone, and they have been replaced by @property declarations. You can decorate @property with additional attributes to express your exact intentions on how the property is to behave. By adding copy to name, the compiler and users of the class know that name is going to be copied. This can simplify the life of programmers using this class, because programmers know they won't need to make a copy of strings they get out of text fields. engine, on the other hand, is managed just by retain/release. If you don't supply either one, the compiler will default to assign, which is generally not what you want with objects.

NOTE

You can use some other decorations, like nonatomic, which makes accessors a bit faster if they won't be used in a multithreaded environment. Desktop machines are so fast that there is no real performance gain by making a property nonatomic, but iPhone developers frequently use it to eke out more performance on that resource-constrained device. You can also use assign if you don't want the attribute object to be retained, to help avoid retain cycles.

Car.m has two major changes. The name and engine accessors are deleted and two @synthesize directives are added:

```
@implementation Car

@synthesize name;
@synthesize engine;
```

And finally, main uses dot notation to set stuff:

```
Car *car = [[Car alloc] init];
car.name = @"Herbie";
...
car.engine = [[Slant6 alloc] init];
```

Appellation Spring

In all the code in this chapter, the name of the property has been the same as the name of an instance variable that backs that property. This pattern is very common and probably one you'll use most of the time. Sometimes, though, you may want one name for the instance variable and another for the public attribute name.

Let's say we want to call the name instance variable in Car something else, like appellation. We just change the name of the instance variable in *Car.h*:

```
@interface Car : NSObject {
    NSString *appellation;
```

```
        NSMutableArray *tires;
        Engine *engine;
}
```

```
@property (copy) NSString *name;
@property (retain) Engine *engine;
```

and then change the synthesize directive:

```
@synthesize name = appellation;
```

The compiler will still create -setName: and -name but will use the appellation instance variable inside of their implementations.

But when you compile, you see a couple of errors. You may recall that we directly accessed the name instance variable, which has been changed. We can choose to do a search and replace on the name, or we can change direct ivar access to use accessors instead. In init, change

```
name = @"Car";
```

to

```
self.name = @"Car";
```

What's that self-dot-name business? It's a bit of disambiguation to let the compiler know that we want to vector through the accessors. If we just use a naked name, the compiler assumes that we're directly modifying an instance variable. To go through the accessors, we can write [self setName:@"Car"]. Remember that the dot is just shorthand for making this exact same call, so self.name = @"Car" is just another way of saying the same thing.

In dealloc, we'll pull a nifty trick:

```
 self.name = nil;
```

This line says to call setName: with an argument of nil. The generated accessor method will automatically release the previous name and replace the name with nil. This method accomplishes the work of releasing the memory for the name. Of course, we could just release name to clean up the memory. If you're clearing out a property outside of dealloc, using the "assign to nil" trick will set the property value to nil, keeping us from having a dangling reference to memory that might have been freed.

Finally, -description needs its first NSLog fixed:

```
NSLog (@"%@ has:", self.name);
```

Now, we can rename `appellation` to something else, like `nickname` or `moniker`. We just need to change the instance variable name and the name used in `@synthesize`.

Read-Only About It

You might have an object with an attribute that is read-only. This attribute might be a value that's computed on the fly, like the surface area of a banana, or might be one that you want other objects to read but not change, like your driver's license number. You can code for these situations with more attributes on `@property`.

By default, properties are mutable: you can read and write them. Properties have a `readwrite` attribute you can use. Since it's the default, you won't usually use it, but it's there if you need it and you want to make your intentions clear. We could have used `readwrite` in *Car.h*:

```
@property (readwrite, copy) NSString *name;
@property (readwrite, retain) Engine *engine;
```

But we didn't, because we generally want to stamp out and abolish and get rid of redundancy and repetition and saying the same thing over again.

Returning to our read-only property discussion, let's say we have a property, such as our license number or shoe size, that we don't want to be changed by anybody. We can use the `readonly` attribute on `@property`. An example class would be something like this:

```
@interface Me : NSObject {
  float shoeSize;
  NSString *licenseNumber;
}
@property (readonly) float shoeSize;
@property (readonly) NSString *licenseNumber;
@end
```

When the compiler sees that `@property` is `readonly`, it generates a getter but not a setter for that attribute. Users of `Me` can call `-shoeSize` and `-licenseNumber`, but if you try to call `-setShoeSize:`, the compiler will complain. You'll get the same behavior when using dot notation.

Alas, Properties Don't Do Everything

You'll notice we didn't convert `Car`'s tire methods to properties:

```
- (void) setTire: (Tire *) tire
         atIndex: (int) index;
- (Tire *) tireAtIndex: (int) index;
```

That's because these methods don't fit into the fairly narrow range of methods that properties cover. Properties will only let you replace -setBlah and -blah methods, but not methods that take extra arguments, like the tire's position on the car.

Summary

In this chapter, we discussed properties, which are a way to reduce the amount of code you have to write (and read later) when doing common operations with object attributes. Use the @property directive to tell the world, "Hey, this object has this attribute of this name of this type." Also use the directive to pass on some information about the property, like its mutability (readonly or readwrite) and object memory management (retain, assign, or copy). Behind the scenes, the compiler automatically generates the method declarations for the setter and getter for the object's attribute.

Use the @synthesize directive to tell the compiler to generate the implementation for the accessors. You can control which instance variable is affected by the generated implementation. If you don't want to use Apple default behavior, you're free to write your own code for the accessors.

Dot notation, although usually presented in the context of properties, is just shorthand for calling the setter and getter for objects. For example, dealie.blah = greeble is exactly the same as [dealie setBlah: greeble], and shronk = dealie.greeble is exactly the same as shronk = [dealie greeble]. Dot notation reduces the amount of typing you have to do and is a little more comfortable for folks coming from other languages.

Coming up next are categories, Objective-C's way of letting you extend existing classes, even if you don't have the code for them! Don't miss that.

Categories

When you write object-oriented programs, you'll often want to add some new behavior to an existing class: you can always create new hoops for objects to jump through. For example, you might have designed a new kind of tire, so you'd subclass `Tire` and add the new cool stuff. When you want to add behavior to an existing class, you'll often create a subclass.

But sometimes, subclassing isn't convenient. For example, you might want to add some new behavior to `NSString`, but you remember that `NSString` is really the front end for a class cluster, which makes it difficult to subclass. In other cases, you might be able to make a subclass, but you're using a toolkit or library that won't be able to handle objects of the new class. For example, your new subclass of `NSString` won't be returned when you make a new string with the `stringWithFormat:` class method.

The dynamic runtime dispatch mechanism employed by Objective-C lets you add methods to existing classes. Hey, that sounds pretty cool! The Objective-C term for these new methods is "categories."

Creating a Category

A **category** is a way to add new methods to existing classes. Want to add a new method to a class? Go right ahead! You can do this to any class, even classes you don't have the source code for.

For example, let's say you are writing a crossword puzzle program that takes a series of strings, determines the length of each string, and puts those lengths into an `NSArray` or `NSDictionary`. You'll need to wrap each length in an `NSNumber` object before adding it into the `NSArray` or `NSDictionary`.

You could write this code:

```
NSNumber *number;
number = [NSNumber numberWithUnsignedInt: [string length]];
// ... do something with number
```

But that would soon get tedious. Instead, you could add a category to NSString that does this work for you. In fact, let's do that. The LengthAsNSNumber project is located in the *12.01 LengthAsNSNumber* project directory and contains the code that adds such a category to NSString.

@interface

The declaration of a category looks a lot like the declaration for a class:

```
@interface NSString (NumberConvenience)

- (NSNumber *) lengthAsNumber;

@end // NumberConvenience
```

You should notice a couple of interesting things about this declaration. First, an existing class is mentioned, followed by a new name in parentheses. This means that the category is called NumberConvenience, and it adds methods to NSString. Another way to say this is, "We're adding a category onto NSString called NumberConvenience." You can add as many categories to a class as you want, as long as the category names are unique.

You indicate the class you're putting the category onto (NSString) and the name of the category (NumberConvenience), and you list the methods you're adding, followed by @end. You can't add new instance variables, so there is no instance variable section as there is with a class declaration.

@implementation

It comes as no surprise that the @interface section has an @implementation companion. You put the methods you're writing in @implementation:

```
@implementation NSString (NumberConvenience)
- (NSNumber *) lengthAsNumber
{
  unsigned int length = [self length];

  return ([NSNumber numberWithUnsignedInt: length]);

} // lengthAsNumber

@end // NumberConvenience
```

Like the @interface for the category, the @implementation has the names of the class and the category, along with the bodies of the new methods.

The lengthAsNumber method gets the length of the string by calling [self length]. You will send the lengthAsNumber message to this string. Then, a new NSNumber is created with the length.

Let's take a quick time-out for one of our new favorite topics: memory management. Is this code correct? Yes! numberWithUnsignedInt is not an alloc, copy, or new method. Because it's not one of those three, it will return an object that we can assume has a retain count of 1 and has been autoreleased. The NSNumber object we create will get cleaned up when the currently active autorelease pool is destroyed.

And here is the new category in action. main() creates a new NSMutableDictionary, adds three strings as the keys and the length of the strings as the values:

```
int main (int argc, const char *argv[])
{
  NSAutoreleasePool *pool;
  pool = [[NSAutoreleasePool alloc] init];

  NSMutableDictionary *dict;
  dict = [NSMutableDictionary dictionary];

  [dict setObject: [@"hello" lengthAsNumber]
        forKey: @"hello"];

  [dict setObject: [@"iLikeFish" lengthAsNumber]
        forKey: @"iLikeFish"];

  [dict setObject: [@"Once upon a time" lengthAsNumber]
        forKey: @"Once upon a time"];

  NSLog (@"%@", dict);

  [pool release];

  return (0);

} // main
```

Let's pull this apart, piece by piece, in our usual fashion. First, we create an autorelease pool, which you're probably tired of hearing about by now:

```
  NSAutoreleasePool *pool;
  pool = [[NSAutoreleasePool alloc] init];
```

Just as a reminder, this pool is where all the autoreleased objects go. In particular, the mutable dictionary will end up in here, as will all of the NSNumbers our category creates.

After making the pool, a new mutable dictionary is created. Recall that this handy Cocoa class lets us store pairs of keys and objects.

```
NSMutableDictionary *dict;
dict = [NSMutableDictionary dictionary];
```

We can't put primitive types like ints into a dictionary, so we have to use a wrapper class like NSNumber. Luckily, our shiny new category makes it easy to embed our string length into an NSNumber. Here is the code that adds the value of 5 to the dictionary, using the key @"hello ":

```
[dict setObject: [@"hello" lengthAsNumber]
        forKey: @"hello"];
```

That code looks weird, but it's actually doing the right thing. Remember that the @"string" kind of strings are actually full-blown NSString objects. They react to messages just like any other NSString object. Because we now have this category on NSString, any string will react to lengthAsNumber, even literal strings like these.

This bears repeating. This bears repeating! *Any* NSString will respond to lengthAsNumber—that includes literal strings, strings from description methods, mutable strings, strings from other parts of the toolkit, strings loaded from files, strings fetched from across the vast reaches of the Internet, and so on. This compatibility is what makes categories a hugely powerful idea. There is no need to subclass NSString to get this behavior—it *just works*.

When you run the program, you'll get output like this:

```
{
    "Once upon a time" = 16;
    hello = 5;
    iLikeFish = 9;
}
```

Bad Categories

Now that you're all high on categories, let's bring you back to earth a bit. Categories have two limitations. The first is that you can't add new instance variables to a class. There's nowhere to put them.

The second limitation concerns name collisions, in which one of your category methods has the same name as an existing method. When names collide, the category wins. Your category method will completely replace the original method, with no way of getting the original back. Some programmers add a prefix to their category methods to make sure there won't be a conflict.

NOTE

> There are techniques for getting around the inability to add new instance variables. For example, you can use a global dictionary to store a mapping between objects and any extra variables you want to associate with them. But you may want to consider if a category is really the best choice for what you're doing.

Good Categories

In Cocoa, categories are used mainly for three purposes: splitting a class's implementation across multiple files or multiple frameworks, creating forward references for private methods, and adding informal protocols to an object. Don't worry if you have no idea what "informal protocol" means. We'll cover that in a little bit.

Splitting an Implementation with Categories

As you saw in Chapter 6, you can put a class's interface into a header file and the implementation into a .m file. But you can't split an @implementation across multiple .m files. If you have a single large class you want to split across multiple .m files, you can use categories to do the job.

Take, for instance, the NSWindow class provided by the AppKit. If you look at the documentation for NSWindow, you'll find hundreds of methods. The NSWindow documentation is over 60 pages long when printed.

Putting all the code for NSWindow into one file would make it huge and unwieldy for the Cocoa development team, not to mention us poor developers. If you look at the header file (which lives at /System/Library/Frameworks/AppKit.framework/Headers/NSWindow.h) and search for "@interface", you'll see the official class interface:

```
@interface NSWindow : NSResponder
```

Then there are a whole bunch of categories, including these:

```
@interface NSWindow(NSKeyboardUI)
@interface NSWindow(NSToolbarSupport)
@interface NSWindow(NSDrag)
@interface NSWindow(NSCarbonExtensions)
@interface NSObject(NSWindowDelegate)
```

This use of categories allows all the keyboard user interface stuff to live in one source file, the toolbar code in another file, drag-and-drop features in yet another, and so on. These categories also break the methods into logical groups, making it easier for folks who are reading the header file. That's what we're going to try but on a smaller scale.

Using Categories in our Project

The CategoryThing project, found in the *12.02 CategoryThing* folder, has a simple class that's spread across a couple of implementation files.

First is *CategoryThing.h*, which has the class declaration and some categories. This file starts with the #import of the Foundation framework, and the class declaration with three integer instance variables:

```
#import <Foundation/Foundation.h>

@interface CategoryThing : NSObject {
    int thing1;
    int thing2;
    int thing3;
}

@end // CategoryThing
```

After the class declaration come three categories, and each category has accessor methods for one instance variable. We'll put the implementation of these into separate files.

```
@interface CategoryThing (Thing1)

- (void) setThing1: (int) thing1;
- (int) thing1;

@end // CategoryThing (Thing1)


@interface CategoryThing (Thing2)

- (void) setThing2: (int) thing2;
- (int) thing2;

@end // CategoryThing (Thing2)


@interface CategoryThing (Thing3)

- (void) setThing3: (int) thing3;
- (int) thing3;

@end // CategoryThing (Thing3)
```

And that's it for *CategoryThing.h*.

CategoryThing.m is pretty simple, containing a description method we can use with the %@ format specifier in NSLog():

```
#import "CategoryThing.h"

@implementation CategoryThing

- (NSString *) description
{
  NSString *desc;
  desc = [NSString stringWithFormat: @"%d %d %d",
          thing1, thing2, thing3];

  return (desc);

} // description

@end // CategoryThing
```

Time for a memory management check. Is `description` doing the right thing? Yes, it is. Because `stringWithFormat` is not an `alloc`, `copy`, or `new`, it returns an object we can assume has a retain count of 1 and has been autoreleased, so it will be cleaned up when the current autorelease pool goes away.

Now for the categories—*Thing1.m* has the implementation for the Thing1 category:

```
#import "CategoryThing.h"

@implementation CategoryThing (Thing1)

- (void) setThing1: (int) t1
{
  thing1 = t1;
} // setThing1

- (int) thing1
{
  return (thing1);
} // thing1

@end // CategoryThing
```

The interesting point to note is that a category can access the instance variables of the class it has been put onto. Category methods are first-class citizens.

The contents of *Thing2.m* are very similar to those of *Thing1.m*:

```
#import "CategoryThing.h"

@implementation CategoryThing (Thing2)
```

```
- (void) setThing2: (int) t2
{
  thing2 = t2;
} // setThing2

- (int) thing2
{
  return (thing2);
} // thing2

@end // CategoryThing
```

After reading this far, you can probably figure out what *Thing3.m* looks like (hint: cut; paste; search; replace).

The *main.m* file contains main(), which actually uses these categories we've been constructing. First come the #import statements:

```
#import <Foundation/Foundation.h>
#import "CategoryThing.h"
```

We need to import the header for CategoryThing so that the compiler can see the class definition and the categories. After that comes main():

```
int main (int argc, const char *argv[])
{
  NSAutoreleasePool * pool;
  pool = [[NSAutoreleasePool alloc] init];

  CategoryThing *thing;
  thing = [[CategoryThing alloc] init];

  [thing setThing1: 5];
  [thing setThing2: 23];
  [thing setThing3: 42];

  NSLog (@"Things are %@", thing);

  [thing release];

  [pool release];

  return (0);

} // main
```

The first two lines of main() are the standard autorelease pool code you've come to know and, uh, love. This pool will end up holding the autoreleased description string that's used by NSLog().

Next, a CategoryThing object is allocated and initialized:

```
CategoryThing *thing;
thing = [[CategoryThing alloc] init];
```

Here's our obligatory report to the memory management police: because this is an alloc, its retain count is 1, and it's not in the autorelease pool, we'll have to arrange to release it when we're done.

Next, some messages are sent to the object to set the values of thing1, thing2, and thing3:

```
[thing setThing1: 5];
[thing setThing2: 23];
[thing setThing3: 42];
```

When you're using an object, it doesn't matter if the methods are declared in the interface, in a superclass, or in a category.

After the thing values have been set, NSLog() prints out the object. As you saw in the description method for CategoryThing, this displays the values of the three thing instance variables:

```
NSLog (@"Things are %@", thing);
```

Because we used alloc to create the thing, we're responsible for releasing it when we're done with it. That happens right now:

```
[thing release];
```

And finally, the autorelease pool is released, and main() returns 0:

```
[pool release];

return (0);

} // main
```

That's it for our little program. Running the program gives these results:

```
Things are 5 23 42
```

Not only can you split a class's implementation across multiple source files, you can divide it among multiple frameworks as well. NSString is a class that lives in the Foundation framework, which has a lot of data-oriented classes, such as strings, numbers, and collections. All the eye candy (windows, colors, drawing, and the like) lives in the AppKit. Even though NSString is declared in Foundation, the AppKit has a category on NSString called NSStringDrawing, which lets you send draw messages to string objects. When you draw a string, the method renders the string's text on the screen. Because this is fancy graphics stuff, it's an AppKit feature. But NSStrings are Foundation objects. The Cocoa designers used categories to put the data functionality into Foundation and the drawing functionality into AppKit. We, as programmers, just deal with NSStrings, and we generally won't care where a particular method comes from.

Making Forward References with Categories

As we've mentioned before, Cocoa doesn't have any truly private methods. If you know the name of a method an object supports, you can call it, even if there is no declaration for that method in a class's @interface.

The compiler, though, tries to be helpful. If it sees you calling a method on an object, and it hasn't seen a declaration or definition for that method yet, it complains like this: warning: 'CategoryThing' may not respond to '-setThing4:'. Generally, this kind of complaint is good, because it will help you catch a lot of your typos.

But the compiler's vigilance can cause problems if you have methods that your implementation uses that aren't listed in the @interface section of your class. There are a lot of good reasons why you don't want to list all your methods there. The methods might be pure implementation details, or you might be playing around with method names to decide which ones you want to use. But if you don't declare your methods before using them, you'll get warnings from the compiler. Fixing all compiler warnings is a good thing, so what can you do?

If you can arrange to define a method before you use it, the compiler will see your definition, and it won't produce a warning. But if that's not convenient to do, or if you're using a non-published method in another class, you'll need to do something else.

Categories to the Rescue!

Declaring a method in a category is enough for the compiler to say, "OK, this method exists. I'm not going to complain if I see the programmer using it." You don't actually have to implement it if you don't want to.

Our technique is often to place a category at the top of the implementation file. Say that Car has a method called rotateTires. We could implement rotateTires in terms of another method called moveTireFromPosition:toPosition: to swap the tires at two locations. This second method is an implementation detail and not something that we want to put into the public interface of the car. By declaring it in a category, rotateTires can use move TireFromPosition:toPosition: without generating any warnings from the compiler. The category would look like this:

```
@interface Car (PrivateMethods)

- (void) moveTireFromPosition: (int) pos1
         toPosition: (int) pos2;

@end // Private Methods
```

When you implement this method, it doesn't have to exist in an @implementation Car (PrivateMethods) block. You can leave it in the @implementation Car section. This lets you separate your methods into categories as an organizational and documentation convenience, while still allowing you to keep all your methods in one big pile in the implementation file. When you're accessing private methods of other classes, you don't even have to supply an implementation of the method. Just having it declared in a category is enough to keep the compiler happy (by the way, you really shouldn't access private methods of other classes, but sometimes, you must to work around bugs in Cocoa or other people's code or to write test code).

Informal Protocols and Delegation Categories

Now, it's time for more of those Big Words and Big Ideas that you often find in object-oriented programming—you know, the ones that sound more complicated than they actually are.

Cocoa classes often use a technique that involves a **delegate**, which is an object asked by another object to do some of its work. For example, the AppKit class NSApplication asks its delegate if it should open an *Untitled* window when the application launches. NSWindow objects ask their delegates if they should allow a window to be closed.

Most often, you will be the one writing the delegate object and giving it to some other object, typically something provided by Cocoa. By implementing specific methods, you can exert control over how the Cocoa object behaves.

Scrolling lists in Cocoa are handled by the AppKit class NSTableView. When the tableView is ready to do some work, such as selecting the row the user just clicked, the object asks its delegate if it can select the row. The tableView sends a message to its delegate:

```
- (BOOL) tableView: (NSTableView *) tableView
        shouldSelectRow: (int) row;
```

The delegate method can look at the tableView and the row and decide whether the row should be selected. If the table includes rows that shouldn't be selected, the delegate might implement the concept of disabled rows that are not selectable.

The ITunesFinder Project

The Cocoa class that lets you find network services published by Bonjour (the technology formerly called Rendezvous) is named NSNetServiceBrowser. You tell the net service browser what service you're looking for and give it a delegate object. The browser object then sends messages to the delegate object telling it when it sees new services.

ITunesFinder, which lives in the *12.03 ITunesFinder* project folder, uses NSNetServiceBrowser to list all the shared iTunes music libraries that it can find.

For this project, we'll start out with main(), which lives in *main.m*. The delegate object is an instance of the class ITunesFinder, so we need to import its header file:

```
#import <Foundation/Foundation.h>
#import "ITunesFinder.h"
```

And then main() starts. We set up the autorelease pool:

```
int main (int argc, const char *argv[])
{
  NSAutoreleasePool *pool;
  pool = [[NSAutoreleasePool alloc] init];
```

Next, a new NSNetServiceBrowser is born:

```
  NSNetServiceBrowser *browser;
  browser = [[NSNetServiceBrowser alloc] init];
```

And then a new ITunesFinder is created:

```
  ITunesFinder *finder;
  finder = [[ITunesFinder alloc] init];
```

Because we're using alloc to create these, we must take responsibility for making sure they'll be released when we're done with them.

Next, we tell the net service browser to use the `ITunesFinder` object as a delegate:

```
[browser setDelegate: finder];
```

Then, we tell the browser to go look for iTunes shares:

```
[browser searchForServicesOfType: @"_daap._tcp"
        inDomain: @"local."];
```

The "_daap._tcp" string tells the net service browser to look for services of type daap ("daap" is short for "Digital Audio Access Protocol") using the TCP networking protocol. This incantation finds libraries published by iTunes. The domain `local.` means to look for the services on the local network. The Internet Assigned Numbers Authority (IANA) maintains a list of Internet protocol families, which usually map to the Bonjour service name.

Next, `main()` logs the fact that it has begun browsing and starts a run loop:

```
NSLog (@"begun browsing");

[[NSRunLoop currentRunLoop] run];
```

A run loop is a Cocoa construct that blocks (that is, doesn't do any processing) until something interesting happens. In this case, "interesting" means that the net services browser discovers a new iTunes share.

In addition to listening for network traffic, run loops handle other things like waiting for user events such as key presses or mouse clicks. The run method actually will not return; it will keep running forever, so the code that follows it won't ever execute. However, we've left it in anyway to let readers of the code know that we're aware of proper memory management (we could construct a run loop that runs only for a specific amount of time, but that code is more complicated and doesn't really contribute to our discussion of delegates). So here's the clean-up code that won't actually get run:

```
[browser release];
[finder release];

[pool release];

return (0);
} // main
```

Now, we have the net service browser and a run loop. The browser sends out network packets looking for particular services, and packets come back saying, "Here I am." When these packets come back, the run loop tells the net service browser, "Here are some packets for you." The browser then looks at the packets, and if they're from a service it hasn't seen before, it sends messages to the delegate object telling it what happened.

Now, it's time to look at the code for our delegate, ITunesFinder. The interface for the ITunesFinder class is minimal:

```
#import <Foundation/Foundation.h>

@interface ITunesFinder : NSObject
@end // ITunesFinder
```

Remember that we don't *have* to declare methods in the @interface. To be a delegate object, we just have to implement the methods we're interested in having called.

The implementation has two methods. First come the preliminaries:

```
#import "ITunesFinder.h"

@implementation ITunesFinder
```

and then the first delegate method:

```
- (void) netServiceBrowser: (NSNetServiceBrowser *) b
          didFindService: (NSNetService *) service
              moreComing: (BOOL) moreComing
{
  [service resolveWithTimeout: 10];

  NSLog (@"found one! Name is %@",
    [service name]);

} // didFindService
```

When an NSNetServiceBrowser finds a new service, it sends the netServiceBrowser: didFindService:moreComing: message to the delegate object. The browser is passed as the first argument (which would be the same as the value of the browser variable in main). If you have multiple service browsers doing searches at the same time, examining this parameter lets you figure out which one has found something.

The NSNetService object passed in the second argument is an object that describes the service that was found, such as an iTunes share. The last argument, moreComing, is used to signal when a batch of notifications is done. Why did the Cocoa designers include this moreComing parameter? If you ran this program on a big college network with a hundred iTunes shares, this method would get called 99 times with moreComing having the value YES and then once with a value of NO. This information is handy to have when constructing the user interface, so you know when to update your window. As new iTunes shares come and go, this method will be called again and again.

[service resolveWithTimeout: 10] tells the Bonjour system to go fetch all the interesting properties about the service. In particular, we want the name of the share, like Scott's Groovy Tunes, so we can print it out. [service name] gets us the name of the share.

iTunes shares can come and go, as people put their laptops to sleep or move off the network. The ITunesFinder class implements a second delegate method that gets called when a network service vanishes:

```
- (void) netServiceBrowser: (NSNetServiceBrowser *) b
           didRemoveService: (NSNetService *) service
                 moreComing: (BOOL) moreComing
{
  [service resolveWithTimeout: 10];

  NSLog (@"lost one! Name is %@",
    [service name]);

} // didRemoveService
```

This is exactly like the didFindService method, except that it logs when a service is no longer available.

Now, run the program, and see what happens. Mark's network has an ancient G4 iMac called iLamp that shares iTunes music around the house. That produces this output:

```
begun browsing
found one! Name is iLamp
```

We start up iTunes on a laptop and share the music under the name markd's music:

```
found one! Name is markd's music
```

After quitting iTunes on the laptop, ITunesFinder tells us

```
lost one! Name is markd's music
```

Delegates and Categories

OK, so what does all this delegate stuff have to do with categories? Delegates highlight another use of categories: the methods that can be sent to a delegate are declared as a category on NSObject. Here is part of the declaration of the NSNetService delegate methods:

```
@interface NSObject
  (NSNetServiceBrowserDelegateMethods)

- (void) netServiceBrowserWillSearch:
      (NSNetServiceBrowser *) browser;
```

```
- (void) netServiceBrowser:
      (NSNetServiceBrowser *) aNetServiceBrowser
    didFindService: (NSNetService *) service
    moreComing: (BOOL) moreComing;

- (void) netServiceBrowserDidStopSearch:
      (NSNetServiceBrowser *) browser;

- (void) netServiceBrowser:
      (NSNetServiceBrowser *) browser
    didRemoveService: (NSNetService *) service
    moreComing: (BOOL) moreComing;
@end
```

By declaring these methods as a category on NSObject, the implementation of
NSNetServiceBrowser can send one of these messages to *any* object, no matter what
class it actually is. This also means that any kind of object can be a delegate, as long as it
implements the method.

NOTE

By putting a category on NSObject like this, any kind of object can be used as a delegate object. There
is no need to inherit from a specialized serviceBrowserDelegate class (like you do in C++) or to
conform to a specific interface (as in Java).

Putting a category on NSObject is called creating an **informal protocol**. As
you know, a "protocol" in computer-speak is a set of rules that govern communication.
An informal protocol is simply a way to say, "Here are some methods you might want
to implement so you can do cool stuff with them." There are methods declared in the
NSNetServiceBrowserDelegateMethods informal protocol that we haven't implemented
in the ITunesFinder. That's OK. With informal protocols, you only implement what you want.

As you might guess, there's also the concept of a formal protocol. We'll cover that in the next
chapter.

Responds to Selectors

You might be asking yourself, "How does NSNetServiceBrowser know if its delegate
can handle those messages that are being sent to it?" You've probably encountered the
Objective-C runtime error that appears when you try sending a message that an object
doesn't understand:

```
 -[ITunesFinder addSnack:]: selector not recognized
```

So how does NSNetServiceBrowser get away with it? It doesn't. NSNetServiceBrowser first checks with the object by asking it, "Can you respond to this selector?" If it can, NSNetServiceBrowser sends the message.

What is a selector? It's just the name of a method, but it's encoded in a special way that's used by the Objective-C runtime for quick lookups. You indicate a selector by using the @selector() compiler directive, with the name of the method nestled in the parentheses. So, the selector for the Car method setEngine: would be

```
@selector(setEngine:)
```

And this would be the selector for the setTire:atIndex: Car method:

```
@selector(setTire:atIndex:)
```

NSObject provides a method called respondsToSelector: that queries an object to see if it will respond to a given message. The following chunk of code uses respondsToSelector:

```
Car *car = [[Car alloc] init];
if ([car respondsToSelector: @selector(setEngine:)]) {
  NSLog (@"yowza!");
}
```

This code prints "yowza!", because a Car object does indeed respond to the setEngine: message.

Now, check out this block of code:

```
ITunesFinder *finder = [[ITunesFinder alloc] init];

if ([finder respondsToSelector:@selector(setEngine:)]) {
  NSLog (@"yowza!");
}
```

There will be no "yowza!" this time. ITunesFinder does not have a setEngine: method.

To find out what it needs to know, NSNetServiceBrowser would call respondsToSelector:@selector(netServiceBrowser:didFindService:moreComing:). If the delegate can respond to that message, the browser will send the message. Otherwise, the browser ignores that delegate for now and just goes on its merry way.

Other Uses for Selectors

Selectors can be passed around and used as arguments to methods and even stored as instance variables. This can lead to some very powerful and flexible constructs.

One of the classes in the AppKit is called `NSTimer`; it can send a message to an object repeatedly, which is very handy in games when you want to move a monster toward the player on a regular basis. When you make a new `NSTimer`, you give it the object you want it to send a message to and a selector saying which method you want it to call. For example, you could have a timer call the `moveMonsterTowardPlayer:` method of your game engine. Or, you could have another timer call an `animateOneFrame:` method.

Summary

We introduced you to categories in this chapter. Categories provide a way to add new methods to existing classes, even if you don't have the source code for those classes.

In addition to adding functionality to existing classes, categories provide a way to split an object's implementation across multiple source files or even across multiple frameworks. For example, think back to `NSString`'s data-handling methods, which are implemented in the Foundation framework, separate from its drawing methods from the AppKit.

Categories let you declare informal protocols. An informal protocol is a category on `NSObject` that lists methods that objects might be able to respond to. Informal protocols are used to implement delegation, a technique that allows you to easily customize the behavior of an object. Along the way, you also learned about selectors, which are a way to indicate a particular Objective-C message in your code.

Coming up next are Objective-C protocols, the formal protocols that are the dressed-up cousins of informal protocols.

Chapter 13

Protocols

*i*n the previous chapter, we talked about the magic of categories and informal protocols. When you use an informal protocol, as you saw in Chapter 12, you implement only the methods you want to respond to. For the NSNetServiceBrowser delegate in Chapter 12, we implemented only the two methods that get called when a new service is added to or removed from the network: we didn't have to implement the six other methods in the NSNetServiceBrowserDelegate informal protocol. We also didn't have to declare anything in our object saying that we're usable as an NSNetServiceBrowser delegate. It all just worked with a minimum of fuss.

As you might guess, Objective-C and Cocoa also include the concept of a formal protocol, and in this chapter, we'll take a look at how those work.

Formal Protocols

A **formal protocol** (like an informal protocol) is a named list of methods. But unlike an informal protocol, a formal one requires that you explicitly adopt the protocol. You **adopt** a protocol by listing the protocol's name in your class's @interface declaration. When you do this, your class is said to **conform** to the protocol (and you thought you were a nonconformist). Adopting a protocol means that you promise to implement all the methods of that protocol. If you don't, the compiler yells at you by generating a warning.

NOTE

> Formal protocols are just like Java interfaces. In fact, Objective-C protocols were the inspiration for Java's interfaces.

Why would you want to create or adopt a formal protocol? It sounds like a lot of work is required to implement every method. Depending on the protocol, some busywork may even be involved. But, more often than not, a protocol has only a small number of methods to implement, and you have to implement them all to gain a useful set of functionality anyway, so the formal protocol requirements are generally not a burden. Objective-C 2.0 has added some nice features that make using protocols much less onerous, which we'll talk about at the end of this chapter.

Declaring Protocols

Let's take a look at a protocol declared by Cocoa, NSCopying. If you adopt NSCopying, your object knows how to make copies of itself:

```
@protocol NSCopying

- (id) copyWithZone: (NSZone *) zone;

@end
```

The syntax looks kind of the same as the syntax for declaring a class or a category. Rather than using @interface, you use @protocol to tell the compiler, "I'm about to show you what a new formal protocol will look like." That statement is followed by the protocol name. Protocol names must be unique.

Next is a list of method declarations, which every protocol adopter must implement. The protocol declaration finishes with @end. There are no instance variables introduced with a protocol.

Let's look at another example. Here's the NSCoding protocol from Cocoa:

```
@protocol NSCoding

- (void) encodeWithCoder: (NSCoder *) aCoder;
- (id) initWithCoder: (NSCoder *) aDecoder;

@end
```

When a class adopts NSCoding, that class promises to implement both of these messages. encodeWithCoder: is used to take an object's instance variables and freeze-dry them into an NSCoder object. initWithCoder: extracts freeze-dried instance variables from an NSCoder and uses them to initialize a new object. These are always implemented as a pair; there's no point in encoding an object if you'll never revive it into a new one, and if you never encode an object, you won't have anything to use to create a new one.

Adopting a Protocol

To adopt a protocol, you list the protocol in the class declaration, surrounded by angle brackets. For example, if Car adopts NSCopying, the declaration looks like this:

```
@interface Car : NSObject <NSCopying>
{
  // instance variables
}

// methods

@end // Car
```

And if Car adopts both NSCopying and NSCoding, the declaration goes like this:

```
@interface Car : NSObject <NSCopying, NSCoding>
{
  // instance variables
}

// methods

@end // Car
```

You can list the protocols in any order; it makes no difference.

When you adopt a protocol, you're sending a message to programmers reading the class declaration, saying that objects of this class can do two very important things: they can encode/decode themselves and copy themselves.

Implementing a Protocol

That's about all there is to know regarding protocols (save a little syntactic detail when declaring variables that we'll discuss later). We'll spend the bulk of this chapter going through the exercise of adopting the NSCopying protocol for CarParts.

Carbon Copies

Let's all chant together the rule of memory management, "If you get an object from an alloc, copy, or new, it has a retain count of 1, and you're responsible for releasing it." We've covered alloc and new already, but we really haven't discussed copy yet. The copy method, of course, makes a copy of an object. The copy message tells an object to create a brand new object and to make the new object the same as the receiver.

Now, we'll be extending CarParts so that you can make a copy of a car (wait until Detroit hears about this). The code for this lives in the *13. 01 - CarParts-Copy* project folder. Along the way, we'll touch on some interesting subtleties involved in implementing the copy-making code.

MAKIN' COPIES

Actually, you can make copies in a bunch of different ways. Most objects refer to—that is, point at—other objects. When you create a **shallow** copy, you don't duplicate the referred objects; your new copy simply points at the referred objects that already exist. NSArray's copy method makes shallow copies. When you make a copy of an NSArray, your copy only duplicates the pointers to the referred objects, not the objects themselves. If you copy an NSArray that holds five NSStrings, you still end up with five strings running around your program, not ten. In that case, each object ends up with a pointer to each string.

A **deep** copy, on the other hand, makes duplicates of all the referred objects. If NSArray's copy was a deep copy, you'd have ten strings floating around after the copy was made. For CarParts, we're going to use a deep copy. This way, when you make a copy of a car, you can change a value it refers to, such as a tire's pressure, without changing the pressure for both cars.

You are free to mix and match deep and shallow copies of your composed objects, depending on the needs of your particular class.

To copy a car, we'll need to be able to make copies of engines and tires too. Programmers, start (with) your engines!

Copying Engines

The first class we'll mess with is Engine. To be able to make a copy of an engine, the class needs to adopt the NSCopying protocol. Here is the new interface for Engine:

```
@interface Engine : NSObject <NSCopying>
@end // Engine
```

Because we've adopted the NSCopying protocol, we have to implement the copyWithZone: method. A **zone** is an NSZone, which is a region of memory from which you can allocate memory. When you send a copy message to an object, it gets turned into copyWithZone: before reaching your code. Back in days of yore, NSZones were more important than they are now, but we're still stuck with them like a small piece of baggage.

Here's Engine's copyWithZone: implementation:

```
- (id) copyWithZone: (NSZone *) zone
{
  Engine *engineCopy;
  engineCopy = [[[self class]
                    allocWithZone: zone]
```

```
        init];

    return (engineCopy);

} // copyWithZone
```

Engine has no instance variables, so all we have to do is make a new engine object. However, that's not quite as easy as it sounds. Look at that complex statement on the right side of
engineCopy. The message sends are nested three levels deep!

The first thing this method does is get the class for self. Then, it sends that class an
allocWithZone: message to allocate some memory and create a new object of that class.
Finally, the init message is sent to this new object to get it initialized. Let's discuss why we
need that complicated nest of messages, especially the [self class] business.

Recall that alloc is a class method. allocWithZone: is a class method too, as you can tell by
the leading plus sign in its method declaration:

```
+ (id) allocWithZone: (NSZone *) zone;
```

We'll need to send this message to a class, rather than an instance. What class do we send it
to? Our first instinct is to send allocWithZone: to Engine, like this:

```
[Engine allocWithZone: zone];
```

That will work for Engine, but not for an Engine subclass. Why not? Ponder Slant6, which
is a subclass of Engine. If you send a Slant6 object the copy message, eventually the code
will end up in Engine's copyWithZone:, because we ultimately use the copying logic from
Engine. And if you send allocWithZone: directly to the Engine class, a new Engine object
will be created, not a Slant6 object. Things can really get confusing if Slant6 adds instance
variables. In that case, an Engine object won't be big enough to hold the additional variables, so you may end up with memory overrun errors.

Now you probably see why we used [self class]. By using [self class], the
allocWithZone: will be sent to the class of the object that is receiving the copy message.
If self is a Slant6, a new Slant6 is created here. If some brand new kind of engine is added
to our program in the future (like a MatterAntiMatterReactor), that new kind of engine
will be properly copied, too.

The last line of the method returns the newly created object.

Let's double-check memory management. A copy operation should return an object with a
retain count of one (and not be autoreleased). We get hold of the new object via an alloc,
which always returns an object with a retain count of one, and we're not releasing it, so we're
A-OK in the memory management department.

That's it for making Engine copy-capable. We don't have to touch Slant6. Because Slant6 doesn't add any instance variables, it doesn't have to do any extra work when making a copy. Thanks to inheritance, and the technique of using [self class] when creating the object, Slant6 objects can be copied too.

Copying Tires

Tires are trickier to copy than Engines. Tire has two instance variables (pressure and treadDepth) that need to be copied into new Tires, and the AllWeatherRadial subclass introduces two additional instance variables (rainHandling and snowHandling) that also must be copied into a new object.

First up is Tire. The interface has grown the protocol-adoption syntax:

```
@interface Tire : NSObject <NSCopying>
{
   float pressure;
   float treadDepth;
}

// ... methods

@end // Tire
```

and now the implementation of copyWithZone::

```
- (id) copyWithZone: (NSZone *) zone
{
   Tire *tireCopy;
   tireCopy = [[[self class] allocWithZone: zone]
                   initWithPressure: pressure
                   treadDepth: treadDepth];

   return (tireCopy);

} // copyWithZone
```

You can see the [[self class] allocWithZone: zone] pattern here, like in Engine. Since we have to call init when we create the object, we can easily use Tire's initWithPressure:treadDepth: to set the pressure and treadDepth of the new tire to be the values of the tire we're copying. This method happens to be Tire's designated initializer, but you don't have to use the designated initializer for copying. If you want, you can use a plain init and use accessor methods to change attributes.

A HANDY POINTER FOR YOU

You can access instance variables directly via the C pointer operator, like this:

```
tireCopy->pressure = pressure;
tireCopy->treadDepth = treadDepth;
```

Generally, we try to use `init` methods and accessor methods in the unlikely event that setting an attribute involves extra work.

Now, it's time for `AllWeatherRadial`. The `@interface` for `AllWeatherRadial` is unchanged:

```
@interface AllWeatherRadial : Tire
{
  float rainHandling;
  float snowHandling;
}

// ... methods
@end // AllWeatherRadial
```

Wait—where's the `<NSCopying>`? You don't need it, and you can probably guess why. When `AllWeatherRadial` inherits from `Tire`, it pulls all of `Tire`'s baggage along, including the conformance to the `NSCopying` protocol.

We'll need to implement `copyWithZone:`, though, because we have to make sure `AllWeatherRadial`'s rain and snow-handling instance variables are copied:

```
- (id) copyWithZone: (NSZone *) zone
{
  AllWeatherRadial *tireCopy;
  tireCopy = [super copyWithZone: zone];

  [tireCopy setRainHandling: rainHandling];
  [tireCopy setSnowHandling: snowHandling];

  return (tireCopy);

} // copyWithZone
```

Because `AllWeatherRadial` is a subclass of a class that can be copied, it doesn't need to do the `allocWithZone:` and `[self class]` jazz we used earlier. This class just asks its super-class for a copy and hopes that the superclass does the right thing and uses `[self class]` when allocating the object. Because `Tire`'s `copyWithZone:` uses `[self class]` to deter-mine the kind of object to make, it will create a new `AllWeatherRadial`, which is just what we want. That code also handles copying the `pressure` and `treadDepth` values for us. Now, isn't that convenient?

The rest of the work is to set the rain and snow-handling values. The accessor methods are good for doing that.

Copying the Car

Now that we can make copies of engines and tires and their subclasses, it's time to make the `Car` itself copiable.

As you'd expect, `Car` needs to adopt the `NSCopying` protocol:

```
@interface Car : NSObject <NSCopying>
{
  NSMutableArray *tires;
  Engine *engine;
}

// ... methods
@end // Car
```

And to fulfill its promise to `NSCopying`, `Car` must implement our old friend `copyWithZone:`. Here is `Car`'s `copyWithZone:` method:

```
- (id) copyWithZone: (NSZone *) zone
{
  Car *carCopy;
  carCopy = [[[self class]
               allocWithZone: zone]
             init];

  carCopy.name = self.name;

  Engine *engineCopy;
  engineCopy = [[engine copy] autorelease];
  carCopy.engine = engineCopy;

  int i;
  for (i = 0; i < 4; i++) {
    Tire *tireCopy;

    tireCopy = [[self tireAtIndex: i] copy];
    [tireCopy autorelease];

    [carCopy setTire: tireCopy
            atIndex: i];
```

```
    }

    return (carCopy);

} // copyWithZone
```

That's a little more code than we've been writing, but all of it is a similar to what you've seen already.

First, a new car is allocated by sending `allocWithZone:` to the class of the object that's receiving this message:

```
Car *carCopy;
carCopy = [[[self class]
              allocWithZone: zone]
            init];
```

CarParts-copy contains no subclasses of `Car`, but it might someday. You never know when someone will make one of those time-traveling DeLoreans. We can future-proof ourselves by allocating the new object using the `self`'s class, as we've done so far.

We need to copy over the car's appellation:

```
carCopy.name = self.name;
```

Remember that the `name` property will copy its string, so the new car will have the proper name.

Next, a copy of the engine is made, and the car copy is told to use that for its engine:

```
  Engine *engineCopy;
  engineCopy = [[engine copy] autorelease];
  carCopy.engine = engineCopy;
```

See that autorelease? Is it necessary? Let's think through memory management for a second. `[engine copy]` will return an object with a retain count of 1. `setEngine:` will retain the engine that's given to it, making the retain count 2. When the car copy is (eventually) destroyed, the engine will be released by `Car`'s `dealloc`, so its retain count goes back to 1. By the time that happens, this code will be long gone, so nobody will be around to give it that last release to cause it to be deallocated. In that case, the engine object would leak. By autoreleasing it, the reference count will be decremented some time in the future when the autorelease pool gets drained.

Could we have done a simple `[engineCopy release]` instead of autoreleasing? Yes. You'd have to do the release after the `setEngine:` call; otherwise, the engine copy would be destroyed before being used. Which way you choose to do it is up to your own tastes. Some programmers like to keep their memory cleanup in one place in their functions, and others like to autorelease the objects at the point of creation so they don't forget to release them later on. Either approach is valid.

After carCopy is outfitted with a new engine, a for loop spins around four times, copying each tire and installing the copies on the new car:

```
int i;
for (i = 0; i < 4; i++) {
  Tire *tireCopy;

  tireCopy = [[self tireAtIndex: i] copy];
  [tireCopy autorelease];

  [carCopy setTire: tireCopy
          atIndex: i];
}
```

The code in the loop uses an accessor method to get the tire at position 0, then position 1, and so on each time through the loop. That tire is then copied and autoreleased so that its memory is handled properly. Next, the car copy is told to use this new tire at the same position. Because we constructed the copyWithZone: methods in Tire and AllWeatherRadial carefully, this code will work correctly with either kind of tire.

Finally, here's main() in its entirety. Most of it is old code you've seen in previous chapters; the groovy new code appears in bold:

```
int main (int argc, const char * argv[])
{
  NSAutoreleasePool *pool;
  pool = [[NSAutoreleasePool alloc] init];

  Car *car = [[Car alloc] init];
  car.name = @"Herbie";

  int i;
  for (i = 0; i < 4; i++) {
    AllWeatherRadial *tire;

    tire = [[AllWeatherRadial alloc] init];

    [car setTire: tire
         atIndex: i];

    [tire release];
  }

  Slant6 *engine = [[Slant6 alloc] init];
```

```
    car.engine = engine;
    [engine release];

    [car print];

    Car *carCopy = [car copy];
    [carCopy print];

    [car release];
    [carCopy release];

    [pool release];

    return (0);

} // main
```

After printing out the original car, a copy is made, and that one is printed out. We should there-fore get two sets of identical output. Run the program and you'll see something like this:

```
Herbie has:
AllWeatherRadial: 34.0 / 20.0 / 23.7 / 42.5
AllWeatherRadial: 34.0 / 20.0 / 23.7 / 42.5
AllWeatherRadial: 34.0 / 20.0 / 23.7 / 42.5
AllWeatherRadial: 34.0 / 20.0 / 23.7 / 42.5
I am a slant-6. VROOOM!
Herbie has:
AllWeatherRadial: 34.0 / 20.0 / 23.7 / 42.5
AllWeatherRadial: 34.0 / 20.0 / 23.7 / 42.5
AllWeatherRadial: 34.0 / 20.0 / 23.7 / 42.5
AllWeatherRadial: 34.0 / 20.0 / 23.7 / 42.5
I am a slant-6. VROOOM!
```

Protocols and Data Types

You can specify protocol names in the data types you use for instance variables and method arguments. By doing this, you give the Objective-C compiler a little more information so it can help error-check your code.

Recall that the id type represents a pointer to any kind of object; it's the generic object type. You can assign any object to an id variable, and you can assign an id variable to any kind of object pointer. If you follow id with a protocol name, complete with angle brackets, you're telling the compiler (and any humans reading the code) that you are expecting any kind of object, as long as it conforms to that protocol.

For example, NSControl has a method called setObjectValue:, which requires an object that conforms to NSCopying:

```
- (void) setObjectValue: (id<NSCopying>) obj;
```

When you compile this, the compiler checks the type of the argument and gives you a warning, like "class 'Triangle' does not implement the 'NSCopying' protocol." Handy!

Objective-C 2.0 Goodies

Apple never leaves well enough alone. Objective-C 2.0 adds two new modifiers for protocols: @optional and @required. Wait a minute. Did we just say that if you conform to a protocol, you're required to implement all of the protocol's methods? Yes, that's true, for older versions of Objective-C. If you have the luxury of Objective-C 2.0, you can do groovy stuff like this:

```
@protocol BaseballPlayer

- (void)drawHugeSalary;

@optional
- (void)slideHome;
- (void)catchBall;
- (void)throwBall;

@required
- (void)swingBat;

@end   // BaseballPlayer
```

So, a class that adopts the BaseballPlayer protocol is required to implement -drawHugeSalary and -swingBat but has the option of sliding home, catching the ball, or throwing the ball.

Why would Apple do this, when informal protocols seem to work OK? It's one more tool in our arsenal to explicitly express our intent in class declarations and our method declarations. Say you saw this in a header file:

```
@interface CalRipken : Person <BaseballPlayer>
```

You know immediately that we're dealing with someone who gets paid a lot and can swing a bat and who might slide home or catch or throw the ball. With an informal protocol, there's no way to say this. Likewise, you can decorate arguments to methods with a protocol:

```
-(void)draft:(Person<BaseballPlayer>);
```

This code makes it obvious what kind of person can get drafted to play baseball. And if you do any iPhone development, you'll notice the things that are informal protocols in Cocoa become formal protocols with a lot of `@optional` methods.

Summary

In this chapter, we introduced the concept of a formal protocol. You define a formal protocol by listing a set of methods inside a `@protocol` block. Objects adopt this formal protocol by listing the protocol name in angle brackets after the class name in an `@interface` statement. When an object adopts a formal protocol, it promises to implement every required method that's listed in the protocol. The compiler helps you keep your promise by giving you a warning if you don't implement all the protocol's methods.

Along the way, we explored some of the nuances that occur with object-oriented programming, particularly the issues that crop up when making copies of objects that live in a hierarchy of classes.

And now, congratulations! You've covered a great majority of the Objective-C language and have delved deeply into a number of topics that come up often in OOP. You have a good foundation for moving on to Cocoa programming or jumping into your own projects. In the next chapter of this book, you'll get a quick taste of writing a graphical Cocoa application using Interface Builder and the AppKit. Interface Builder and AppKit are the soul of Cocoa programming and are the central topic of most Cocoa books and projects—and they're also a lot of fun. After that, we'll delve more into some of Cocoa's lower-level features.

Chapter 14

Introduction to the AppKit

S
o far in this book, all our programs have used the Foundation Kit and have communicated with us through the time-honored method of sending text output to the console. That's fine for getting your feet wet, but the real fun begins when you see a Mac-like interface that includes things you can click and play with. We'll take a detour in this chapter to show you some highlights of the Application Kit (or AppKit), Cocoa's user-interface treasure trove.

The program we'll construct in this chapter is called CaseTool, and you can find it in the *14.01 CaseTool* project folder. CaseTool puts up a window that looks like the screenshot shown in Figure 14-1. The window has a text field, a label, and a couple of but-

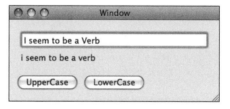

Figure 14-1. *The finished product*

tons. When you type some text into the field and click a button, the text you entered is converted to uppercase or lowercase. Although that's very cool indeed, you'll no doubt want to add additional useful features before you post your application on VersionTracker with a $5 shareware fee.

Making the Project

You'll be using Xcode and Interface Builder, and we'll lead you though the step-by-step process of building this project. The first thing to do is create the project files. Then, we'll lay out the user interface, and finally, we'll make the connections between the UI and the code.

Let's get started by going to XCode and making a new Cocoa Application project. Run XCode; choose **New Project** from the **File** menu; select **Cocoa Application** (as shown in Figure 14-2); and give your new project a name (see Figure 14-3).

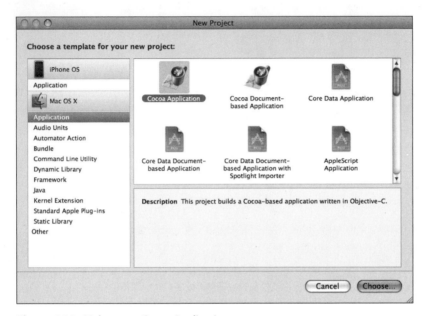

Figure 14-2. *Make a new Cocoa Application.*

Now, we add a new Objective-C class file, which we'll call *AppController*, so named because it will be the controlling object for our application. Select the *Sources* folder in the **Groups & Files** pane of the project window. Choose **New File** from the **File** menu. Figure 14-4 depicts XCode asking for the kind of file you want to create (in this case, an *Objective-C class*), and Figure 14-5 shows naming the file. Make sure the *Also create AppController.h* checkbox is checked.

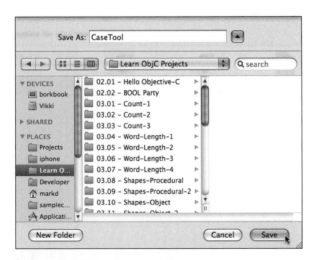

Figure 14-3. *Name the new project.*

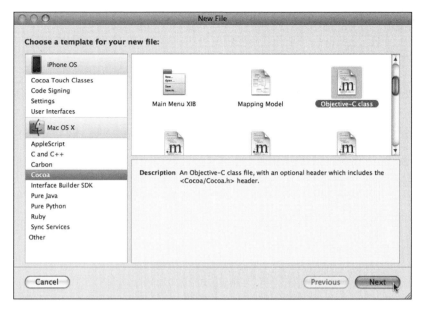

Figure 14-4. *Create a new Objective-C class.*

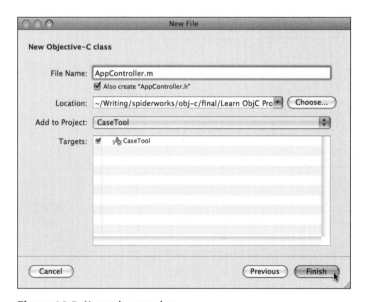

Figure 14-5. *Name the new class.*

Making the AppController @interface

We'll use the Interface Builder application to lay out the window's contents and hook up various connections between AppController and the user interface controls. Interface Builder is also used to lay out iPhone applications, so time in Interface Builder is well spent no matter which platform you'll end up programming for. We'll add stuff to the AppController class, and then Interface Builder will notice our additions and let us build the user interface.

First, we'll set up the header file for AppController:

```
#import <Cocoa/Cocoa.h>

@interface AppController : NSObject {
   IBOutlet NSTextField *textField;
   IBOutlet NSTextField *resultsField;
}

- (IBAction) uppercase: (id) sender;
- (IBAction) lowercase: (id) sender;

@end // AppController
```

There are two new quasi-keywords in there: IBOutlet and IBAction. These are actually just #defines provided by the AppKit. IBOutlet is defined to be nothing, so it disappears when we compile. IBAction is defined to be void, which means the return type of the methods declared in AppController will be void (that is, returning nothing).

If IBOutlet and IBAction don't do anything, why are they even there? The answer is that they're not there for the compiler: IBOutlet and IBAction are actually flags to Interface Builder, as well as the humans who read the code. By looking for IBOutlet and IBAction, Interface Builder learns that AppController objects have two instance variables that can be connected to stuff, and AppController provides two methods that can be the target of button clicks (and other user interface actions). We'll talk about how this works in a little bit.

In Interface Builder, we'll connect the textField instance variable to an NSTextField object. This text field is where users will type strings to be converted, which is the typical role for an NSTextField.

resultsField will be connected to a read-only NSTextField. When in read-only mode, an NSTextField acts like a text label. This text label is where the uppercase or lowercase version of the string will be displayed.

`uppercase:` will be the method that gets called when the *UpperCase* button is clicked. The argument, `sender`, is the `NSButton` object the user clicked. Sometimes, you can look at the `sender` argument for an action to get additional information about what happened. But not this time: we'll be ignoring it for CaseTool.

`lowercase:` is the method that's called when the *LowerCase* button is clicked.

Interface Builder

Now, it's time to crank up Interface Builder, affectionately known as IB to its friends. We want to edit the *MainMenu.xib* file that comes along with the project. This file is outfitted with a menu bar, along with a window we can put user controls into.

In the Xcode project window, find and double-click *MainMenu.xib* (see Figure 14-6).

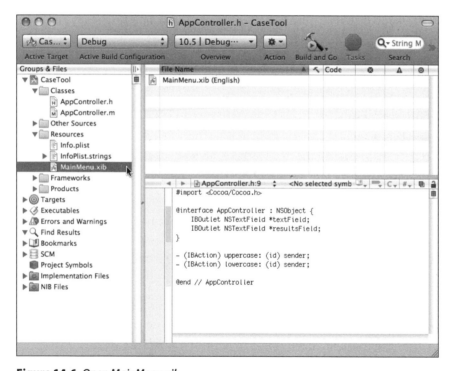

Figure 14-6. *Open MainMenu.xib.*

This launches Interface Builder to open the file. Even though the file extension is *.xib*, we call these *nib files*. "Nib" is an acronym for NeXT Interface Builder, an artifact of Cocoa's heritage as part of a company called NeXT. Nib files are binary files that contain freeze-dried objects, and *.xib* files are nib files in XML format. They get compiled into nib format at compile time.

Once IB opens the file, you'll see something like the four windows shown in Figure 14-7. Looking first at the upper-left, we see the IB *Dock* window, which holds icons representing the contents of the nib file. This is the main window for the nib file. Below that is the very short (don't miss it!) menu bar for the application. You can add new menus and menu items and edit existing items. We won't be messing with that for this program.

Below the menu bar is an empty window where we'll put the text fields and buttons. This real, live window corresponds to the miniature window-shaped icon down in the *Dock* window. Double-click that icon at any time to open the window. To the right of everything is the IB *Library* palette. This palette contains objects you can drag out into your window. There's a lot of stuff in there. You can type some text in the search box at the bottom to pare down what's shown in the library. For your convenience, a description is provided for each kind of object you can play with.

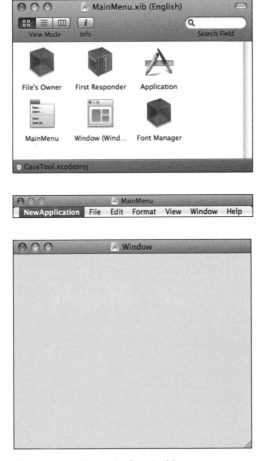

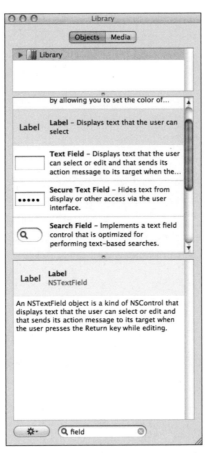

Figure 14-7. *Meet Interface Builder*

Now, let's start using Interface Builder to continue with our program. We're going to tell Interface Builder to create one of our AppController objects. When the program runs, Cocoa will load the nib file, and we'll have a new AppController object there for us to work with. But first, we need to create the AppController.

Drag an NSObject from the library into the *CaseTool.xib Dock* window. It will have the very creative name of *Object*, as shown in Figure 14-8.

Figure 14-8. *After dragging an object from the library*

Make sure your object is selected (has a gray box behind it), and choose **Tools ➤ Identity Inspector** (or you can use the keyboard shortcut ⌘6. This brings up the inspector window, which lets you tweak all sorts of attributes about the objects you have selected. We want to change the class to AppController, so choose it from the drop-down menu, as shown in Figure 14-9.

If you look at the *Dock* window now, the object has magically renamed itself to *AppController*, as shown in Figure 14-10.

Figure 14-9. *Change the object's class.*

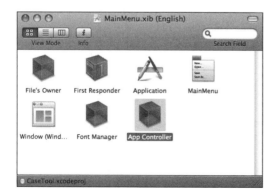

Figure 14-10. *Poof! It's an AppController!*

Laying Out the User Interface

Now, it's time to lay out the user interface. Find a *Text Field* (not a *Text Field Cell*) in the library, and drag it into the window, as shown in Figure 14-11. As you drag things around in the window, you'll see blue guidelines appear. These help you lay out your objects according to Apple user interface specifications.

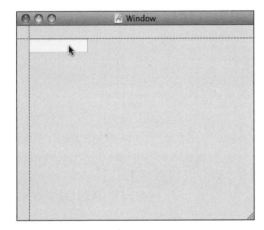

Figure 14-11. *Drag out an editable text field.*

Now, we'll drag out a *Label*. Grab a *Label* object from the library, and drag it into the window, as shown in Figure 14-12. This is where the uppercase and lowercase results will go.

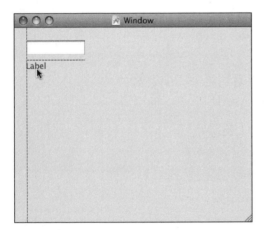

Figure 14-12. *Drag out a label.*

Next, find the push button in the Library, and drag that over. Position it under the label as shown in Figure 14-13. This is pretty cool, isn't it?

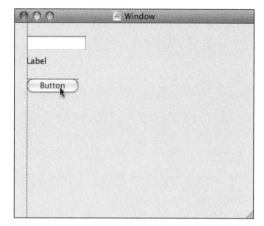

Figure 14-13. *Drag a button into the window.*

Now, double-click the newly deposited button. The label becomes editable. Type *UpperCase*, and press return to accept the edit. Figure 14-14 shows the button editing in action.

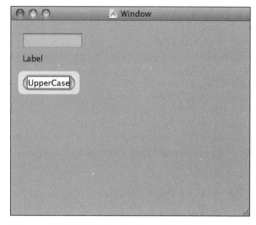

Figure 14-14. *Edit the button's label.*

Now, drag another button from the palette and change its label to *LowerCase*. Figure 14-15 shows the window after the second button has been added.

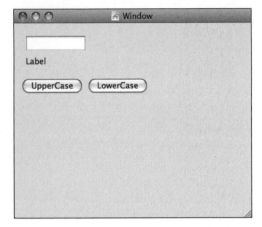

Figure 14-15. *All the items have been added.*

Next, we did a little interior decorating, resizing the text fields and the window itself to make it a little nicer, as shown in Figure 14-16. We also resized the *Label* to span the width of the window. The label must be wide enough to display whatever text you type into the field. Now, the window is just the way we want it.

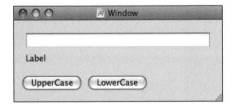

Figure 14-16. *The window is cleaned up.*

Making Connections

In this section, we'll show you how to wire up your code to the lovely user interface elements we just finished creating.

Hook Up the Outlets

Now, it's time to hook up some connections. First, we need to tell the AppController object which NSTextField its textField and resultsField instance variables should point to.

First, arrange the windows so that both the *MainMenu.xib Dock* window and your window with the text fields are visible at the same time. Next, hold down the control key and drag from *AppController* to the text field. A blue line follows your mouse pointer. Drag over to the text field, as shown in Figure 14-17. You should see a little *Text Field* label appear once you drag over the text field.

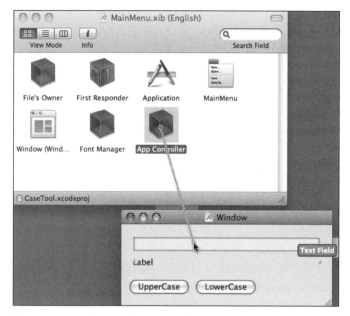

Figure 14-17. *Starting the connection*

When you release the mouse button, a menu containing the possible IB *Outlets* appears. Choose the *textField* option, as shown in Figure 14-18.

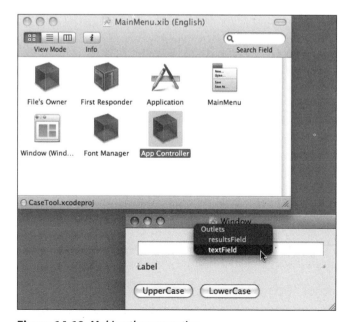

Figure 14-18. *Making the connection*

Now, do the same thing, but this time, control-drag from the *AppController* to the *Label*, and choose the *resultsField* item to make that connection.

Double-check your work by choosing the *Connections* panel of the inspector or by using the keyboard short-cut ⌘5. You should see both connections at the top of the inspector, as shown in Figure 14-19.

Figure 14-19. *Double-checking the connections*

Hook Up the Actions

Now, we're ready to wire the buttons to actions so they'll trigger our code. We'll control-drag again to make our love connections, this time from the button to the AppController.

> ## NOTE
>
> Knowing which way to drag the connection is a common source of confusion when using Interface Builder. The direction of the drag is *from* the object that needs to know something *to* the object it needs to know about.
>
> AppController needs to know which NSTextField to use for the user's input, so the drag is from AppController to the text field.
>
> The button needs to know which object to tell, "Hey! Someone pushed me!" So you drag from the button to AppController.

Control-click the *UpperCase* button, and drag a wire to *AppController*, as shown in Figure 14-20.

One you've drawn the wire from the button to *AppController*, select uppercase: in the inspector, as shown in Figure 14-21.

Now, whenever the button is clicked, the uppercase: message will be sent to the AppController instance, just like we always wanted it to. We can then do whatever we want in our uppercase: method.

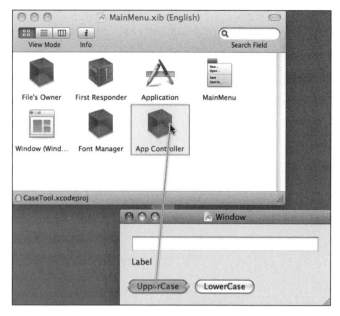

Figure 14-20. *Connecting the UpperCase button*

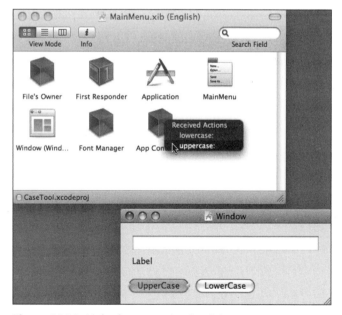

Figure 14-21. *Make the connection (again)*

Finally, we make the last connection by hooking up the *LowerCase* button. Control-drag from the *LowerCase* button to *AppController,* and select `lowercase:`. And now we're done in Interface Builder. Save your nib file and, if you want, quit Interface Builder.

Chances are you moved along fairly slowly laying out the objects and making the connections. Don't worry about it—with practice, you'll get a lot faster. An experienced IB jockey can zip through all these steps in less than a minute.

AppController Implementation

Now, let's get back to coding. It's time to implement `AppController`. But first, a little bit on how `IBOutlets` work.

When a nib file is loaded—*MainMenu.nib* is loaded automatically when the application starts, and you can create your own nib files and load them yourself—any objects that were stored in the nib file are re-created. This means that an `alloc` and an `init` both take place under the hood. So, when the application starts, an `AppController` instance is allocated and initialized. During the `init` method, all the `IBOutlet` instance variables are nil. Only after *all* the objects in the nib file are created (and this includes the window and text fields and buttons) will all the connections be set up.

Once all the connections are made (which simply involves putting the address of the `NSTextField` objects into the `AppController`'s instance variables), the message `awakeFromNib` is sent to every object that was created. A very, very common error is to try to do some work with `IBOutlets` in the `init` method. Because all the instance variables are nil, all messages to them are no-ops, so any work you try to do in `init` will silently fail (this is one of the places where Cocoa can let you down and cost you some debugging time). If you're wondering, why this is not working, use `NSLog` to print the values of your instance variables and see if they're all nil. There's also no predefined order in which the objects are created, and no predefined order in which `awakeFromNib` messages are sent.

Let's get on with `AppController`'s implementation. Here are the necessary preliminaries:

```
#import "AppController.h"

@implementation AppController
```

Next is an `init` method to show the value of the `IBOutlet` instance variables at `init` time (they'll be nil; trust us on this one):

```
- (id) init
{
  if (self = [super init]) {
    NSLog (@"init: text %@ / results %@",
           textField, resultsField);
```

```
    }

    return (self);

} // init
```

To have a nicer user interface, we should set the text fields to some reasonable default value, rather than *Label*. True, it's an accurate default value, but it's not terribly interesting. We'll put *Enter text here* into the text field, and the results field will be preset to *Results*. awakeFromNib is the ideal place for this:

```
- (void) awakeFromNib
{
  NSLog (@"awake: text %@ / results %@",
         textField, resultsField);

  [textField setStringValue: @"Enter text here"];
  [resultsField setStringValue: @"Results"];

} // awakeFromNib
```

NSTextField has a method called setStringValue:, which takes an NSString as its parameter and changes the contents of the text field to reflect that string value. That's the method we're using to change the text fields to something more interesting for users to look at.

Now for the action methods—first is uppercase:

```
- (IBAction) uppercase: (id) sender
{
  NSString *original;
  original = [textField stringValue];

  NSString *uppercase;
  uppercase = [original uppercaseString];

  [resultsField setStringValue: uppercase];

} // uppercase
```

We get the original string from the textField using the stringValue message, and we make an uppercase version. NSString provides us with the handy uppercaseString method, which creates a new string built from the contents of the receiving string, but with every letter kicked to uppercase. That string is then set as the contents of the resultsField.

Time for our obligatory memory management check: is everything groovy? You betcha. Both of the new objects that are created (the original string and the upper case string) come from methods that are not alloc, copy, or new, so they're in the autorelease pool and will get cleaned up. It's the responsibility of setStringValue: to either copy or retain the incoming string. What setStringValue: does is its own business. But we know our memory management is correct.

lowercase: is just like uppercase:, but on the down-low:

```
- (IBAction) lowercase: (id) sender
{
  NSString *original;
  original = [textField stringValue];

  NSString *lowercase;
  lowercase = [original lowercaseString];

  [resultsField setStringValue: lowercase];

} // lowercase
```

And that's it! When you run the program, you'll see the window appear. Type in a string and change its case, just like in Figure 14-22.

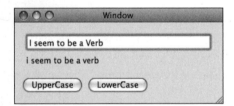

Figure 14-22. *The finished CaseTool program does what it does.*

Summary

This chapter has been a whirlwind tour that just touched the surface of Interface Builder and the Application Kit. We used only one AppKit class directly (NSTextField) and a couple of classes indirectly (NSButton, which powers the buttons, and NSWindow, which is the object controlling the window). There are over 100 different classes in the AppKit for you to play with, many of which appear in Interface Builder.

At this point, you're fully qualified to dive into a Cocoa book or project. We'll continue in the next chapter with an exploration of some of the low-level features of the Foundation Kit.

File Loading and Saving

*m*ost computer programs (applications) end up creating some kind of semi-permanent artifact of the user's work. Maybe it's an edited photo. Maybe it's a chapter of a novel. Maybe it's your band's cover of "Free Bird." In each of these cases, the user ends up with a file on a disk.

The standard C library provides function calls to create, read, and write files, such as open(), read(), write(), fopen(), and fread(). These functions are well documented elsewhere, so we won't talk about them. Cocoa provides Core Data, which handles all this file stuff behind the scenes for you. We won't be talking about this either.

So what does that leave us? Cocoa provides two general classes of file handling: property lists and object encoding, which we'll talk about here.

Property Lists

In Cocoa, there is a class of objects known as **property list** objects, frequently abbreviated as **plist**. These lists contain a small set of objects that Cocoa knows how to do stuff with, in particular, how to save them to files and load them back. The property list classes are NSArray, NSDictionary, NSString, NSNumber, NSDate, and NSData, along with their mutable counterparts if they have any.

You've seen the first four before but not the last two. We'll chat about those before we start filing things away. You can find all the code for this part of the chapter in the project *15.01 PropertyListing*.

NSDate

Time and date handling are pretty common in programs. iPhoto knows the date when you took that picture of your dog, and your personal accounting application knows the closing date when reconciling your bank statement. NSDate is the fundamental class in Cocoa's date and time handling.

To get the current date and time, use [NSDate date], which gives you an autoreleased object. So this code

```
NSDate *date = [NSDate date];
NSLog (@"today is %@", date);
```

would print something like this

```
today is 2008-08-23 11:32:02 -0400
```

There are methods you can use to compare two dates, so you can sort lists. There are also methods to get a date as a delta from the current time. For instance, you might want the date for exactly 24 hours ago:

```
NSDate *yesterday =
  [NSDate dateWithTimeIntervalSinceNow: -(24 * 60 * 60)];
NSLog (@"yesterday is %@", yesterday);
```

The preceding code prints out

```
yesterday is 2008-08-22 11:32:02 -0400
```

+dateWithTimeIntervalSinceNow: takes an argument of an NSTimeInterval, which is a typedef of a double representing some interval of seconds. This lets you specify a time displacement in the future with a positive time interval or in the past with a negative time interval, as we're doing here.

NSData

A common idiom in C is passing buffers of data around to functions. To do this, you usually pass to a function the pointer to the buffer and the length of the buffer. Plus, memory management issues may arise in C. For example, if the buffer has been dynamically allocated, who is responsible for cleaning it up when it's no longer useful?

Cocoa provides us the NSData class that wraps a hunk of bytes. You can get the length of the data and a pointer to the start of the bytes. Because NSData is an object, the usual memory management behaviors apply. So, if you're passing a hunk of data to a function or method, you can pass an autoreleased NSData instead without worrying about cleaning it up. Here is an NSData object that will hold an ordinary C string, which is just a sequence of bytes, and print out the data:

```
const char *string = "Hi there, this is a C string!";
NSData *data = [NSData dataWithBytes: string
                           length: strlen(string) + 1];
NSLog (@"data is %@", data);
```

Here are the results:

```
data is <48692074 68657265 2c207468 69732069 73206120 43207374 72696e67 2100>
```

That's, uh, special. But, if you have an ASCII chart handy (you can find one by firing up the terminal and typing the command man ascii), you can see that this chunk of hexadecimal is actually our string. 0x48 is "H", 0x69 is "i", and so on. The -length method gives us the number of bytes, and the -bytes method gives us a pointer to the beginning of the string. Notice the + 1 in the +dataWithBytes: call? That's to include the trailing zero-byte that C strings need. Also notice the 00 at the end of the results of the NSLog. By including the zero-byte, we can use the %s format specifier to print the string:

```
NSLog (@"%d byte string is '%s'",
       [data length], [data bytes]);
```

which results in the following output:

```
30 byte string is 'Hi there, this is a C string!'
```

NSData objects are immutable. Once you create them, that's it. You can use them, but you can't change them. NSMutableData, though, lets you add and remove bytes from the data's contents.

Writing and Reading Property Lists

Now that you have seen all of the property list classes, what can we do with them? The collection property list classes (NSArray, NSDictionary) have a method called -writeToFile: atomically:, which writes the property lists to files. NSString and NSData also have a writeToFile:atomically: method, but it just writes out strings or blobs of data.

So, we could load up an array with strings and then save it:

```
NSArray *phrase;
phrase = [NSArray arrayWithObjects: @"I", @"seem", @"to",
   @"be", @"a", @"verb", nil];
[phrase writeToFile: @"/tmp/verbiage.txt" atomically: YES];
```

Now, look at the file */tmp/verbiage.txt*, and you should see something like this:

```
<?xml version="1.0" encoding="UTF-8"?>
<!DOCTYPE plist PUBLIC "-//Apple//DTD PLIST 1.0//EN"
  "http://www.apple.com/DTDs/PropertyList-1.0.dtd">
<plist version="1.0">
<array>
    <string>I</string>
    <string>seem</string>
    <string>to</string>
    <string>be</string>
    <string>a</string>
    <string>verb</string>
</array>
</plist>
```

This code, while a bit verbose, is exactly what we tried to save: an array of strings. These property list files can be arbitrarily complex, with arrays of dictionaries containing arrays of strings and numbers and dates. Xcode also includes a property list editor, so you can poke around plist files and modify them. If you look around the operating system, you'll find lots of property list files, like all of your preference files in *Library/Preferences* in your home directory and system configuration files like those in */System/Library/LaunchDaemons*.

NOTE

Some property list files, especially the preferences files, are stored in a compressed binary format. You can convert these files to something human-readable using the `plutil` command: `plutil -convert xml1 filename.plist`.

Now that we have our *verbiage.txt* file sitting on disk, we can read it in with `+arrayWithContentsOfFile:` method, like this:

```
NSArray *phrase2 = [NSArray arrayWithContentsOfFile: @"/tmp/verbiage.txt"];
NSLog (@"%@", phrase2);
```

And our output happily matches what we saved earlier:

```
(
  I,
  seem,
  to,
  be,
  a,
  verb
)
```

NOTE

Did you notice the word "atomically" in our `writeToFile:` method? Are these calls radioactive? Nope. The `atomically:` argument, which takes a BOOL, tells Cocoa whether it should save the contents of the file in a temporary file first and, later, swap this temporary file with the original file when the file save is successful. This argument is a safety mechanism—if something bad happens during the save, you won't clobber the original file. But that safety does come at a price: you're consuming double the disk space while the save happens since the original file is still there. Unless you're saving huge files that might fill the user's hard drives, you should save your files atomically.

If you can boil your data down to property list types, you can use these very convenient calls to save stuff to disk and read it back later. When you're playing around with new ideas or bootstrapping a new project, you can use these conveniences to get your programs up and running quickly. Even if you just want to save a blob of data to disk and you're not using objects at all, you can use NSData to ease the work. Just wrap your data in an NSData object and call `writeToFile:atomically:` on the NSData object.

One downside to these functions is that they don't return any error information. If you can't load a file, you'll just get a nil pointer back from the method, without any idea of what went wrong.

Encoding Objects

Unfortunately, you can't always express your objects' information as property list classes. If we could express everything as dictionaries of arrays, we wouldn't need our own classes. Luckily, Cocoa has machinery for letting objects convert themselves into a format that can be saved to disk. Objects can encode their instance variables and other data into a chunk of data, which can be saved to disk. That chunk of data can be read back into memory later, and new objects can be created based on the saved data. This process is called **encoding and decoding**, or **serialization and deserialization**.

If you remember our foray into Interface Builder in the last chapter, we dragged objects out of the library and into the window, and things were saved to the nib file. In other words, the NSWindow and NSTextField objects were serialized and saved to disk. When the nib file was loaded into memory when the program ran, the objects were deserialized, and new NSWindow and NSTextField objects were created and hooked together.

As you can probably guess, you can do the same thing with your own objects by adopting the NSCoding protocol. The protocol looks like this:

```
@protocol NSCoding
- (void) encodeWithCoder: (NSCoder *) aCoder;
- (id) initWithCoder: (NSCoder *) aDecoder;
@end
```

By adopting this protocol, you promise to implement both of these methods. When your object is asked to save itself, -encodeWithCoder: will be called. When your object is asked to load itself, -initWithCoder: will be called.

So what's this coder thing? An NSCoder is an abstract class that defines a bunch of useful methods for converting your objects into an NSData and back. You never create a new NSCoder because it doesn't actually do much. But there are a couple of concrete subclasses of NSCoder that you actually use to encode and decode your objects. We'll be using two of them, NSKeyedArchiver and NSKeyedUnarchiver.

Probably the easiest way to understand these guys is with an example. You can look in the project *15.02 SimpleEncoding* for all of the code.

Let's start off with a simple class with some instance variables:

```
@interface Thingie : NSObject <NSCoding> {
  NSString *name;
  int magicNumber;
  float shoeSize;
  NSMutableArray *subThingies;
}
@property (copy) NSString *name;
@property int magicNumber;
@property float shoeSize;
@property (retain) NSMutableArray *subThingies;

- (id)initWithName: (NSString *) n
      magicNumber: (int) mn
         shoeSize: (float) ss;

@end // Thingie
```

This should be pretty familiar. We have four instance variables of object and scalar types, including one collection. Properties default to readwrite, so we did not mention that in the property definitions. There are public properties for each of them and a handy one-stop-shopping init method to create a new Thingie from scratch.

Notice that `Thingie` adopts `NSCoding`. That means we're going to provide an implementation for the encodeWithCoder and initWithCoder methods. For now, we'll make those two
empty.

```
@implementation Thingie
@synthesize name;
@synthesize magicNumber;
@synthesize shoeSize;
@synthesize subThingies;

- (id)initWithName: (NSString *) n
       magicNumber: (int) mn
          shoeSize: (float) ss {
  if (self = [super init]) {
    self.name = n;
    self.magicNumber = mn;
    self.shoeSize = ss;
    self.subThingies = [NSMutableArray array];
  }

  return (self);
}

- (void) dealloc {
  [name release];
  [subThingies release];

  [super dealloc];

} // dealloc


- (void) encodeWithCoder: (NSCoder *) coder {
  // nobody home
} // encodeWithCoder


- (id) initWithCoder: (NSCoder *) decoder {
  return (nil);
} // initWithCoder


- (NSString *) description {
  NSString *description =
  [NSString stringWithFormat: @"%@: %d/%.1f %@",
      name, magicNumber, shoeSize, subThingies];
```

```
    return (description);

} // description

@end // Thingie
```

This chunk of code will initialize a new object, clean up any messes we have made, create the stub methods to make the compiler happy over us adopting NSCoding, and return a description.

Notice that in the `init` method we're using `self.attribute` on the left-hand side of the assignments. Remember that this actually means that we're calling the accessor methods for those attributes, and these methods were created by `@synthesize`. We're not doing a direct instance variable assignment. This object creation technique will get us proper memory management for the passed in `NSString` and for the `NSMutableArray` we create, so we don't have to provide it explicitly.

So, inside of `main()`, make a `Thingie`, and print it:

```
Thingie *thing1;
thing1 = [[Thingie alloc]
            initWithName: @"thing1"
            magicNumber: 42
            shoeSize: 10.5];

NSLog (@"some thing: %@", thing1);
```

The preceding code will print out this:

```
some thing: thing1: 42/10.5 (
)
```

That was fun. Now let's archive this object. Implement `Thingie`'s `encodeWithCoder:` like this:

```
- (void) encodeWithCoder: (NSCoder *) coder {
    [coder encodeObject: name
          forKey: @"name"];
    [coder encodeInt: magicNumber
          forKey: @"magicNumber"];
    [coder encodeFloat: shoeSize
          forKey: @"shoeSize"];
    [coder encodeObject: subThingies
          forKey: @"subThingies"];

} // encodeWithCoder
```

We'll be using NSKeyedArchiver to do all of the work of archiving our objects into an NSData. The keyed archiver, as its name implies, uses key/value pairs to hold an object's information. Thingie's -encodeWithCoder encodes each instance variable under a key that matches the instance variable name. You don't have to do this. You could encode the name under the key flarblewhazzit, and nobody would care. Keeping the key names similar to the instance variable names makes it easy to know what maps to what.

You're welcome to use naked strings like this for your encoding keys, or you can define a constant to prevent typos. You can do something like #define kSubthingiesKey @"subThingies", or you can have a variable local to the file, like static NSString *kSubthingiesKey = @"subThingies";

Notice that there's a different encodeSomething:forKey: for each type. You need to make sure you use the proper method to encode your types. For any Objective-C object type, you use encodeObject:forKey:

When you're restoring an object, you'll use decodeSomethingForKey methods:

```
- (id) initWithCoder: (NSCoder *) decoder {
  if (self = [super init]) {
    self.name = [decoder decodeObjectForKey: @"name"];
    self.magicNumber = [decoder decodeIntForKey: @"magicNumber"];
    self.shoeSize = [decoder decodeFloatForKey: @"shoeSize"];
    self.subThingies = [decoder decodeObjectForKey: @"subThingies"];
  }

  return (self);

} // initWithCoder
```

initWithCoder: is like any other init method. You need to have your superclass initialize things before you can do your stuff. You have two ways to do this, depending on what your parent class is. If your parent class adopts NSCoding, you should call [super initWithCoder: decoder]. If your parent class does not adopt NSCoding, then you just call [super init]. NSObject does not adopt NSCoding, so we do the simple init.

When you use decodeIntForKey:, you pull an int value out of the decoder. When you use decodeObjectForKey:, you pull an object out of the decoder, recursively using initWithCoder: on any embedded objects. Memory management works the way you would expect: you're getting objects back from a method that's not called alloc, copy, or new, so you can assume the objects are autoreleased. Our property declarations make sure that all memory management is handled correctly.

You'll notice that we have the encoding and decoding in the same order as the instance variables. You don't have to do that, it's just a handy habit to make sure that you're encoding and decoding everything and haven't skipped something. That's one of the reasons for using keys with the call—you can put them in and pull them out in any order.

Now, let's actually use this stuff. We have thing1 we created earlier. Let's archive it:

```
NSData *freezeDried;
freezeDried = [NSKeyedArchiver archivedDataWithRootObject: thing1];
```

The +archivedDataWithRootObject: class method encodes that object. First, it creates an NSKeyedArchiver instance under the hood; it then passes it to the -encodeWithCoder method of the object thing1. As thing1 encodes its attributes, it can cause other objects to be encoded, like the string and the array, and any contents we might put in that array. Once the entire pile of objects has finished encoding keys and values, the keyed archiver flattens everything into an NSData and returns it.

We can save this NSData to disk if we want by using the -writeToFile:atomically: method. Here, we're just going to dispose of thing1, re-create it from the freeze-dried representation, and print it out:

```
[thing1 release];
thing1 = [NSKeyedUnarchiver unarchiveObjectWithData: freezeDried];
NSLog (@"reconstituted thing: %@", thing1);
```

It prints out the exact same thing we saw earlier:

```
reconstituted thing: thing1: 42/10.5 (
)
```

Seeing a gun on the wall in the first act of a Chekhov play makes you wonder, and, similarly, you're probably wondering about that mutable array called subThingies. We can put objects into the array, and they will get encoded automatically when the array gets encoded. NSArray's implementation of encodeWithCoder: invokes encodeWithCoder on all of the objects, eventually leading to everything being encoded. Let's add some subThingies to thing1:

```
Thingie *anotherThing;

anotherThing = [[[Thingie alloc]
     initWithName: @"thing2"
     magicNumber: 23
     shoeSize: 13.0] autorelease];
[thing1.subThingies addObject: anotherThing];
anotherThing = [[[Thingie alloc]
     initWithName: @"thing3"
     magicNumber: 17
     shoeSize: 9.0] autorelease];
```

```
[thing1.subThingies addObject: anotherThing];

NSLog (@"thing with things: %@", thing1);
```

And this prints out thing1 and the subthings:

```
thing with things: thing1: 42/10.5 (
    thing2: 23/13.0 (
    ),
    thing3: 17/9.0 (
    )
)
```

Encoding and decoding works exactly the same:

```
freezeDried = [NSKeyedArchiver archivedDataWithRootObject: thing1];

thing1 = [NSKeyedUnarchiver unarchiveObjectWithData: freezeDried];
NSLog (@"reconstituted multithing: %@", thing1);
```

and prints out the same logging seen previously.

What happens if there are cycles in the data being encoded? For example, what if thing1 is in its own subThingies array? Would thing1 encode the array, which encodes thing1, which encodes the array, which encodes thing1 again, over and over again? Luckily, Cocoa is clever in its implementation of the archivers and unarchivers so that object cycles can be saved and restored.

To test this out, put thing1 into its own subThingies array:

```
[thing1.subThingies addObject: thing1];
```

Don't try using NSLog on thing1, though. NSLog isn't smart enough to detect object cycles, so it's going to go off into an infinite recursion trying to construct the log string, eventually dropping you into the debugger with thousands upon thousands of -description calls.

But, if we try encoding and decoding thing1 now, it works perfectly fine, without running off into the weeds:

```
freezeDried = [NSKeyedArchiver archivedDataWithRootObject: thing1];
thing1 = [NSKeyedUnarchiver unarchiveObjectWithData: freezeDried];
```

Summary

As you saw in this chapter, Cocoa provides two ways of loading and saving files. Property list data types are a collection of classes that know how to load and save themselves. If you have a collection of objects that are all property list types, you can use handy convenience functions for saving them to disk and reading them back in.

If, like most Cocoa programmers, you have your own objects that aren't property list types, you can adopt the NSCoding protocol and implement methods to encode and decode the objects: You can turn your own pile of objects into an NSData, which you can then save to disk and read back in later. From this NSData, you can reconstruct the objects.

Coming next is key-value coding, which lets you interact with your objects on a higher plane of abstraction.

Chapter 16

Key-Value Coding

One idea we keep coming back to is indirection. Many programming techniques are based on indirection, including this whole object-oriented programming business. In this chapter, we'll look at another indirection mechanism. This is not an Objective-C language feature, but one provided by Cocoa.

So far, we've been changing an object's state directly by calling methods directly or via a property's dot-notation or by setting instance variables. Key-value coding, affectionately known as KVC to its friends, is a way of changing an object's state indirectly, by using strings to describe what piece of object state to change. This chapter is all about key-value coding.

Some of the more advanced Cocoa features, like Core Data and Cocoa Bindings (which we'll not talk about in this book), use KVC as cogs in their fundamental machinery.

A Starter Project

We'll be working with our old friend CarParts again. Check out the project called *16.01 Car-Value-Coding* for the goodies. To get things rolling, we've added some attributes to the Car class, like the make and model, to play around with. We renamed `appellation` back to `name` to make things more uniform:

```
@interface Car : NSObject <NSCopying> {
    NSString *name;
    NSMutableArray *tires;
    Engine *engine;

    NSString *make;
    NSString *model;
    int modelYear;
    int numberOfDoors;
```

```
        float mileage;
}

@property (readwrite, copy) NSString *name;
@property (readwrite, retain) Engine *engine;
@property (readwrite, copy) NSString *make;
@property (readwrite, copy) NSString *model;
@property (readwrite) int modelYear;
@property (readwrite) int numberOfDoors;
@property (readwrite) float mileage;
...
@end // Car
```

And we've added the @synthesize directives so that the compiler will automatically gener-ate the setter and getter methods:

```
@implementation Car

@synthesize name;
@synthesize engine;
@synthesize make;
@synthesize model;
@synthesize modelYear;
@synthesize numberOfDoors;
@synthesize mileage;
...
```

We've also updated the -copyWithZone method to move the new attributes over:

```
- (id) copyWithZone: (NSZone *) zone
{
    Car *carCopy;
    carCopy = [[[self class]
                    allocWithZone: zone]
                init];

    carCopy.name = name;
    carCopy.make = make;
    carCopy.model = model;
    carCopy.numberOfDoors = numberOfDoors;
    carCopy.mileage = mileage;
    // plus copying tires and engine, code in chapter 13.
```

And we changed the -description to print out these new attributes and to leave out the Engine and Tire printing:

```
- (NSString *) description {
    NSString *desc;
```

```
    desc = [NSString stringWithFormat:
               @"%@, a %d %@ %@, has %d doors, %.1f miles, and %d tires.",
               name, modelYear, make, model, numberOfDoors, mileage, [tires
count]];

    return desc;

} // description
```

Finally, in main, we'll set these properties for the car and print them out. We've also used autorelease along with the alloc and init so that all memory management is kept in one place.

```
int main (int argc, const char * argv[])
{
    NSAutoreleasePool *pool;
    pool = [[NSAutoreleasePool alloc] init];

    Car *car = [[[Car alloc] init] autorelease];
    car.name = @"Herbie";
    car.make = @"Honda";
    car.model = @"CRX";
    car.numberOfDoors = 2;
    car.modelYear = 1984;
    car.mileage = 110000;

    int i;
    for (i = 0; i < 4; i++) {
        AllWeatherRadial *tire;

        tire = [[AllWeatherRadial alloc] init];

        [car setTire: tire
             atIndex: i];

        [tire release];
    }

    Slant6 *engine = [[[Slant6 alloc] init] autorelease];
    car.engine = engine;

    NSLog (@"Car is %@", car);

    [pool release];

    return (0);

} // main
```

After running the program, you get a line like this:

```
Car is Herbie, a 1984 Honda CRX, has 2 doors, 110000.0 miles, and 4 tires.
```

Introducing KVC

The fundamental calls in key-value coding are `-valueForKey:` and `-setValue:forKey:`. You send the message to an object and pass in a string, which is the key for the attribute of interest.

So, we can ask for the name of the car:

```
NSString *name = [car valueForKey:@"name"];
NSLog (@"%@", name);
```

This gives us `Herbie`. Likewise, we can get the make:

```
NSLog (@"make is %@", [car valueForKey:@"make"]);
```

`valueForKey:` performs a little bit of magic and figures out what the value of the make is and returns it.

`valueForKey:` works by first looking for a getter named after the key: `-key` or `-isKey`. So for these two calls, `valueForKey:` looks for `-name` and `-make`. If there is no getter method, it looks inside the object for an instance variable named `_key` or `key`. If we had not supplied accessor methods via `@synthesize`, `valueForKey` would look for the instance variables `_name` and `name` or `_make` and `make`.

That last bit is huge: `-valueForKey` uses the metadata in the Objective-C runtime to crack open objects and poke inside them looking for interesting information. You can't really do this kind of stuff in C or C++. By using KVC, you can get values where there are no getter methods and without having to access an instance variable directly via an object pointer.

The same technique works for the model year:

```
NSLog (@"model year is %@", [car valueForKey: @"modelYear"]);
```

which would print out `model year is 1984`.

Hey, wait a minute! `%@` in NSLog prints out an object, but `modelYear` is an `int`, not an object. What's the deal? For KVC, Cocoa automatically boxes and unboxes scalar values. That is, it automatically puts scalar values (`int`s, `float`s, and some `struct`s) into NSNumbers or NSValues when you use `valueForKey`, and it automatically takes scalar values out of these objects when you use `-setValueForKey`. Only KVC does this autoboxing. Regular method calls and property syntax don't do this.

In addition to retrieving values, you can set values by name by using `-setValue:forKey:`:

```
[car setValue: @"Harold" forKey: @"name"];
```

This method works the same way as `-valueForKey:`. It first looks for a setter for name, like `-setName` and calls it with the argument `@"Harold"`. If there is no setter, it looks in the class for an instance variable called name or _name and then assigns it.

WE MUST UNDERSCORE THIS RULE

> Both the compiler and Apple reserve instance variable names that begin with an underscore, promising dire consequences to you and your dog if you try to use one. There's no actual enforcement of this rule, but there might be someday, so disobey at your own risk.

If you're setting a scalar value, before calling `-setValue:forKey:`, you need to wrap it up (box it):

```
[car setValue: [NSNumber numberWithFloat: 25062.4]
    forKey: @"mileage"];
```

And `-setValue:forKey:` will unbox the value before it calls `-setMileage:` or changes the mileage instance variable.

A Path! A Path!

In addition to setting values by key, key-value coding allows you to specify a key path, which, like a file system path, lets you follow a chain of relationships.

To give us something to dig into, how about we add some horsepower to our engines? We'll add a new instance variable to Engine:

```
@interface Engine : NSObject <NSCopying> {
    int horsepower;
}

@end // Engine
```

Notice that we're not adding any accessors or properties. Usually, you'll want to have accessors or properties for interesting object attributes, but we'll avoid them here to really show you that KVC digs into objects directly.

We're adding an init method so that the engine starts off with a nonzero horsepower:

```
- (id) init {
    if (self = [super init]) {
```

```
        horsepower = 145;
    }

    return (self);

} // init
```

We also added copying of the horsepower instance variable in -copyWithZone so that copies will get the value, and we added it to the -description, which is pretty old hat by now,
so we'll leave out further explanation.

Just to prove we can get and set the value, the following code

```
NSLog (@"horsepower is %@", [engine valueForKey: @"horsepower"]);
[engine setValue: [NSNumber numberWithInt: 150]
        forKey: @"horsepower"];
NSLog (@"horsepower is %@", [engine valueForKey: @"horsepower"]);
```

prints out

```
horsepower is 145
horsepower is 150
```

What about those key paths? You specify different attribute names separated by dots. By
asking a car for its "engine.horsepower", you get the horsepower value. In fact, let's try
accessing key paths using the -valueForKeyPath and -setValueForKeyPath methods.
We'll send these messages to the car instead of the engine:

```
[car setValue: [NSNumber numberWithInt: 155]
     forKeyPath: @"engine.horsepower"];
NSLog (@"horsepower is %@", [car valueForKeyPath: @"engine.horsepower"]);
```

These key paths can be arbitrarily deep, depending on the complexity of your object graph
(which is just a fancy way of saying your collection of related objects); you can have key
paths like "car.interior.airconditioner.fan.velocity". In some ways, digging into
your objects can be easier with a key path than doing a series of nested method calls.

Aggregated Assault

One cool thing about KVC is that if you ask an NSArray for a value for a key, it will actually
ask every object in the array for the value for that key and then pack things up in another
array, which it gives back to you. The same works for arrays that are inside of an object (recall
composition?) that you access by key path.

NSArrays that are embedded in other objects are known in the KVC vernacular as having to-many relationship. For instance, a car has a relationship with many (well, four) tires. So we can say that Car has a to-many relationship with Tire. If a key path includes an array attribute, the remaining part of the key path is sent to every object in the array.

OUT OF MANY, ONE

Since you now know about to-many relationships, you're probably wondering what a to-one relationship is. Ordinary object composition is a to-one relationship. A car has a to-one relationship with its engine, for instance.

Remember that Car has an array of tires, and each tire has its air pressure. We can get all of the tire pressures in one call:

```
NSArray *pressures = [car valueForKeyPath: @"tires.pressure"];
```

After making the following call

```
NSLog (@"pressures %@", pressures);
```

we can print out these results:

```
pressures (
    34,
    34,
    34,
    34
)
```

What's happening here exactly, aside from us being vigilant about our tire maintenance? valueForKeyPath: breaks apart your path and processes it from left to right. First, it asks the car for its tires. Once it has the tires in hand, it asks the tires object for its valueForKeyPath: with the rest of the key path, "pressure" in this case. NSArray implements valueForKeyPath: by looping over its contents and sending each object the message. So the NSArray sends each tire it has inside itself a valueForKeyPath: using "pressure" for the key path, which results in the tire pressure being returned, boxed up in an NSNumber. Pretty handy!

Unfortunately, you can't index these arrays in the key path, such as by using "tires[0]. pressure" to get to the first tire.

Pit Stop

Before we head to the next bit of key-value goodness, we'll be adding a new class, called Garage, which will hold a bunch of classic cars. You can find all this stuff in the project named *16.02 Car-Value-Garaging* Here's Garage's interface:

```
#import <Cocoa/Cocoa.h>

@class Car;

@interface Garage : NSObject {
    NSString *name;
    NSMutableArray *cars;
}

@property (readwrite, copy) NSString *name;

- (void) addCar: (Car *) car;

- (void) print;

@end // Garage
```

Nothing's new here. We're forward-declaring Car, because all we need to know is that it's an object type to use as an argument to the -addCar: method. The name is a property, and the @property statement says that users of Garage can access and change the name. And there's a method to print out the contents. To implement a collection of cars, we've got a mutable array behind the scenes.

The implementation is similarly straightforward:

```
#import "Garage.h"

@implementation Garage

@synthesize name;

- (void) addCar: (Car *) car {
    if (cars == nil) {
        cars = [[NSMutableArray alloc] init];
    }
    [cars addObject: car];

} // addCar

- (void) dealloc {
    [name release];
    [cars release];
```

```
    [super dealloc];
} // dealloc

- (void) print {
    NSLog (@"%@:", name);

    for (Car *car in cars) {
        NSLog (@"  %@", car);
    }

} // print

@end // Car
```

We include the *Garage.h* header file as usual and @synthesize the name accessor methods.

–addCar: is an example of lazy initialization of the cars array; we only create it when neces-sary. –dealloc cleans up the name and the array, and –print walks through the array and prints out the cars.

We've also totally overhauled the main *Car-Value-Garage.m* source file compared to previous versions of the program. This time, the program makes a collection of cars and puts them into the garage.

First off are the necessary #imports for the objects we're going to be using:

```
#import <Foundation/Foundation.h>

#import "Car.h"
#import "Garage.h"
#import "Slant6.h"
#import "Tire.h"
```

Next, we have a function to make a car from a pile of attributes. We could have made a class method on Car, or made some kind of factory class, but Objective-C is still C, so we can use functions. Here, we're using a function, because it keeps the code for assembling a car close to where it is actually being used.

```
Car *makeCar (NSString *name, NSString *make, NSString *model,
              int modelYear, int numberOfDoors, float mileage,
              int horsepower) {
    Car *car = [[[Car alloc] init] autorelease];

    car.name = name;
    car.make = make;
    car.model = model;
    car.modelYear = modelYear;
    car.numberOfDoors = numberOfDoors;
```

```
        car.mileage = mileage;

        Slant6 *engine = [[[Slant6 alloc] init] autorelease];
        [engine setValue: [NSNumber numberWithInt: horsepower]
                forKey: @"horsepower"];
        car.engine = engine;


        // Make some tires.
        int i;
        for (i = 0; i < 4; i++) {
            Tire * tire= [[[Tire alloc] init] autorelease];
            [car setTire: tire atIndex: i];
        }

        return (car);

} // makeCar
```

Little of this should be unfamiliar by now. A new car is made and autoreleased per Cocoa convention, because the folks who will be getting the car from this function won't themselves be calling new, copy, or alloc. Then, we set some properties—remember that this technique is different from KVC, since we're not using setValue:forKey. Next, we make an engine and use KVC to set the horsepower, since we didn't make an accessor for it. Finally, we make some tires and put those on the car. At last, the new car is returned.

And here's the new version of main():

```
int main (int argc, const char * argv[])
{
    NSAutoreleasePool *pool;
    pool = [[NSAutoreleasePool alloc] init];

    Garage *garage = [[Garage alloc] init];
    garage.name = @"Joe's Garage";

    Car *car;
    car = makeCar (@"Herbie", @"Honda", @"CRX", 1984, 2, 110000, 58);
    [garage addCar: car];

    car = makeCar (@"Badger", @"Acura", @"Integra", 1987, 5, 217036.7,
                    130);
    [garage addCar: car];

    car = makeCar (@"Elvis", @"Acura", @"Legend", 1989, 4, 28123.4, 151);
    [garage addCar: car];
```

```
    car = makeCar (@"Phoenix", @"Pontiac", @"Firebird", 1969, 2, 85128.3,
                    345);
    [garage addCar: car];

    car = makeCar (@"Streaker", @"Pontiac", @"Silver Streak", 1950, 2,
                    39100.0, 36);
    [garage addCar: car];

    car = makeCar (@"Judge", @"Pontiac", @"GTO", 1969, 2, 45132.2, 370);
    [garage addCar: car];

    car = makeCar (@"Paper Car", @"Plymouth", @"Valiant", 1965, 2, 76800,
                    105);
    [garage addCar: car];

    [garage print];

    [garage release];

    [pool release];

    return (0);

} // main
```

main() does some bookkeeping, makes a garage, and builds a small stable of cars to be kept there. Finally, it prints out the garage and then releases it.

Running the program gives this terribly exciting output:

```
Joe's Garage:
   Herbie, a 1984 Honda CRX, has 2 doors, 110000.0 miles, 58 hp and 4 tires
   Badger, a 1987 Acura Integra, has 5 doors, 217036.7 miles, 130 hp and 4
tires
   Elvis, a 1989 Acura Legend, has 4 doors, 28123.4 miles, 151 hp and 4
tires
   Phoenix, a 1969 Pontiac Firebird, has 2 doors, 85128.3 miles, 345 hp and
4 tires
   Streaker, a 1950 Pontiac Silver Streak, has 2 doors, 39100.0 miles, 36 hp
 and 4 tires
   Judge, a 1969 Pontiac GTO, has 2 doors, 45132.2 miles, 370 hp and 4 tires
   Paper Car, a 1965 Plymouth Valiant, has 2 doors, 76800.0 miles, 105 hp
and 4 tires
```

Now, we have the foundation for the next bit of key-value goodness we promised.

Smooth Operator

Key paths can refer to more than object values. A handful of operators can be stuck into the key paths to do things like getting the average of an array of values or returning the minimum and maximum of those values.

For example, here's how we count the number of cars:

```
NSNumber *count;
count = [garage valueForKeyPath: @"cars.@count"];
NSLog (@"We have %@ cars", count);
```

When we run this, it prints out We have 7 cars.

Let's pull apart this key path, "cars.@count". cars says to get the cars property, which we know is an NSArray, from garage. Well, OK, we know it's an NSMutableArray, but we can consider it just to be an NSArray if we're not planning on changing anything. The next thing is @count. The at sign, as you know, is a signal that there's some magic coming up. For the compiler, @"blah" is a string, and @interface is the introduction for a class. Here, @count tells the KVC machinery to take the count of the result of the left-hand part of the key path.

We can also get the sum of a particular value, like the total number of miles our fleet has covered. The following snippet

```
NSNumber *sum;
sum = [garage valueForKeyPath: @"cars.@sum.mileage"];
NSLog (@"We have a grand total of %@ miles", sum);
```

prints out We have a grand total of 601320.6 miles, which gets us from the Earth to the moon and back, with some spare change.

So how does this work? The @sum operator breaks the key path into two parts. The first part is treated as a key path to some to-many relationship, the cars array in this case. The other part is treated like any key path that has a to-many relationship in the middle. It is treated as a key path used against each object in the relationship. So mileage is sent to every object in the relationship described by cars, and the resulting values are added up. Of course, each of these key paths can be of arbitrary length.

If we wanted to find out the average mileage per car, we can divide this sum by the count. But there's an easier way—the following lines

```
NSNumber *avgMileage;
avgMileage = [garage valueForKeyPath: @"cars.@avg.mileage"];
NSLog (@"average is %.2f", [avgMileage floatValue]);
```

print out

---

average is 85902.95

Pretty simple, huh? Without all this key-value goodness, we'd have to write a loop over the cars (assuming we could even get hold of the cars array from the garage), ask each car for its mileage, accumulate that into a sum, and then divide by the count of cars—not hard stuff but still a small pile of code.

Let's pull apart the key path we used this time: "cars.@avg.mileage". Like @sum, the @avg operator splits the key path into two parts, the part that comes before it, cars in this case, is a key path to the to-many relation for cars. The part after @sum is another key path, which is just the mileage. Under the hood, KVC happily spins a loop, adds up the values, keeps a count, and does the division.

There are also @min and @max operators, which do the obvious things:

```
NSNumber *min, *max;
min = [garage valueForKeyPath: @"cars.@min.mileage"];
max = [garage valueForKeyPath: @"cars.@max.mileage"];
NSLog (@"minimax: %@ / %@", min, max);
```

with the result of minimax: 28123.4 / 217036.7.

KVC IS NOT FOR FREE

KVC makes digging around in collections pretty easy. So why not use KVC for everything, then, and forget about accessor methods and writing code? There's never a free lunch, unless you work at some of the wilder Silicon Valley technology companies. KVC is necessarily slower, because it needs to parse strings to figure out what it is you want. There is also no error checking by the compiler. You might ask for karz.@avg. millage: the compiler has no idea that's a bad key path, and you'll get a runtime error when you try to use it.

Sometimes, you have an attribute that can take on only a small set of values, like the make of all of the cars. Even if we had a million cars, we would have a small number of unique makes. You can get just the makes from your collection with the key path "cars.@distinctUnionOfObjects.make":

```
NSArray *manufacturers;
manufacturers =
  [garage valueForKeyPath: @"cars.@distinctUnionOfObjects.make"];
NSLog (@"makers: %@", manufacturers);
```

When the preceding code is run, you get this:

```
makers: (
    Honda,
    Plymouth,
    Pontiac,
    Acura
)
```

The operator there in the middle of this key path, with the distinctly scary name of "@ distinctUnionOfObjects", does just what it says. It applies the same logic as the other operators: it takes the collection specified on the left and uses the key path on the right against each object of that collection, then turns the resulting values into a collection. The "union" part of the name refers to taking the union of a bunch of objects. The "distinct" part of the name weeds out all of the duplicates. There are a couple other operators along the lines of this one, but we'll leave them for you to discover. Also, you can't add your own operators. Bummer.

Life's a Batch

KVC has a pair of calls that let you make batch changes to objects. The first is dictionaryWithValuesForKeys:. You give it an array of strings. The call takes the keys, uses valueForKey: with each of the keys, and builds a dictionary with the key strings and the values it just got.

Let's pick a car from the garage and get a dictionary of some of its attributes:

```
car = [[garage valueForKeyPath: @"cars"] lastObject];
NSArray *keys = [NSArray arrayWithObjects: @"make", @"model",
                                           @"modelYear", nil];
NSDictionary *carValues = [car dictionaryWithValuesForKeys: keys];
NSLog (@"Car values : %@", carValues);
```

Running this gives us some information from Paper Car:

```
Car values : {
    make = Plymouth;
    model = Valiant;
    modelYear = 1965;
}
```

And we can change these values turning our Valiant into something new and (arguably) improved—a Chevy Nova:

```
NSDictionary *newValues =
[NSDictionary dictionaryWithObjectsAndKeys:
     @"Chevy", @"make",
     @"Nova", @"model",
     [NSNumber numberWithInt:1964], @"modelYear",
     nil];
[car setValuesForKeysWithDictionary: newValues];
NSLog (@"car with new values is %@", car);
```

And after we run these lines of code, we see it's actually a new car:

```
car with new values is Paper Car, a 1964 Chevy Nova, has 2 doors, 76800.0
miles, and 4 tires.
```

Notice that some values have changed (make, model, and year), but others haven't, like the name and mileage.

This tool isn't terribly useful for this program, but it allows you to do some nifty tricks in user interface code. For example, you could have something like Apple's Aperture Lift and Stamp tool, which lets you move some, but not all, alterations you made to a picture onto other pictures. You could lift all of the attributes using `dictionaryWithValuesForKeys` and let the contents of the dictionary drive all the stuff displayed in the user interface. The user can take stuff out of the dictionary and then use this modified dictionary to change the other pictures using `setValuesForKeysWithDictionary`. If you design your user interface classes the right way, you can use the same lift and stamp panel with disparate things like photos, cars, and recipes.

You might wonder what happens with nil values, such as a car with no name, because dictionaries can't contain nil values. Think back to Chapter 7, where [NSNull null] is used to represent nil values. The same thing happens here. For a no-name car, [NSNull null] will be returned under the @"name" when you call `dictionaryWithValuesForKeys`, and you can supply [NSNull null] for a `setValuesForKeysWithDictionary` to do the same, but in reverse.

The Nils Are Alive

This discussion of nil values brings up an interesting question. What does "nil" mean for a scalar value, like for mileage. Is it zero? Is it –1? Is it pi? There's no way for Cocoa to know. You can try like this:

```
[car setValue: nil forKey: @"mileage"];
```

But Cocoa gives you the smack-down:

```
'[<Car 0x105740> setNilValueForKey]: could not set nil as the value for the
key mileage.'
```

To fix this problem, you override -setNilValueForKey and provide whatever logic makes sense. We'll make an executive decision and say that nil mileage means to zero out the car's mileage, rather than using some other value like –1:

```
- (void) setNilValueForKey: (NSString *) key {
    if ([key isEqualToString: @"mileage"]) {
        mileage = 0;
    } else {
        [super setNilValueForKey: key];
    }
} // setNilValueForKey
```

Notice that we call the superclass method if we get an unexpected key. That way, if someone tries to use key-value coding for a key we don't understand, the caller will get the proper complaint. Generally, unless there's a rare, good reason not to (like a specific action you're intentionally trying to avoid), always invoke the superclass method when you're overriding.

Handling the Unhandled

The last stop on our key-value tour (three-hour tour?) is handling undefined keys. If you've tried your hand at any KVC and mistyped a key, you've probably seen this:

```
'[<Car 0x105740> valueForUndefinedKey:]: this class is not key value
coding-compliant for the key garbanzo.'
```

This basically says that Cocoa can't figure out what you mean by using that key, so it gives up.

If you look closely at the error message, you notice it mentions the method valueForUndefinedKey:. As you can probably guess, we can handle undefined keys by overriding this method. You also can probably guess that there's a corresponding setValue:forUndefinedKey:, if you try to change a value with an unknown key.

If the KVC machinery can't find a way to do its magic, it falls back and asks the class what to do. The default implementation just throws up its hands, as you saw previously. We can change that behavior, though. Let's turn Garage into a very flexible object that lets us set and get any key. We start by adding a mutable dictionary:

```
@interface Garage : NSObject {
    NSString *name;
    NSMutableArray *cars;
    NSMutableDictionary *stuff;
}
...
@end // Garage
```

Next, we add the valueForUndefinedKey methods:

```
- (void) setValue: (id) value forUndefinedKey: (NSString *) key {
    if (stuff == nil) {
        stuff = [[NSMutableDictionary alloc] init];
    }
    [stuff setValue: value forKey: key];
} // setValueForUndefinedKey

- (id) valueForUndefinedKey:(NSString *)key {
    id value = [stuff valueForKey: key];
    return (value);
} // valueForUndefinedKey
```

and release the dictionary in -dealloc.

Now, you can set any arbitrary values on the garage:

```
[garage setValue: @"bunny" forKey: @"fluffy"];
[garage setValue: @"greeble" forKey: @"bork"];
[garage setValue: [NSNull null] forKey: @"snorgle"];
[garage setValue: nil forKey: @"gronk"];
```

and get them back out:

```
NSLog (@"values are %@ %@ %@ and %@",
    [garage valueForKey: @"fluffy"],
    [garage valueForKey: @"bork"],
    [garage valueForKey: @"snorgle"],
    [garage valueForKey: @"gronk"]);
```

This NSLog prints out

```
values are bunny greeble <null> and (null)
```

Notice the difference between <null> and (null). <null> is an [NSNull null] object, and (null) is a real live nil value that we got back because "gronk" was not in the dictionary. Also notice we used the KVC method setValue:forKey: when using the stuff dictionary. Using this method allows callers to pass in a nil value without requiring us to check for it in the code. The NSDictionary setObject:forKey: will complain if you give it nil, while setValue:forKey: with a nil value on a dictionary will remove that key from the dictionary.

Summary

Key-value coding includes a lot more than we can cover in this chapter, but you should now have a solid foundation for exploring other aspects of KVC. You've seen examples of setting and getting of values with a single key, where KVC looks for setter and getter methods to accomplish what you ask. If it can't find any methods, KVC digs directly into an object and change values.

You've also seen key paths, which are dot-separated keys that specify a path through a network of objects. These key paths may look a lot like they're accessing properties, but they are actually very different mechanisms. You can stick various operators in a key path to have KVC do extra work on your behalf. Last, we looked at several methods you can override to customize corner-case behavior.

Next up, we explore the truth—Cocoa's predicate feature.

Chapter 17

NSPredicate

a fairly common operation when writing software is to take a collection of objects and evaluate them against some kind of known truth. You hang on to objects that conform to the truth and throw out objects that don't, leaving you with a pile of interesting objects to play with.

You see this all the time with software you use, like iPhoto. If you tell iPhoto to show you only pictures with a rating of three stars or better, the truth you've specified is "photo must have a rating of three stars or better." All of your photos are run through this filter. Those that have a rating of three or more stars pass through it, and the rest don't. iPhoto then shows you all your good pictures.

Similarly, iTunes has its search box. The truth you're seeking might be that the artist is Marilyn Manson or Barry Manilow. So all of your non-head-banging and noncrooning music will be hidden, allowing you to create one of the strangest dance mixes around.

Cocoa provides a class called NSPredicate that lets you specify these truth filters. You can create NSPredicate objects that describe exactly what you think is the truth and run each of your objects through the predicate to see if they match.

"Predicate" in this sense is different than the "predicate" you might have learned about in an English grammar class. "Predicate" here is used in the mathematical and computer science sense: a function that evaluates to a true or false value.

NSPredicate is Cocoa's means of describing queries, like you might use with a database. You can use NSPredicates with database-style APIs like Core Data and Spotlight, although we won't be covering either of those here (but you can apply much of what's in this chapter to those two technologies as well as to your own objects). You can think of NSPredicate as yet another means of indirection. You can use a predicate object that does your checking, rather than asking explicitly in code, "Are these the droids I'm looking for?" By swapping predicate objects around, you can have common code sift through your data without hard-coding the conditions you're looking for. This is another application of the Open/Closed Principle that you met back in Chapter 3.

Creating a Predicate

Before you can use an NSPredicate against one of your objects, you need to create it, which you can do in two fundamental ways. One involves creating a lot of objects and assembling them. This requires a lot of code and is handy if you're building a general user interface for specifying searches. The other way involves query strings you put into your code. These are much easier to deal with when just getting started, so we'll concentrate on query strings in this book. The usual caveats with string-oriented APIs apply here, especially lack of error checking by the compiler and, sometimes, curious runtime errors.

There is no escape from CarParts—we'll be basing this chapter's examples on the garage of cars built in the last chapter. You can find everything in the *17.01 Car-Part-Predicate* project.

To start, we'll look at just one car:

```
Car *car;
car = makeCar (@"Herbie", @"Honda", @"CRX", 1984, 2, 110000, 58);
[garage addCar: car];
```

Recall that we wrote the makeCar function to build up a car and give it an engine and some tires. In this case, we have Herbie, a two-door 1984 Honda CRX with a 58-horespower engine with 110,000 miles on it.

Now, let's make a predicate:

```
NSPredicate *predicate;
predicate = [NSPredicate predicateWithFormat: @"name == 'Herbie'"];
```

Let's pull this apart. predicate is one of our usual Objective-C object pointers, which will point to an NSPredicate object. We use the NSPredicate class method +predicateWithFormat: to actually create the predicate. We give it a string, and +predicateWithFormat: takes that string and builds a tree of objects behind the scenes that will be used to evaluate the predicate.

predicateWithFormat sounds a lot like stringWithFormat, provided by NSString, which lets you plug in stuff using printf-style format specifiers. As you'll see later, you will be able to do the same thing with predicateWithFormat. Cocoa has consistent naming schemes—it's nice like that.

This predicate string looks like a standard C expression. On the left-hand side is a key path, name. Next comes an operator for equality, ==, and a quoted string on the right-hand side. If a chunk of text in the predicate string is not quoted, it is treated as a key path. If it's quoted, it's treated as a literal string. You can use single quotes or double quotes (as long as they're balanced). Usually, you'll use single quotes; otherwise, you'll have to escape each double quote in the string.

Evaluate the Predicate

OK, so we've got a predicate. What now? We evaluate it against an object!

```
BOOL match = [predicate evaluateWithObject: car];
NSLog (@"%s", (match) ? "YES" : "NO");
```

-evaluateWithObject: tells the receiving object (the predicate) to evaluate itself with the given object. In this case, it takes the car, applies valueForKeyPath: using name as the key path to get the name. Then, it compares it for equality to "Herbie". If the name and "Herbie" are the same, -evaluateWithObject: returns YES, otherwise NO. The NSLog uses the ternary operator to convert the numerical BOOL to a human-readable string.

Here's another predicate:

```
predicate = [NSPredicate predicateWithFormat: @"engine.horsepower > 150"];
match = [predicate evaluateWithObject: car];
```

The predicate string has a key path on the left-hand side. This key path digs into the car, finds the engine, and then finds the horsepower of the engine. Next, it compares that value with 150 to see if it's larger.

After we evaluate this against Herbie, match has the value of NO, because little Herbie's horsepower (58) is not greater than 150.

Checking an object against a particular predicate's truth is all well and good, but things get more interesting when you have collections of objects. Say we wanted to see which cars in our garage are the most powerful. We can loop through the cars and test each one with this predicate:

```
NSArray *cars = [garage cars];
for (Car *car in [garage cars]) {
    if ([predicate evaluateWithObject: car]) {
        NSLog (@"%@", car.name);
    }
}
```

We get the cars from the garage, loop over them all, and evaluate each one against the predicate. This chunk of code prints the cars with highest horsepower:

```
Elvis
Phoenix
Judge
```

Makes sense, no? Before we go on, let's make sure we're clear about all the pieces of syntax involved. Take a good look at the car name call in the NSLog. That's using the Objective-C 2.0 dot syntax and is the equivalent of call [car name];. There's no magic involved. The predicate string here is "engine.horsepower > 150". engine.horespower is a key path, which might involve all sorts of magic under the hood.

Fuel Filters

One famous virtue/vice of programmers is laziness. Wouldn't it be nice if we didn't have to write that for loop and if statement? It's only a couple of lines of code, but zero lines of code would be even better. Luckily, a couple of categories add predicate filtering methods to Cocoa's collection classes.

-filteredArrayUsingPredicate: is a category method on NSArray that will spin through the contents of the array, evaluate each object against a predicate, and accumulate objects that evaluate to YES into a new array that is returned:

```
NSArray *results;
results = [cars filteredArrayUsingPredicate: predicate];
NSLog (@"%@", results);
```

This produces the following results:

```
(
    Elvis, a 1989 Acura Legend, has 4 doors, 28123.4 miles, 151 hp and 4
tires,
    Phoenix, a 1969 Pontiac Firebird, has 2 doors, 85128.3 miles, 345 hp
and 4 tires,
    Judge, a 1969 Pontiac GTO, has 2 doors, 45132.2 miles, 370 hp and 4
tires
)
```

OK, so these results are not identical to the previous ones. This is an array of cars; in the previous example, we had names. We can use KVC (key-value coding) to extract the names, remembering that when `valueForKey:` is sent to an array, the key is applied to all elements of the array:

```
NSArray *names;
names = [results valueForKey:@"name"];
```

If we print out `names`, we'll see this:

```
(
    Elvis,
    Phoenix,
    Judge
)
```

Let's say you have a mutable array, and you want to yank out all the items that don't belong. NSMutableArray has a method `-filterUsingPredicate`, which, handily enough, will do just the yanking we're looking for:

```
NSMutableArray *carsCopy = [cars mutableCopy];
[carsCopy filterUsingPredicate: predicate];
```

If you print out `carsCopy`, it will be the set of three cars we saw earlier.

You can still use `-filteredArrayUsingPredicate:` with an `NSMutableArray` to make a new (nonmutable) array because `NSMutableArray` is a subclass of `NSArray`. `NSSets` have similar calls, too.

As we mentioned with KVC, using predicates is really convenient, but it runs no faster than writing all the code yourself. That's because there's no way to avoid looping over all the cars and doing some work with each of them. For the most part, this looping is no big deal, because computers are very fast these days. Go ahead and write the most convenient code possible and then measure your performance using Apple's tools like Shark or Instruments if you run into speed problems. iPhone programmers, though, should pay very close attention to program performance at all times.

Format Specifiers

Experienced programmers know that hard-coding isn't necessarily a good idea. What if we wanted to know which cars have over 200 horsepower and then later which cars have over 50 horsepower? We could have predicate strings like "`engine.horsepower > 200`" and "`engine.horsepower > 50`", but we'd have to recompile the program and get back to the bad world we escaped in Chapter 3.

We can put varying stuff into our predicate format strings in two ways: format specifiers and variable names. First, we'll take a look at format specifiers. You can put in numerical values with %d and %f like you're familiar with:

```
predicate =
    [NSPredicate predicateWithFormat: @"engine.horsepower > %d", 50];
```

Of course, rather than using 50 right there in your code, you could have that value driven by the user interface or some external mechanism.

In addition to the usual printf specifiers, you can also use %@ to insert a string value. %@ is treated just like a quoted string:

```
predicate = [NSPredicate predicateWithFormat: @"name == %@", @"Herbie"];
```

Notice that the %@ is not quoted in the format string here. If you quoted %@, like with "name == '%@'", the characters % and @ would be in the predicate string.

NSPredicate strings also let you use %K to specify a key path. This predicate is the same as the others, using name == 'Herbie' as the truth:

```
predicate =
    [NSPredicate predicateWithFormat: @"%K == %@", @"name", @"Herbie"];
```

Using format specifiers is one way to have flexible predicates. The other involves putting variable names into the string, similar to environment variables:

```
NSPredicate *predicateTemplate =
    [NSPredicate predicateWithFormat:@"name == $NAME"];
```

Now that we have a predicate with a variable in it, we can make new specialized predicates using the predicateWithSubstitutionVariables call. You create a dictionary of key/value pairs, in which the key is the variable name (without the dollar sign), and the value is what should be plugged into the predicate:

```
NSDictionary *varDict;
varDict = [NSDictionary dictionaryWithObjectsAndKeys:
                @"Herbie", @"NAME", nil];
```

This uses the string "Herbie" for the value under the key "NAME". So make this the new predicate:

```
predicate =
    [predicateTemplate predicateWithSubstitutionVariables: varDict];
```

This predicate works exactly like the other ones you've seen.

You can use different kinds of objects for the variable values, like NSNumbers, with this predicate that filters for engine power:

```
predicateTemplate =
  [NSPredicate predicateWithFormat: @"engine.horsepower > $POWER"];
varDict = [NSDictionary dictionaryWithObjectsAndKeys:
          [NSNumber numberWithInt: 150], @"POWER", nil];
predicate =
  [predicateTemplate predicateWithSubstitutionVariables: varDict];
```

This creates a predicate whose truth is an engine horsepower that's more than 150.

In addition to NSNumbers and NSStrings, you can use [NSNull null] for nil values, and you can even use arrays, as you'll see a little later in this chapter. Note that you can't use $VARIABLE for key paths, only values. If you want to vary key paths programmatically when using predicate format strings, you'll need to use the %K format specifier.

No type checking is done by the predicate machinery. You can accidentally plug in a string where a number was expected, which might end up as an error message complaint at runtime or just baffling behavior.

Hello Operator, Give Me Number 9

NSPredicate's format string includes a lot of different operators you can use. We'll touch on most of the operators and give a quick example of each one. The rest can be found in Apple's online documentation.

Comparison and Logical Operators

The predicate string syntax supports some of your favorite operators from C, such as the equality operators == and =.

The inequality operators come in various flavors:

> >: Greater than

> >= *and* =>: Greater than or equal to

> <: Less than

> <= *and* =<: Less than or equal to

> != *and* <>: Not equal

The syntax also supports parenthetical expressions (really!) and the AND, OR, and NOT logical operators or their C-looking equivalents &&, ||, and !.

Here's an example. You can filter out the most and least powerful cars, leaving the midrange ones:

```
predicate = [NSPredicate predicateWithFormat:
                @"(engine.horsepower > 50) AND
                  (engine.horsepower < 200)"];
results = [cars filteredArrayUsingPredicate: predicate];
NSLog (@"%@", results);
```

And if we actually apply this to our fleet, we get the following results:

```
    Herbie, a 1984 Honda CRX, has 2 doors, 34000.0 miles, 58 hp and 4
tires,
    Badger, a 1987 Acura Integra, has 5 doors, 217036.7 miles, 130 hp and
  4 tires,
    Elvis, a 1989 Acura Legend, has 4 doors, 28123.4 miles, 151 hp and
  4 tires,
    Paper Car, a 1965 Plymouth Valiant, has 2 doors, 76800.0 miles, 105 hp
  and 4 tires
```

Operators in predicate strings are case-insensitive. You can use AnD, ANd, AND, or and at your whim. We'll be using all capitals here, but you don't have to in real code.

The inequalities work with numeric values and string values as well. To see all the cars from the beginning of the alphabet, use this predicate:

```
predicate = [NSPredicate predicateWithFormat: @"name < 'Newton'"];
results = [cars filteredArrayUsingPredicate: predicate];
NSLog (@"%@", [results valueForKey: @"name"]);
```

```
(
    Herbie,
    Badger,
    Elvis,
    Judge
)
```

Array Operators

The predicate string "(engine.horsepower > 50) OR (engine.horsepower < 200)" is a pretty common pattern. We're looking for horsepower values between these two numbers. Wouldn't it be cool if we could use an operator to see what's BETWEEN two values? Turns out we can:

```
predicate = [NSPredicate predicateWithFormat:
            @"engine.horsepower BETWEEN { 50, 200 }"];
```

The curly braces denote an array, and BETWEEN treats the first element of the array is the lower bound and the second element as the upper bound.

You can plug in your own NSArrays by using the %@ format specifier:

```
NSArray *betweens = [NSArray arrayWithObjects:
                        [NSNumber numberWithInt: 50],
                        [NSNumber numberWithInt: 200], nil];
predicate = [NSPredicate predicateWithFormat:
    @"engine.horsepower BETWEEN %@", betweens];
```

You can use variables too:

```
predicateTemplate =
    [NSPredicate predicateWithFormat: @"engine.horsepower BETWEEN $POWERS"];
varDict =
    [NSDictionary dictionaryWithObjectsAndKeys: betweens, @"POWERS", nil];
predicate =
    [predicateTemplate predicateWithSubstitutionVariables: varDict];
```

Arrays have more uses than just specifying the endpoints of an interval. You can use the IN operator to see if a particular value is contained in an array. This should be familiar to programmers with SQL experience:

```
predicate = [NSPredicate predicateWithFormat:
    @"name IN { 'Herbie', 'Snugs', 'Badger', 'Flap' }"];
```

We have cars named Herbie and Badger, so those will survive a filtering:

```
results = [cars filteredArrayUsingPredicate: predicate];
NSLog (@"%@", [results valueForKey: @"name"]);
```

Sure enough, this only returns two:

```
(
    Herbie,
    Badger
)
```

SELF Sufficient

Sometimes, you'll be applying predicates to simple values, like plain old string strings, rather than fancy objects that can be manipulated with key paths. Say we have an array of the car names, and we want to apply the same filter we used previously. What would we use in place of name, since NSString does not react well when you ask it for a name?

SELF to the rescue! SELF refers to the object being evaluated by the predicate. In fact, we can express all of our key paths in the predicates as being relative to SELF. This predicate is exactly the same as the previous one:

```
predicate = [NSPredicate predicateWithFormat:
  @"SELF.name IN { 'Herbie', 'Snugs', 'Badger', 'Flap' }"];
```

Now, back to that array of strings. How do we tell if a string is also in that array of names? Let's take a look.

First, you'll need that array of just the names from somewhere. Since we're already hip-deep in CarParts, we'll deal with those, using the KVC trick of getting the valueForKey: against an array:

```
NSArray *names = [cars valueForKey: @"name"];
```

This is an array of strings containing all the names of the cars we own. Next, make a predicate:

```
predicate = [NSPredicate predicateWithFormat:
  @"SELF IN { 'Herbie', 'Snugs', 'Badger', 'Flap' }"];
```

and then evaluate it:

```
results = [names filteredArrayUsingPredicate: predicate];
```

If you look at results now, it's the same two names we've seen before: Herbie and Badger.

Here's a quiz. What output is produced by the following?

```
NSArray *names1 = [NSArray arrayWithObjects:
  @"Herbie", @"Badger", @"Judge", @"Elvis", nil];
NSArray *names2 = [NSArray arrayWithObjects:
  @"Judge", @"Paper Car", @"Badger", @"Finto", nil];

predicate = [NSPredicate predicateWithFormat: @"SELF IN %@", names1];
results = [names2 filteredArrayUsingPredicate: predicate];
NSLog (@"%@", results);
```

Here's the answer:

```
(
    Judge,
    Badger
)
```

This is a clever way of taking the intersection of two arrays. OK, so how does it work? The predicate includes the contents of the first array, so it looks something like

```
SELF IN {"Herbie", "Badger", "Judge", "Elvis"}
```

Now, the second name array is filtered with this predicate. Strings that are in both arrays will be in `names2` and will cause the `SELF IN` clause to say it's true, and so the string will be in the results array. Objects only in the second array will get dropped on the floor, since they won't match any of the strings in the predicate. Strings only in the first array will just sit there, waiting to be compared against, and will never make it into the results.

String Operations

The relational operators we saw before work with strings. There are also some that are string-specific:

- `BEGINSWITH`: Check whether a string begins with another string.

- `ENDSWITH`: Check whether a string ends with another string.

- `CONTAINS`: Check whether a string lives somewhere inside another string.

Using relational operators lets you do tricks like using `"name BEGINSWITH 'Bad'"` to match "Badger", `"name ENDSWITH 'vis'"` to match "Elvis", and `"name CONTAINS udg"` to match "Judge".

What happens if you write a predicate string like `"name BEGINSWITH 'HERB'"`? This won't match "Herbie" or anything else, because these matches are case-sensitive. Likewise, `"name BEGINSWITH 'Hérb'"` won't match, because the "e" has an accent. To relax the rules for name matching here, we can decorate these operators with `[c]`, `[d]`, or `[cd]`. The c stands for "case insensitive," the d for "diacritic insensitive" (that is, without accents), and `[cd]` for both. Usually, you'll use `[cd]` unless there's a good reason to be case- and accent-sensitive. You never know when a user will have a sticky caps lock key and end up talking to your application IN ALL CAPS.

This predicate string will match Herbie: `"name BEGINSWITH[cd] 'HERB'"`

Like, Fer Sure

Sometimes, doing string matches at the beginning or end (or middle) of a string isn't powerful enough. For these situations, the predicate format string includes the LIKE operator. With this operator, a question mark matches one character and an asterisk matches any number of characters. SQL and Unix shell programmers will recognize this behavior (sometimes called "globbing").

The predicate string "name LIKE '*er*'" will match any name that has "er" in the middle of it. This is equivalent to CONTAINS.

The predicate string "name LIKE '???er*'" will match "Paper Car", because it has three characters, an "er", and any number of characters after the "er". It does not match "Badger" because that has four characters before the "er".

LIKE also accepts the [cd] decoration for case and diacritic insensitivity.

If you're into regular expressions, you can use the MATCHES operator. Give it a regular expression, and the predicate will evaluate it.

EXPRESS YOURSELF

Regular expressions are a very powerful, very compact way of specifying string-matching logic. Sometimes, regular expressions can become dense and obscure, and entire books have been written on the subject. The NSPredicate regular expressions use the International Components for Unicode (ICU) syntax, which you can learn about with the help of your favorite Internet search engine.

While regular expressions are powerful, they also can be computationally expensive. If you have simpler operations in your predicate, such as the basic string operators and comparison operators, perform those first before using MATCHES. That should give you a speed boost.

That's All, Folks

This discussion of predicates wraps up *Learn Objective-C*. We've covered a lot of ground, from indirection and the basics of object-oriented programming, all the way through sophisticated tools like key-value coding and filtering objects with NSPredicate. Congratulations on surviving this entire book! You are now officially ready to tackle the next stage of your Mac programming career. Thank you for joining us.

Coming to Objective-C from Other Languages

*m*any programmers come to Objective-C and Cocoa from other languages and have a hard time learning Objective-C because it behaves differently from most other popular languages. New Objective-C programmers often assert that Objective-C is a bad language because it does not have behaviors X, Y, Z, which TheirFavoriteLanguage has. And feature checklists aside, let's face it: in some respects, Objective-C is just plain weird.

The advice we can offer new Objective-C and Cocoa programmers—even those with years of experience in other languages and other platforms—is to set aside any preconceived notions of how things are *supposed to* work and accept Objective-C, Cocoa, and Xcode on their own terms for a while. Work through a few books and tutorials. Once you have some Objective-C experience under your belt, you can see which techniques and approaches from other languages apply to Cocoa and Objective-C and which ones don't. No language is ideal for all circumstances, and no toolkit is perfect for every job. The best things to do are to learn enough to decide if a particular language and toolkit will do what you need and be aware of the tradeoffs involved.

In this appendix, we'll present some information that should help smooth your transition from other popular languages to Objective-C.

Coming from C

Objective-C is just plain old C with a few additional features for handling object orientation. The bulk of this book describes these extra features, so we won't repeat everything here, but a couple of interesting topics are worth covering.

Remember that Objective-C programmers get access to all the goodies that come with C, such as the standard C library. For example, you are welcome to use `malloc()` and `free()` to deal with dynamic memory or `fopen()` and `fgets()` for handling files.

Occasionally, someone on the Cocoa mailing lists asks, "I'm calling an ANSI C library that uses callbacks to do its work. How can I have it call a method instead?" This question also comes up when you're using low-level Apple frameworks like Core Foundation and Core Graphics.

The short answer is, "You can't." The callbacks work only for C functions that have the signature required by the library. The functions that implement Objective-C methods need to have the self and selector arguments first, so they'll never match the required signatures.

Most callback-oriented libraries let you supply some user data or a pointer. You can think of this as a rock under which you can hide. You give the library some meaningful pointer when you register your callback, and the library gives you back your pointer when it calls your callback.

All Objective-C objects are dynamically allocated, so it's safe to use the address of an object as this context pointer. You don't need to worry about some stack-allocated object disappearing underneath you. Inside the callback, you cast the context pointer into your object type and then start sending it messages.

For example, let's say you're using an imaginary C API XML parsing library, and you feed data to a class called `TreeWalker` as the XML file is parsed. Make a new `TreeWalker`:

```
TreeWalker *walker = [[TreeWalker alloc] init];
```

Then, make the XML parser:

```
XMLParser parser;
parser = XMLParserLoadFile ("/tmp/badgers.xml");
```

Set the callback function (a C function) for the parser, and use the `TreeWalker` object as the context:

```
XMLSetParserCallback (parser, elementCallback, walker);
```

Then, as the XML file is parsed, the callback is called:

```
void elementCallback (XMLParser *parser,
          XMLElement *element,
          userData *context)
```

```
{
  TreeWalker *walker = (TreeWalker *) context;

  [walker handleNewElement: element
          inParser: parser];

} // someElementCallback
```

You can see that the context pointer is cast to an object pointer, and messages are sent to that object.

Coming from C++

C++ has a lot of features that Objective-C lacks: multiple inheritance, namespaces, operator overloading, templates, class variables, abstract classes, STL (Standard Template Library), and so on. If you miss these, Objective-C has features and techniques that can replace, or at least simulate, them.

For example, you can use categories and protocols as a form of multiple inheritance or for implementing abstract base classes. One common use for multiple inheritance is to provide an interface so that other code can invoke particular methods on your object. Categories and protocols are perfect for this situation. You can use protocols to provide pure abstract base classes.

Categories and protocols won't help you if you're using multiple inheritance to bring in extra instance variables (called **member variables** in C++). To do this, you can use composition to include an object in another object and then use stub methods to redirect messages to the second object (which is a common technique in Java). You can also simulate multiple inheritance by overriding the forwardInvocation: method. This method gets called if a message is received that the object doesn't know how to handle. By examining the NSInvocation object, you can see if it should be forwarded on to your "multiply inherited" object and then send it if necessary. This technique saves you from having to write a lot of little stub methods. However, it's much slower than real multiple inheritance and can be a pain to set up.

Other conventions can replace still more C++ features, such as stub methods that call abort for abstract classes that shouldn't be instantiated, though some features have weak replacements, such as name prefixes instead of namespaces.

C++ vtable vs. Objective-C Dynamic Dispatch

One of the biggest differences between C++ and Objective-C is the mechanism of dispatching methods (or **member functions**, as they're known in C++). C++ uses a vtable-based mechanism for determining what code to invoke for virtual functions.

You can think of each C++ object as having a pointer to an array of function pointers. When the compiler sees that the code wants to invoke a virtual function, it calculates an offset from the start of the vtable, emits machine code to take the function pointer at that offset from the start of the vtable, and uses that as the chunk of code to execute. This process requires the compiler to know, at compile time, the type of the object that is calling the member function so that it can calculate the correct offset into the vtable. This kind of dispatch is very fast, requiring just a couple of pointer operations and one read to get the function pointer.

The Objective-C way, described in detail in Chapter 3, uses a runtime function to poke around in the various class structures searching for the code to invoke. This technique can be several times slower than the C++ route.

Objective-C adds flexibility and convenience at the expense of speed and safety, which is a classic trade-off. With the C++ model, the member function dispatch is fast. It is also very safe because the compiler and linker make sure that the object being used can handle that method. But the C++ method can also be inflexible, because you can't really change the kind of object you're dealing with. You have to use inheritance to allow different classes of objects to react to the same message.

A lot of information about a class is not retained by the C++ compiler, such as its inheritance chain, the members that compose it, and so on. At runtime, the ability to treat objects generically is limited. The most you can do at runtime is a dynamic cast, which tells you if an object is a specific kind of subclass of another object.

The C++ inheritance hierarchy can't be changed at runtime. Once the program has been compiled and linked, it's pretty much set in stone. Dynamic loading of C++ libraries is frequently problematic, due in part to the complexities of C++ name mangling—the way it performs type-safe linking using the primitive Unix linkers it has to work with.

In Objective-C, an object needs only a method implementation for it to be callable, which allows arbitrary objects to become data sources and/or delegates for other objects. The lack of multiple inheritance can be an inconvenience, but one that is greatly eased by the ability to send any message to any object without having to worry about its inheritance pedigree.

Of course, this ability to send any message to any object makes Objective-C less type safe than C++. You can get runtime errors if the object being sent a message can't handle it. There are no type-safe containers in Cocoa. Any object can be put into a container.

Objective-C carries around a lot of metadata about a class, so you can use reflection to see if an object responds to a particular message. This practice is very common for objects that have data sources or delegates. By first checking to see if the delegate responds to a message, you can avoid some of the runtime errors you might get. You can also use categories to add methods to other classes.

Because of this metadata, it's easier to reverse engineer the classes used in a program. You can determine the instance variables, their layout in the object structure, and the methods defined by the class. Even stripping the executable of its debugging information doesn't remove the Objective-C metadata. If you have highly confidential algorithms, you may want to implement them in C++ or at least obfuscate their names—don't use class or method names like `SerialNumberVerifier`, for example.

In Objective-C, you can send messages to the nil (zero) object. There is no need to check your message sends against `NULL`. Messages to nil are no-ops. The return values from messages sent to nil depend on the return type of the method. If the method returns a pointer type (such as an object pointer), the return value will be nil, meaning you can safely chain messages to a nil object—the nil will just propagate. If the method returns an `int` the same size of a pointer or smaller, it will return zero. If it returns a float or a structure, you will have an undefined result. Because of this, you can use a nil object pattern to keep you from having to test object pointers against `NULL`. On the other hand, this technique can mask errors and cause bugs that are difficult to track down.

All objects in Objective-C are dynamically allocated. There are no stack-based objects and no automatic creation and destruction of temporary objects or automatic type conversion between class types, so Objective-C objects are more heavyweight than C++ stack-based objects. That's one of the reasons why small lightweight entities (like `NSPoint` and `NSRange`) are structures instead of first-class objects.

Finally, Objective-C is a very loose language. Where C++ has public, protected, and private member variables and member functions, Objective-C has some basic support for protected instance variables, which are easy to circumvent, but no protection at all for member functions. Anyone who knows the name of a method can send that message to the object. Using the Objective-C reflection features, you can see all the methods supported by a given object. Methods are callable even if they never appear in a header file, and you have no reliable way to figure out which object is calling the method, because message sends can come from C functions (as discussed earlier in this appendix).

As you've seen, you don't have to redeclare methods you override in subclasses. There are two schools of thought on whether this is a good idea. One camp says that redeclaring provides information to the reader about which changes the class makes to its superclasses, while the other faction says that these are just implementation details that class users don't have to be bothered with and are not worth causing recompilations of all dependent classes when a new method is overridden.

Objective-C has no class variables. You can simulate them by using file-scoped global variables and providing accessors for them. An example class declaration might look like this (other stuff, like declarations for instance variables and method declarations, is included):

```
@interface Blarg : NSObject
{
}

+ (int) classVar;
+ (void) setClassVar: (int) cv;

@end // Blarg
```

And then the implementation would look like this:

```
#import "Blarg.h"

static int g_cvar;

@implementation Blarg

+ (int) classVar
{
   return (g_cvar);
} // classVar

+ (void) setClassVar: (int) cv
{
   g_cvar = cv;
} // setClassVar

@end // Blarg
```

The Cocoa object hierarchy has a common ancestor class: NSObject. When you create a new class, you'll almost always subclass NSObject or an existing Cocoa class. C++ object hierarchies tend to be several trees with distinct roots.

Objective-C++

There is a way to have the best of both worlds. The GCC compiler that comes with Xcode supports a hybrid language called Objective-C++. This compiler lets you freely mix C++ and Objective-C code, with a couple of small restrictions. You can get type safety and low-level performance when you need them, and you can use Objective-C's dynamic nature and the Cocoa toolkit where it makes sense.

A common development scenario is to put all of the application's core logic into a portable C++ library (if you're building a cross-platform application) and write the user interface in the platform's native toolkit. Objective-C++ is a great boon to this style of development. You get the performance and type safety of C++, and the users get applications created with the native toolkit that fit in seamlessly with the platform.

To have the compiler treat your code as Objective-C++, use the *.mm* file extension on your source. The *.M* extension also works, but the Mac's HFS+ file system is case insensitive but case preserving, so it's best to avoid any kind of case dependency.

Like matter and antimatter, the Objective-C and C++ object hierarchies cannot mix. So you can't have a C++ class that inherits from NSView, and you can't have an Objective-C class inheriting from std::string.

You can put pointers to Objective-C objects into C++ objects. Since all Objective-C objects are dynamically allocated, you can't have complete objects embedded in a class or declared on a stack. You'll need to alloc and init any Objective-C objects in your C++ constructors (or wherever it's convenient) and release them in your destructors (or somewhere else). So this would be a valid class declaration:

```
class ChessPiece {
  ChessPiece::PieceType type;
  int row, column;
  NSImage *pieceImage;
};
```

You can put C++ objects into Objective-C objects:

```
@interface SWChessBoard : NSView
{
    ChessPiece *piece[32];
}

@end // SWChessBoard
```

C++ objects embedded in Objective-C objects, rather than having a pointer relationship, will have their constructors called when the Objective-C object is allocated and will have their destructors called when the Objective-C object is deallocated.

Coming from Java

Like C++, Java has numerous features that Objective-C does not have or implements in different ways. For instance, classic Objective-C has no garbage collector but has retain/release and the autorelease pool. You can turn on garbage collection in your Objective-C programs if you wish.

Java interfaces are like Objective-C formal protocols, as they both require the implementation of a set of methods. Java has abstract classes, but Objective-C does not. Java has class variables, while in Objective-C, you use static file-scoped global variables and provide accessors to them, as shown in the "Coming from C++" section. Objective-C is pretty loose with public and private methods. As we've noted, any method that an object supports can be invoked, even if it doesn't appear in any external form, such as a header file. Java lets you declare classes final, preventing any subclasses from being made. Objective-C goes to the other extreme by letting you add methods to any class at runtime.

Class implementations in Objective-C are usually split into two files: the header file and the implementation itself. This separation isn't required, though, for small private classes, as you've seen with some of the code in this book. The header file (with a .h extension) holds the public information related to the class, such as any new enums, types, structures, and objects that will be used by the code that uses this class. Other bodies of code import this file with the preprocessor (using #import). Java lacks the C preprocessor, which is a textual substitution tool that automatically processes C, Objective-C, and C++ source code before it is given to the compiler. When you see directives that start with #, you know that line is a command to the preprocessor. The C preprocessor actually knows nothing about the C family of languages; it just does blind text substitutions. The preprocessor can be a very powerful—and dangerous—tool. Many programmers consider the lack of the preprocessor in Java to be a feature.

In Java, almost every error is handled with exceptions. In Objective-C, error handling depends on the API you're using. The Unix API typically returns a –1 value and a global error number (errno) is set to a specific error. The Cocoa APIs typically throw exceptions only on programmer errors or situations where cleanup is not possible. The Objective-C language provides exception handling features similar to Java and C++: @try, @catch, and @finally.

In Objective-C, the null (zero) object is termed *nil*. You can send messages to nil and not have to worry about a NullPointerException. Messages to nil are no-ops, so there is no need to check your message sends against NULL. Messages to nil are discussed earlier in the "Coming from C++" section.

In Objective-C, you can change a class's behavior at runtime by adding methods to existing classes using categories. There are no such things as final classes in Objective-C; you can subclass anything, as long as you have a header file for it, because the compiler needs to know how big an object the superclass defines.

In practice, you end up doing a lot less subclassing in Objective-C than in Java. Through mechanisms like categories and the dynamic runtime that allows sending any message to any object, you can put functionality into fewer classes, and you can also put the functionality into the class that makes the most sense. For instance, you can put a category on NSString to add a feature, such as reversing a string or removing all white space. Then, you can invoke that method on any NSString, no matter where it comes from. You're not restricted to your own string subclass to provide those features.

Generally, the only times you need to subclass in Cocoa are when you are creating a brand new object (at the top of an object hierarchy), fundamentally changing the behavior of an object, or working with a class that requires a subclass because it doesn't do anything useful out of the box. For instance, the NSView class used by Cocoa for making user interface components has no implementation for its drawRect: method. You need to subclass NSView and override that method to draw in the view. But for many other objects, delegation and data sources are used. Because Objective-C can send any message to any object, an object does not need to be of a particular subclass or to conform to a particular interface, so a single class can be a delegate and data source to any number of different objects.

Because data source and delegate methods are declared in categories, you don't have to implement all of them. Cocoa programming in Objective-C has few empty stub methods, or methods that turn around and invoke the same method on an embedded object just to keep the compiler quiet when adopting a formal protocol.

With power comes responsibility, of course. With Objective-C's manual retain, release, and autorelease memory management system, it's easy to create tricky memory errors. Placing categories on other classes can be a very powerful mechanism, but if abused, it can make your code difficult to untangle and impossible to give to someone else. Plus, Objective-C is based on C, so you get all of C's baggage, along with its dangers when using the preprocessor, including the possibility of pointer-related memory errors.

Coming from BASIC

Many programmers learned how to program using Visual Basic or REALbasic, and their transition to Cocoa and Objective-C can be a confusing one.

BASIC (Visual and REAL) environments provide an integrated development environment that makes up the complete workspace. Cocoa splits the development environment into two parts: Interface Builder and Xcode. You use Interface Builder to create the user interface and to tell the user interface the name of the methods to invoke on a particular object, and then you put your control logic into source code edited in Xcode (or TextMate, BBEdit, emacs, or whichever text editor is your favorite).

In BASIC, the user interface items and the code they work with are tightly integrated. You put chunks of code into the buttons and text fields to make them behave the way you want. You can factor this code out into a common class and have the code in the buttons talk to that class, but for the most part, BASIC programming involves putting code on user interface items. If you're not careful, this style can lead to messy programs with the logic scattered across a lot of different items. BASIC programming typically involves changing properties of objects to get them to behave the way you want.

In Cocoa, you find a clear separation between the interface and the logic that goes on behind that interface. You have a collection of objects that talk to each other. Rather than setting a property on an object, you ask the object to change its property. This distinction is subtle but important. The bulk of the think-time you have in Cocoa is figuring out what message you need to send rather than what property you need to set.

BASIC has a very rich market in third-party controls and support code. Frequently, you can buy something off the shelf and integrate it into your codebase rather than build it yourself.

Coming from Scripting Languages

Programmers coming from scripting languages, such as Perl, PHP, Python, and Tcl, will probably have the hardest transition to the Objective-C and Cocoa world.

Scripting languages excel in programmer conveniences, such as very robust string handling and processing, automatic memory management (whether by reference counting or garbage collection under the hood), very quick turnaround in development, flexible typing (being able to move between numbers, strings, and lists with ease), and a plethora of packages you can download and use. The runtime environment is often very flexible in scripting languages too, letting you design your own object types and control structures at will.

If you're coming from a scripting language, in many ways Objective-C will seem like a big step backward in time. It is a language of the '80s, compared to scripting languages that evolved in the '90s. String handling can be painful, since there is no built-in regular expression capability. Making strings with `printf()` style formats is about as fancy as Cocoa gets. Even though Objective-C has grown garbage collection, a lot of existing code you'll see on the Internet uses the manual memory management techniques with `retain` and `release`. Development includes a compile and link phase, causing a delay between making a code change and seeing the result. You have to manually deal with distinct types, such as integers, character arrays, and string objects. Plus, you have all the baggage C brings along, such as pointers, bitwise operations, and easy-to-make memory errors.

Why go through this pain to use Objective-C? Performance is one reason: depending on the kind of application, Objective-C can perform better than a scripting language. Access to the native user interface toolkit (Cocoa) is another important advantage. Most scripting languages support the Tk toolkit originally developed for the Tcl language. This package is workable, but it doesn't have the depth and breadth of user interface features that you get with Cocoa. And, importantly, applications built with Tk typically don't look and feel like Mac programs.

You can have the best of both worlds, though, by using scripting bridges. There are bridges between Objective-C and Python (called PyObjC) and Ruby (RubyObjC), so both of those scripting languages can be first-class citizens. When you use these bridges, you can subclass Cocoa objects in Python or Ruby and have access to all of Cocoa's features.

Summary

Objective-C and Cocoa aren't like any other programming language and toolkit. Objective-C has some neat features and behaviors that derive from its dynamic runtime dispatch qualities. You can do things in Objective-C that you can't do in other languages.

Objective-C lacks some niceties that have been added to other languages over the years. In particular, robust string handling, name spaces, and metaprogramming are features in these other languages that you don't have in Objective-C.

Everything in programming comes down to trade-offs. You have to decide whether what you would gain in Objective-C compared to your current language of choice is worth what you would lose. For us, being able to use Cocoa for building applications more than pays for the time and effort it took to get familiar with Objective-C.

Index

You Need the Companion eBook

Your purchase of this book entitles you to buy the companion PDF-version eBook for only $10. Take the weightless companion with you anywhere.

We believe this Apress title will prove so indispensable that you'll want to carry it with you everywhere, which is why we are offering the companion eBook (in PDF format) for $10 to customers who purchase this book now. Convenient and fully searchable, the PDF version of any content-rich, page-heavy Apress book makes a valuable addition to your programming library. You can easily find and copy code—or perform examples by quickly toggling between instructions and the application. Even simultaneously tackling a donut, diet soda, and complex code becomes simplified with hands-free eBooks!

Once you purchase your book, getting the $10 companion eBook is simple:

❶ Visit **www.apress.com/promo/tendollars/**.

❷ Complete a basic registration form to receive a randomly generated question about this title.

❸ Answer the question correctly in 60 seconds, and you will receive a promotional code to redeem for the $10.00 eBook.